MEMOIRS OF AN ANTI-SEMITE

Gregor von Rezzori was born in the Bukovina in 1914. He studied at the University of Vienna and for a time lived in Bucharest. In Germany, after World War II, he became active as a writer and in radio broadcasting and filmmaking activities. Mr. Rezzori's first books included *Tales from Maghrebinia* (1953) and *Oedipus Triumphs at Stalingrad* (1954). Another novel, *Ein Hermelin in Tschernopol,* appeared in the United States under the title *The Hussar* in 1960. American readers first discovered him as a writer in English, however, with the appearance of his story "Memoirs of an Anti-Semite" in *The New Yorker* in 1969, which appears in this volume as "Troth" and which was composed in English. Mr. Rezzori's most recent major work is the novel *The Death of My Brother Abel* (1976), soon to be published in English. Gregor von Rezzori lives with his wife, Beatrice Monti, in Tuscany.

Memoirs of an Anti-Semite

Gregor von Rezzori

PENGUIN BOOKS

Penguin Books Ltd, Harmondsworth,
Middlesex, England
Penguin Books, 625 Madison Avenue,
New York, New York 10022, U.S.A.
Penguin Books Australia Ltd, Ringwood,
Victoria, Australia
Penguin Books Canada Limited, 2801 John Street,
Markham, Ontario, Canada L3R 1B4
Penguin Books (N.Z.) Ltd, 182–190 Wairau Road,
Auckland 10, New Zealand

Originally published in Germany under the title
Memoiren eines Antisemiten by Verlag Steinhausen GmbH, München, 1979
This English-language edition first published in
the United States of America by The Viking Press 1981
Published in Penguin Books 1982·

Copyright © Gregor von Rezzori, 1969, 1981
Memoiren eines Antisemiten copyright © Verlag Steinhausen GmbH,
München, 1979
Translation copyright © Viking Penguin Inc., 1981
All rights reserved

LIBRARY OF CONGRESS CATALOGING IN PUBLICATION DATA
Rezzori, Gregor von.
Memoirs of an anti-semite.
Translation of: Memoiren eines Antisemiten.
I. Title.
PT2635.E98M4513   1982   833'.912   82-516
ISBN 0 14 00.6224 6   AACR2

Printed in the United States of America by
Offset Paperback Mfrs., Inc., Dallas, Pennsylvania
Set in Linotron Janson

The stories "*Skushno*," "Youth," and "*Pravda*" were translated from the German by
Joachim Neugroschel. The English of "Löwinger's Rooming House" and "Troth" is
the author's own.

"Troth" originally appeared in *The New Yorker*, in slightly different form, under the
title "Memoirs of an Anti-Semite."

Contents

Memoirs of an Anti-Semite

Skushno

S *kushno* is a Russian word that is difficult to translate. It means more than dreary boredom: a spiritual void that sucks you in like a vague but intensely urgent longing. When I was thirteen, at a phase that educators used to call the awkward age, my parents were at their wits' end. We lived in the Bukovina, today an almost astronomically remote province in southeastern Europe. The story I am telling seems as distant—not only in space but also in time—as if I'd merely dreamed it. Yet it begins as a very ordinary story.

I had been expelled by a *consilium abeundi*—an advisory board with authority to expel unworthy students—from the schools of the then Kingdom of Rumania, whose subjects we had become upon the collapse of the Austro-Hungarian Empire after the first great war. An attempt to harmonize the imbalances in my character by means of strict discipline at a boarding school in Styria (my people still regarded Austria as our cultural homeland) nearly led to the same ignominious end, and only my pseudo-voluntary departure from the institution in the nick of time prevented my final ostracism from the privileged ranks of those for whom the path to higher education was open. Again in the jargon of those assigned the responsible task of raising children to become "useful members of society," I was a "virtually hopeless case." My parents, blind to how the contradictions within me had grown out of the highly charged difference between their own natures, agreed with the schoolmasters: the mix of neurotic sensitivity and a tendency to violence, alert perception and inability to learn, tender need for support and lack of adjustability, would only develop into something criminal.

One of the trivial aphorisms my generation owes to Wilhelm Busch's *Pious Helene* is the homily "Once your reputation's done / You can live a life of fun." But this optimistic notion results more from wishful thinking than from practical experience. In my case, had anyone asked me about my state of mind, I would have sighed and answered, *"Skushno!"* Even though rebellious thoughts occasionally surged within me, I dragged myself, or rather I let myself be dragged, listlessly through my bleak existence in the snail's pace of days. Nor was I ever free of a sense of guilt, for my feeling guilty was not entirely foisted upon me by others; there were deep reasons I could not explain to myself; had I been able to do so, my life would have been much easier.

I see myself in that difficult period as in a snapshot taken by one of those precision-engineered cameras blessed with a wealth of tiny screws and levers, gaping lenses, and pleated black-leather bellows which one pulled like an accordion from gleaming nickel scissor supports, cameras that were produced by the same *Zeitgeist*—still close to the horse-and-buggy world—as the clear-angled, high-wheeled automobiles that so aroused my boyhood fantasy. I envied my classmates—the well-behaved ones whom I left behind when I was sent from school—when they received such photographic apparatuses as birthday or Christmas rewards for success in their schoolwork, though I did not much value the photographs they gave me now and then.

I can see one snapshot now: it is of a boy with the rounded, defiant face of violated and soon assassinated childhood; his glum resolve, focusing exclusively on himself, is a bit ridiculous, and it deceives us about the earnest ordeal of adolescence, which—awkward in this respect too—can find no better expression of its genuine agonies. The day is overcast. I am sitting on a log, wearing a windbreaker of stiff, waterproof linen with a military belt and large pockets, the kind of jacket sported in the late 1920s by members of ideological associations, whether of the far left or the extreme right. In my case, of course, I was remote from anything philosophical, and I simply used the jacket on long rambles I took whenever I could, wandering lonesome and aimless into the countryside around Czernowitz. In the sunshine-basking seasons, the landscape with its vast horizon was as beautiful as a park; under a wintry sky, aswarm with crows, it offered only melancholy leagues of farmland, plowed up into black clods; far away, beyond the snowy strips that marked the hollows in the rolling terrain, the black lines of woodlands stretched all the way to the mountains, twilight blue and barely visible at the milk-glass edge of the sky dome. It was just such a day, in late winter, that corresponded best to my mood of *skushno*.

I have no hat; my hair is tousled by the wind. Smooth as a seal, my dachshund Max sits at my feet, worshipfully gazing up at me. He is my sole playmate and buddy, my friend, my comforter, in whom I find if not instant understanding then certainly unconditional love and unreserved approval of anything I do.

This photo does not exist—I must quickly point out—for I kept to myself so completely that no one could have snapped it; the schoolmates I have spoken of were now far away. Max and I bummed around the countryside near Czernowitz like a pair of tramps. Morally, too, we were rather footloose. We had a tacit agreement that any guinea hen venturing too far from its home coop was fair game; likewise any cat caught mousing in the furrows. Felines were my special prey, for, much to my sorrow, Max, despite all his other praiseworthy qualities, was not fierce. He would quite eagerly, indeed hysterically, rush at his game, but if it stood up to him, at the slightest nick on his nose he would turn tail, retreat yowling behind my heels, and yelp ignobly from his refuge. I comforted myself with the thought that he was still young and I was probably asking too much of him. Anyway, I carried a good slingshot and a handful of lead pellets in the pocket of my nonpolitical windbreaker, and my aim was almost as good as that of a circus marksman. Even the most tenacious tom reeled off in a daze when the bean-sized bullet struck his skull. Max then had a much easier time of it.

Today, dogs and cats share my home peaceably. But in those days I regarded the enmity between them as a law of nature; and, being a dog-lover, I was of course a cat-hater. I was the son of a man to whom hunting meant everything; the necessity of annihilating prey was as established a fact for me as the categorical imperative was for my teachers; and everyone knows that in shooting grounds, cats are pests. As for attacking the guinea fowl, that was a deliberate iniquity, an act of defiance. Raised according to the strictest rules of sportsmanship, I found a painful satisfaction in being a chicken thief. I was flouting the etiquette of venery, thus to a certain extent sullying my father's name. For the sheaf of thoughtfully severe punishments that were to make me conscious of my waywardness included, alas, the penalty of not being allowed to go hunting with my father. Every spring and summer since early boyhood, I had been permitted to accompany my father in the seasonal cycle of sporting joys: tracking woodcock and snipe at Eastertide, and, in my summer vacations, stalking bucks. Then, later, growing more robust, I had occasionally been taken along on the principal part of the annual hunt, during the rutting season of the deer in autumn and the wild-boar hunt in winter. But now I ran, straight out of Czernowitz and then on aimlessly cross-country, to escape the afflicting temptations that would have been unendurable at home: the nostalgic images of the mountain forests where my father hunted, resounding with the mating cries of blackcocks and woodcocks along the margins of the forests and, when everything was green again, the billy goats' gamboling in the first summer heat, the air alive with dancing gnats. This year, I was forbidden these pleasures.

The stubblefields underfoot were still wet from snow that had only recently melted away. Buds were gleaming on the brookside willows, and you could count on your fingers the days remaining until spring: the buds would soon be breaking open into furry catkins, the sky would be blue again and striped with wet white clouds, the cuckoo would be calling everywhere. But I was chained to my guilt. My moral delinquencies were not the only sins I had to make amends for. I dragged around the syllabus I had missed and now had to make up as a convict the iron ball on his ankle. I knew—after all, it was droned into me every day—that if I passed the makeup exam in the fall, I would be reprieved: that is I would have one last chance for scholastic rehabilitation. Even though I knew this would mean nothing but one more year of boarding-school exile, far from home, far from my beloved country, from hunting, and from my dachshund Max, I was nevertheless resolved to do everything in my power to pass this examination.

My power was woefully dissipated, however. Outside, a thawing wind blew through tree branches which, still bare and transparent, were spun into the silky gray of the sky. I could hear the blackbirds panicking at twilight, drops falling, mice rustling in the dry leaves around the underbrush—all the small noises that almost startle a hunter when he listens for a sign of his prey. . . . I sat in my room, in front of my schoolbooks, absorbing not a word of what I read, not the simplest question. Seeking a surrogate for the missing hunting ventures with my father, I had plunged into hunting literature with all the passion of a starved imagination; soon, without quite realizing it myself, I was able to read in the original the classic French book on hunting by Gaston de Foix. But this achievement had garnered me no praise or even recognition. On the contrary: it was now considered proven that sheer wickedness rather than genuine slow-wittedness made me unwilling to fulfill my duties. This, in turn, embittered me so deeply that I gave up deciphering old French texts and did nothing but run around in the open air, with *skushno* in my heart.

The dynamics of such pedagogical quarrels are well known. The case histories are all too similar, and I need not bother to narrate mine in greater detail. Soon salvation came from relatives—an elderly, childless couple who put an end to the lamentations about me for the time being. They offered to take in the problem child for the summer.

Uncle Hubert and Aunt Sophie had been told about me early on, and about the progress, or rather problems, I was making. My parents were not without an ulterior motive: legacy-angling, I suppose, for these kin had no closer family ties than us and they were well to do. They lived in the country—more precisely, they lived as feudal lord and lady in one of those out-of-the-way hamlets with tongue-twisting names which, on maps of the European southeast, make the riverine regions along the Prut or Dniester seem like civilized territories. One should not forget, of course, the immensity of that territory, as well as the quite discordant and not always deeply rooted *kind* of civilization one finds there. East and West meet there unchanged in architecture, language, and customs, even in the smallest village. But I was born and bred in that part of the world, so I did not expect a walled town rich in gables and oriels, with arched sandstone arcades around the Roland's fountain in the town-hall square. And I knew that my uncle and aunt were not to be pictured as the baron and baroness of an ivy-covered stronghold towering over such a scene.

The townlet in which my relatives lived and where they were the most important employers was a settlement in the marches of colonial territory on the European continent—it had sprung up out of windblown cultural sand, as it were, and would melt away again. Especially at night, when you approached it from a distance, its forlornness under the starry sky touched you to the quick: a handful of lights scattered over a flat-topped hill at the bend of a river, tied to the world solely by the railroad tracks, which glistened in the goat's milk of the moonlight. The firmament was as enormous as the huge mass of the earth, against whose heavy darkness these signals of human presence asserted themselves with a bravery that could scarcely be called reasonable. The sight was poignant in a sentimental way, like certain paintings of Chagall's. With *skushno* in the heart, one could experience it as devastatingly beautiful.

During the day, the town was generally stripped of such poetry. It consisted of a rustic depot and a few zigzagging streets trodden into the loam and lined with plain houses, some with gardens, as in a village, and some stark by the roadside and covered with sheet metal to eye level. Thistles and scrubby camomile ran riot along the verge of open ditches; swarms of sparrows twittered in the hazel bushes along the fences and scuffled over the straw clusters in the stable dung that lay randomly at farm gates. Wheel tracks of heavy carts, often drawn by oxen, cut deep into the dust or mire, depending on the season. At the point where the tracks ran together, in a square of chestnut trees around a thinly graveled marketplace, a building presented itself to the main road, its façade plastered with posters and announcements from the front steps all the way up to the gutters under the roof. This town hall was a stereotypical municipal administration building; its gable bore a stumpy tower from whose skylight window a flag dangled on national holidays. Three shops lurked around the square, waiting for customers; on market days, a tavern with a bakery was packed with peasants, who had driven their cartloads of pigs, calves, poultry, and vegetables in from the countryside; the apothecary's shop announced itself by way of a hanging lamp, in the form of a glass red cross, within a stone's throw of the street urchins.

At the end of the main road, the vanishing point of its short perspective, lay a fenced-in plot; behind boxwood boskets, neglected for decades, where dozens of roving cats

7

napped, loomed an edifice built of delicately assembled bright-red bricks. Startling, crazy—turreted, merloned, and orieled—it had a sheet-metal roof with edges serrated like a doily and dragon-head gargoyles at each eave, and it was richly decked out with pennons, halberds, and little weather vanes. This was the "villa" of the physician Dr. Goldmann. A showpiece of architectural romanticism from the 1890s, it was proffered as a curiosity by Uncle Hubert and Aunt Sophie to anyone visiting for the first time. Next to the down-to-earth toy-brick box of the Armenian Catholic church and the plain domical synagogue, the only other sight worth seeing was the lovely old onion-tower church of the Orthodox monastery, set in a grove of spruces on the gentle hilltop. All these buildings stood shamelessly, as it were, under a sky that, heedless of human vanity, stretched eastward to the Kirghiz Steppe and way beyond to Tibet. On weekdays, the place was almost lifeless, if we disregard the straggling gangs of lice-ridden Jewish children who romped among the sparrows in the dusty roads.

In the summer, the sun burned mercilessly upon the bare rooftops, and the air over them quivered blurrily. In winter, biting frost took the world into its white tongs, icicles barred the small windows of the houses, and in the river meadow the trees stood as if spun out of glass. At times—mostly unexpected—something picturesque erupted: a Jewish funeral, for instance, when, like dark, bizarre flowers, male shapes in long black caftans and red fox-fur caps suddenly emerged from the ground among the skew and sunken gravestones, under the pale birches and weeping willows of the small, out-of-the-way Jewish cemetery. Some of these figures were slightly hunched, with speech as soft and hoarse as if they were about to clear their throats, and they had long earlocks and white or chestnut beards; others had gaping eyes and heads thrown back, framed by the blazing fox-fur caps, and protruding abdomens and loud voices. Or, on the anniversary of the saint who lay in an embossed silver coffin at the Orthodox church, the monastery courtyard and the grove in front of it filled with male and female peasants wearing gaudily embroidered blouses, lambskin jackets, and laced sandals, with carnations behind their ears or in their strong white teeth. The polyphonic chanting of the monks alternated with the droning of the Talmud students at the synagogue.

Uncle Hubert and Aunt Sophie's house lay like a baronial manor at the edge of the village. Although the entrance could be locked, the huge wrought-iron gate was usually open and the driveway lay free under huge old acacias. A spacious courtyard, framed by lindens, separated the house from the farm buildings and stables and a small brewery that was operated along with the farm. In back you could hear the rustling of the beeches and alders, the spruces, birches, and mountain ash of a spacious park that merged imperceptibly into the open countryside.

I had known this estate since childhood, and I felt as much at home here as in my parents' house and garden in Czernowitz, or as in the Carpathian hunting lodge where I was no longer allowed to visit. I especially loved to stay with my relatives because I had been allowed to spend vacations here, sometimes even for several months when my mother's physicians diagnosed her as needing rest—exceptional periods, in any case, which in childhood are always taken to be festive. For my relatives, my sporadic visits were just rare and brief enough for them to enjoy me. When the problems of my upbringing arose, Uncle Hubert and Aunt Sophie were downright astonished, not without a gentle suggestion that perhaps one should take into account a certain inadequacy in the educational methods, if not in the educators themselves: "Why, that's absolutely incredible. The boy is so sweet and merry and well behaved with us, such a sensible child, so good-natured and obedient. This sort of thing could never happen in our home."

No wonder, then, that for me, Aunt Sophie's exceedingly ample bosom, tightly laced and covered by dependably sportive blouses and rough tweed jackets, signified warm maternalism far more than did my mother's elegant and poetically sentimental, unfortunately all too high-strung, untouchability. And Uncle Hubert, too, represented in my early years something incomparably more stable, more focused on concrete things, hence more calming, than my father's increasingly gloomy, increasingly disillusioned daydreams, as he fled deeper and deeper into his monomaniacal passion for the hunt.

Of course, Uncle Hubert and Aunt Sophie themselves inhabited a disunited world. The remote spot in the eastern borderland of the former Habsburg—and hence ancient Roman—Empire where they played the role of virtual cultural viceroy was located at a meeting point (or chafing point, if you will) between two civilizations. One, the Western, had not endured long enough to bless the land and people with more than an infrastructure (as it would be called today) geared to technological colonization; it had then promptly girded itself to destroy what little there was of the indigenous culture. The other, likewise at the defenseless mercy of the steppe winds from the east, opposed the Western in the spirit of a fatalistic resignation to destiny; but along with that it had, alas, a propensity for letting things go, run to seed, degenerate into slovenliness. Still, both Uncle Hubert and Aunt Sophie were of a piece —prototypical provincial aristocrats such as can be found in Wales or the Auvergne, in Jutland or Lombardy: by no means narrow-minded, much less uneducated, in some respects even surprisingly enlightened; yet an easygoing life in secure circumstances and natural surroundings, a life of clear-cut duties and constantly reiterated tasks, gave their thoughts and emotions, their language and conduct, a simplicity that might easily strike a casual observer as simplemindedness. The very next look would suffice—at least in the case of my relatives—to ascertain a discreet warmheartedness and a deeply humane tact, which in more sophisticated types are not necessarily the rule.

It was taken for granted that not a single word would be

spoken to remind me of my duty to cram for my makeup examination. My uncle and aunt tacitly assumed I would do this of my own accord, with my own common sense—and my own ambition. When and how was left entirely up to me. For the moment at least, I was officially on vacation; I could sleep as long as I liked and loaf about wherever I wished. I had been given permission to bring my dachshund Max, and Uncle Hubert spoke with such lively and joyous anticipation of the annual quail and snipe hunt to take place later in the summer that no doubts assailed me as to whether I would be allowed to go along. There was only one thing that I could take as a gentle admonition—and it only heightened my bliss: instead of putting me near Aunt Sophie's bedroom, as they had in earlier years, they put me into the so-called tower with Max. "You'll be more undisturbed here," they said, without the least suggestion of a hint.

The tower, naturally, was no tower. This was the name for makeshift quarters located over the brewery office and accessible from the garden by way of a steep ladder. During the great winter hunts, out-of-town guests were housed here, especially Uncle Hubi's most intimate bachelor friends: sportsmen who could drink anyone under the table. For the rest of the year, the tower normally remained empty. Its three garret rooms strung out under the eaves, where a dusty smell of disuse and infrequent ventilation lingered, enjoyed a legendary reputation. There was talk of events that were better merely hinted at in the presence of children, although, of course, everyone knew these were mostly humorous exaggerations. Yet they kept popping up over and over again, if only as jocosely cited proof of Aunt Sophie's sympathetic and comradely tolerance and her model team-work marriage with Uncle Hubert.

I felt as if I had grown one hand taller overnight. By moving into the tower, I had gone among the men. At last I had outgrown the tormenting solicitude of my mother, the apron strings of governesses and tutors, whose extension into a collective was what the hated discipline of boarding school had been for me. Here, in the tower, free men dwelled, sovereigns who forged their own destinies, who knew the science of weapons, the last heroes and warriors. I settled, I breathed my way, into their rugged world.

In the mustiness of the attic rooms, you could still sniff cigar butts, and it did not take much imagination to picture the rest: the darkness of winter mornings with a wood fire crackling, the early bustle in the house and the courtyard, the jittery whimpering of the hounds, and the fragrance of strong coffee and toast, bacon and fried eggs. They all announced the hunting day: a long day, eagerly lived, a day of self-oblivion and pulse-throbbing suspense, with surprises at any moment, minutes of the most thrilling expectation, swiftest decision, actions as sure as in a dream . . . tingling alternations of triumph and disappointment, the breath flying with the second hand, the hours that paint the heavens from the clear, light-budding mother-of-pearl rosiness of the rising morn to the bloodbath of the evening. . . . The hunt is over, the lungs burst with stinging fresh air, the blood courses keenly through the veins, the hunters are going home, the runners of their sleighs crunching beneath them: burning cold on your cheeks and your body, snugly warm in your weatherproof gear, the night throwing its black cloth over the beautiful world, filling the woods with darkness as they loom up mightily on either side of the road, the horses steaming along, lifting their tails as they trot, the unscrewed rosettes of their anuses dropping moist, warm, smoking balls that remain between the gliding marks of the runners as nourishment for famished birds: a mysterious world of starry, spatial coldness and muck-born life—your hand has sown death today, this makes you feel alive. . . . A rumbling return to the festively illuminated house, the mug of grog glowing in your fingers, a well-turned compliment to the gracious femininity of the lady of the house, a nimble grab at the parlor maid's behind when she brings hot water, delicious unwinding of the limbs in the bath, the delight of fresh white linen, of the light shoes for the evening dress suit, the grand meal, the many wines, the bag of hundreds of murdered creatures: stiff, hairy, blood-encrusted plunder that was playing at life a bare few hours ago, a flitting shadow play, lusterless eyes, outflared by torchlight, the blares of the hunting horn fading away in the cold mist of the night, then cognac in snifters, the men talking, reliving their experiences, the jokes, the teasing, the booming laughter. . . . All these things were waiting for me; soon they would be my life, my being.

I was all the happier because this male world quite obviously had a playful streak, belying the claim that we rather pitiably grow out of the wonder-fraught life-dreams of childhood into the earnestness of momentous tasks and duties that make adulthood somber, burdening it with responsibilities. On the contrary: I felt as if I had suffered through the ordeals of youthful boredom, tormenting restraint, and incessant vexation, finally to reach a never-never land of liberty, of equality among equals, of lighthearted fraternity. In the tower was gathered anything that had become superfluous in the house or, for reasons of good taste, had been sifted out of the house. Everything around me—from the carved-buckhorn furniture to the cheerfully gaudy crazy-quilt carpet, from the ashtray, presenting a deceptive porcelain replica of a cigarette butt and a half-spread hand of cards, to the ivory skull functioning as a letter weight on the desk—all these things parodied the usual furnishings, as in artists' studios and student digs. The huge bearskin before the fireplace with its lifelike stuffed head, the glass case suspended over the mantel with a collection of unwontedly huge tropical butterflies, the English beer pots in the shape of seated drinkers, the cast-iron clothes tree, were likewise ironically exaggerated in their purpose. The last, like a Roman general's trophy, was an emblem clustering together all the paraphernalia of hunting—nets, horns, shotguns, game bags, bowie knives. To me, at least, the tower seemed to express the cheerfully lived-out play instinct, these adults' true sense of life, the true essence of their existence. This essence was only flimsily camouflaged by gestures of earnest morality—duty-laden, charity-conscious—and it was always near the edge of danger, of death.

Previously, when I had had my room next to Aunt Sophie's boudoir, the dramatics of existence, especially childhood existence, had been presented to me in sentimental engravings that illustrated *Paul et Virginie*. I had often acted out the individual scenes—but it was a literary dramatics. The adventures of Paul and Virginie were events I could picture vividly in my imagination but I knew would never happen to me in real life. Here in the tower, however, the walls were covered with prints of the legendary equestrian feats of Count Sàndor (no one ever failed to mention that he was the father of Princess Pauline, daughter-in-law of Chancellor Metternich). These feats could be immediately enacted: I could go into the stable, have a horse saddled, and try to emulate the count. The jeopardy was no less mortal than in the calvary of Paul and Virginie, but it was easily sought out and thereby spiritualized into playfulness. The daredevil count would make his horse climb to the window-sill and gracefully lean upon it with one hoof while the rider calmly chatted with the beautiful damsel leaning out the casement. The possibility of his breaking his neck was as great as during a leap over a hurdle with a loosened girth, so that the horse well-nigh sprang away from under him, while the rider, keeping his perfect posture, remained in the stirrups and saddle, like Baron von Münchhausen on the flying cannonball. This image tallied perfectly with the ubiquitous souvenirs of the Great War, the shell cases and grenade splinters and heavy sabers and Uncle Hubert's Uhlan shako, which had been shot straight through during the fighting in Galicia. (This circumstance provided his friends with matter for endless joking, although the incident had been quite serious: one half centimeter lower and the bullet would have not just singed his hair and scalp but pierced his brain.)

14

Often, I would stand motionless in one of the tower rooms for hours at a time, listening into the silence. If I had claimed to be working, they would probably have interpreted my answer as insolent and rebuked me. But it was true: I was working my way into a man's existence. I did it instinctively, in the fashion of mystics—by trying to become as one with the things around me; after all, these objects contained the spirit of virile existence and thus had to have something of its substance.

This was not difficult to do among the temperas that showed mounted skirmishes between Uhlans and Cossacks in Galicia during the early years of the Great War. Exciting events could be relived effortlessly. But how could one penetrate the mystery of what it was that made a piece of furniture—for instance, a full-length mirror, a so-called *psyché*—quite unmistakably masculine, while a similar piece in Aunt Sophie's bedroom, made in the same severe Empire neoclassic style, was just as unmistakably feminine? Piercing to the essence, the entity, of this maleness demanded such intense spiritual activity, such subtle mobilizing of the senses, that I was often virtually numbed and so oddly frightened that I had to flee from myself, out into the open.

Something was now surprisingly revealed to me, namely Uncle Hubi's bachelor days. These opened up to me as a new dimension not just of Uncle Hubi but of the whole world. What gave me most food for thought was the realization that this adolescence and early manhood of my uncle-by-marriage, this period whose mementos had found refuge here, was absolutely masculine, yet masculine in a girlishly sentimental and poetic way that did not fundamentally contradict the rough-tough tone of the "last heroes and warriors." The symbol of that period was two student rapiers crisscrossed and entwined by a divided apple-green and peach-red ribbon. Above the point of intersection hung a "little keg," a brimless cap of the same colors as the ribbon, with a fraternity cipher embroidered on it in gold; emphatically terminated by an exclamation point, the cipher contained the initials of the fraternity name as well as those of the motto *Vivat, crescat, floreat!* The letters twisted into an arabesque: the musical key signature for the atmospheric motif of the reality to which these objects bore symbolic witness.

I realized now the meaning of certain hints in the teasing, mocking tone that made the relationship between Uncle Hubi and his friends and kinfolk cozily amusing, allusions I had never especially heeded and of course never understood. As a former Austrian, Uncle Hubi openly hated Prussia and despised the states of the old Austro-Hungarian empire that had gone so far as to form a new and hybrid empire under the crown of the Hohenzollerns. Nonetheless, my uncle had attended the University of Tübingen, taking active part in a dueling fraternity there, and (presumably in concordance with his brothers, but counter to the prohibition of political activity among corpsmen) he had committed himself, in fraternal enthusiasm, to the notion of a Greater Germany— an anti-Semite and a Wagnerian, as well as an ardent disciple of his political idol Georg von Schönerer. The latter, having forced his way into the editorial office of the *Neues Wiener Tagblatt* (in March 1888, this "Jew gazette" had incorrectly spread the news of Kaiser Wilhelm I's death), had received a prison sentence and forfeited his title of nobility. I had heard about the incident at home. My father never failed to remind Uncle Hubi of it in his occasional fits of caustic humor, which invariably hit the target: Uncle Hubi was still able to wax indignant about a harshness that had almost brought him to the barricades as a young man—and usually Aunt Sophie seconded him: "If there's one thing Hubi just can't bear, it's injustice. You just *have* to understand!"

What I now understood—or rather re-created—was Uncle Hubi's youth. I almost physically grasped the burning passion that a blast of the *Zeitgeist* had kindled in him, so fiery that it devoured everything to which he had been reared and educated—his highly civilized Old Austrian skepticism, its loathing of exuberance and impetuousness, the love of tradition and the respectful loyalty to the state—and devoured all this as thoroughly as it had the other elements that were in his blood, as it were, derived from the land where he had been born and bred: Balkan cunning and its all-defusing sense of humor, Oriental mellowness and its phlegm. I tried to track down the tinder of this passion, and I found it in a book with a simple—but no less demanding—title: *The Bible*. Needless to say, this was not the Holy Writ of the Old and the New Testaments. It was a "drinking book" for the student fraternities, a collection of lyrics from which, along with the spirit of the German nineteenth century, everything else leaped out at me: everything that was regarded as truly and essentially German by myself—and presumably by any other German-speaking person who was descended, like me and my family, from colonial settlers of the old empire and was living in a remote area of Eastern Europe. It all leaped out at me like a fiery wind.

The spring was at its height when I came to Uncle Hubert and Aunt Sophie; melted water shot through the ditches, making the brooks overflow into the meadows; and it seems to me that I must have carried on in an equally effusive way. The title page of the "Bible" sported a colored emblem: a group of merry students boating down the Rhein, wearing a costume that corps members don even today on festive occasions—a braid-trimmed, black-velvet jacket, snug white trousers, and high boots, plus the "little keg," the fraternity cap. One student lies stretched out in the stern; a second one stands in the bow, crooning; the others ply the oars. The hills on the opposite bank are crowned with the ruins of castles. I was so moved by this little picture and its gaily romantic mood that I yearned for nothing so much as to run around in that outfit myself. Aunt Sophie had always had a maternal sympathy for my childhood extravagances. A few years before, she had given me an unforgettably beautiful Christmas present: a lushly fringed Indian outfit, with moccasins imaginatively embroidered by her own hand.

And now, kind Aunt Sophie rummaged through all the plunder boxes in the attic, looking for something similar enough to the braided velvet jacket to pass for a fraternity costume after a few alterations. Fortunately, Geib, the old butler, remembered that a deceased brother of his brother-in-law (the blacksmith at the brewery) had been a foreman in a manganese mine on the Bistriţa River, and perhaps the widow still had his miner's jacket.

I was on good terms with this blacksmith, whose name was Haller. I liked hanging around his smithy, especially to melt out the lead core from old rifle bullets. I cast the lead into pellets for my slingshot and used the copper shells as tips for my arrows. Envious and admiring, I would watch Haller remove the white-hot bullets from the fire with his tongs, letting the lead run out and quickly rolling the empty shells over the horny calluses of his hand without getting burned. I tried to imitate him once, and wound up with some bad blisters. In any case, Haller liked me, and he spoke to his brother's widow: the jacket became mine. It reeked of camphor and was much too large; but Aunt Sophie, who always had a couple of seamstresses working in a back room, had them take in the jacket at the seams so that it more or less fitted. It barely differed from the student getup and even had small epaulets in the bargain.

So far, so good. But it was harder to rig up the lower part of the gear: the snug white trousers and the black boots reaching way past the knees. I staunchly refused to pull on some cotton hunting drawers of Uncle Hubi's; but—only after some inner reluctance—I did accept a silk leotard that Aunt Sophie had worn under her costume at some masquerade in long-past days of slender youthfulness. A pair of black rubber boots, forgotten by some hunting guest, only went up to my calves, spaciously wobbling around them. But to compensate, good Aunt Sophie dug up a black-velvet biretta, crowning it all by twisting a genuine red foxbrush around it, just like on the proud headgear of the "fox major," who oversees the first-year pledges in a dueling corps.

18

When, all tackled up at last, I faced the looking glass in Aunt Sophie's boudoir (the *psyché* in Empire style), the Rumanian chambermaid Florica, who had helped my aunt and the old housekeeper Katharina with the preparations, was overcome by such a convulsive fit of the giggles that she had to be sent from the room.

I viewed myself alone and thoroughly a few times more in the manlier full-length mirror in the tower. At thirteen, after all, it is easy to stand in front of a mirror with a sheaf of chicken feathers in your hair and see Chief Buffalo Horn, with the noble savage's aquiline nose and his full war paint. It is easier still to project a few deft scars into a round boyish face, a long pipe into the energetically compressed childish mouth, and a foaming stein of beer into the small fist. But my goal was not the hale and hearty fraternity life. What I was trying to experience for myself, feel for myself—in this presumably highly comical imitation of a costume that was nothing so much as the fashionable expression of a senti-ment—what I was after was the Germanhood of the corpsmen.

It had to be something corresponding to my own state, my own mood: a sensation composed of the same sentimental elements that kept me tense and restless, a similar urgent yearning with no goal. No, there *was* a goal: a German *skushno*, in a word. The songs in the drinking book stemmed from many different eras, but they all shared the same restlessness, the same mood of departure no matter where to, and the same bitterness of anticipated futility.

I got Aunt Sophie to play the "Bible" songs I liked most for their purest utterance of this mood. She was a fine musician; in her youth, she had dreamed of becoming a concert pianist. Poor Uncle Hubi had a tin ear, but his help was indispensable when we did not know some melody, for he claimed to have them all fresh in his memory from his fraternity days. As is often the case with people who cannot carry a melody, he himself could not hear how tunelessly he sang; nonetheless, he deployed bombast and volume to replace whatever struck him subconsciously as being off key. For even the simplest ditty, he would blow up his chest like a Wagnerian singer, gesticulating as he bellowed to the four winds, not even pausing when Aunt Sophie threw her hands over her ears and shouted, "For heaven's sake, Hubi, stop! You sound like a bull being slaughtered!" Nor would he stop if she and I, shaking with mirth, collapsed in each other's arms, our eyes flooding with tears, our lungs gasping for air. He was too kindhearted, had too great a sense of humor, to resent this.

And so our "musical archaeology," as he dubbed it, became a sort of rite. Every evening before dinner—at which I was allowed to appear in my improvised uniform— the three of us swooped upon the "Bible" and picked out the songs we liked best, or tried to re-create in their presumed original form the songs that Uncle Hubi's resuscitation had only inadequately resurrected. Thus arose a family intimacy I had never known in my parental home. I was very happy, and I believe that Uncle Hubert and Aunt Sophie were likewise happy in their way: they had found, albeit belatedly, the son who had been denied to them.

Such harmony with my surroundings, which I promptly took for an ultimate harmony with the entire world, contributed to the enthusiasm that glowed through me for our newly discovered Germanhood. Hitherto, I had lived in the Old Austrian skepticism, to which, after the collapse of the Dual Monarchy, resignation had been added. I was still surrounded by much older and old-born people. The high civilization of my milieu (especially here, at its outermost fringes, where it was being ground down by another culture) was not in keeping with my age. The ever-polite tempering, the "after you" for anybody at any time, the ironic reflection, the mournful certainty that one lived in a decaying world, the shoulder-shrugging resignation—these were all in physiological contradiction to my age, so to speak. The contradiction was simply unbearable. I experienced this in my repugnance toward a man named Stiassny, who had been a permanent guest in my uncle's home for decades.

Stiassny was a kind of genius *manqué*, encyclopedically educated, a doctor in all sorts of occult sciences, a ruins-rummager and fragment-gatherer, "an heir to decay," as he styled himself. He came from Prague, and his family had once been extremely rich. If you visited him in his room, which was crammed with bizarre objects and rare books, you could inspect the catalogue of the auction at which, shortly after 1919, the family's entire property had gone under the gavel—not only all the household effects, furnishings, coaches, servant liveries, but also his father's important art collection. The most interesting pieces were doubtless an early Raphael Madonna and the parlor car in which the Stiassnys had traveled. One brother had shot himself after the auction.

Stiassny did not regard this family misfortune as a stroke of personal fate. "Why, it's merely one part of the universal dissolution," he would say with an ashy smile. And it struck him as both natural and logical that he was thus reduced to total poverty and compelled to find refuge "wherever this dissolution has not yet been achieved—or at least not in visible form." Besides, in our area of the world, in homes of some prosperity it was not unusual for someone to remain as a guest for years and ultimately decades if some unhappy twist of luck had left him in circumstances forcing him to lay claim to unrestricted hospitality.

Russia was a short hike away, beyond the Dniester River; the Revolution of 1917 had washed swarms of refugees toward us; whole families had been taken in by relatives or magnanimous friends. Stiassny exacted this kind helpfulness as a privilege, however, and sometimes he was even rather insolent about it. He caviled at the housekeeping, inserting sarcastic remarks and clauses everywhere; he carped at the food, the service, indeed the behavior, the inadequate education, and the provinciality of his host and hostess and their less lingering guests; and he bawled out the domestics. Yet, he also felt obliged to deploy ironical servility, which garnered him the nickname of "Stiassny Who-am-I." As though it were a self-tormenting pleasure to act innately humble, merely tolerated in this existence, he began every other sentence with the phrase "But then who am I to expect . . ." or "But then who am I to permit myself . . ."—all this merely to introduce some subtly perfidious malice, or some denunciation with a first gradual but ultimately all the more destructive aftereffect. "But then who am I to say that I do not love my fellowmen?" he would say. "I owe my existence in every respect to the generosity of others. It began with my conception—*nicht wahr?*—a highly unexpected act of mutual generosity between my parents, who quite explicitly despised one another and normally did not undertake such chores together, vigorously as they may have blessed outsiders."

I must confess I was afraid of him—as one might secretly fear a conjuror with all-too-sinister grimaces. Yet I believe that my blend of repugnance and admiration was something he must have aroused in everyone—except, of course, Aunt Sophie, who had taken him under her care like any creature in need of protection: a jackdaw with a broken wing; a superannuated dray horse that was supposed to be driven to the slaughterhouse; the gardener's feebleminded son, who could, after all, perform a few useful services, like peeling potatoes for the kitchen or carrying firewood. My father, in contrast, had no sympathy whatsoever for Stiassny's dichotomous nature, and he bluntly despised him, mistreating him whenever he visited my uncle's house; even though I felt it served Stiassny right, my father's rudeness tormented me.

Withdrawn as Stiassny was in the household, he was pushy in that he was always around. Normally, he was not to be seen. He sat in his room over books and all kinds of weird studies. For instance, he cast the horoscopes of all the servants, explaining to Aunt Sophie that their character defects came from inauspicious constellations; or he tinkered

22

on an apparatus for counterbalancing the harmful earth radiation under Aunt Sophie's and Uncle Hubi's marriage bed. Allegedly, he sometimes consulted ghosts or at least could conjure them up. All these activities took place in sensational secrecy, which made him generally present in an abstract way. But at mealtime, Stiassny appeared fully in person and with impressive punctuality. No matter how small or makeshift the meal—a quick snack before a long outing, a cup of tea and some sandwiches for someone coming home late—Stiassny was there waiting, as inevitably as if he belonged with edibles, as a knife and fork belong with eating and a glass with drinking.

He stood with eyes lowered and hands folded in clerical modesty, wearing his dark, well-tailored, but dreadfully stained suit, the shirt with frayed cuffs and collar, and the skew and sloppily knotted tie; yet his elegance was undeniable. His tall stature and well-proportioned frame, the distinguished head with the blazing white hair and the very beautiful red lips, were as attractive as the rest of him was repulsive—his terribly ruined teeth; his dark-brown fingers tanned by incessant smoking; the pale, decayed, and overfed flesh bloated from his stay-at-home existence. As long as his almost colorless light eyes between the half-closed lids scrutinized the all-too-familiar furniture in the dining room and the usually quite sumptuously laden table, they expressed scornful irony. But barely had they encountered the eyes of the host, the hostess, or one of the other guests when they faded; abruptly they seemed like a blind man's eyes, even though they must have perceived as sharply as before; and Stiassny's face resumed a look of the most servile self-denial, as though he were about to say, "But then who am I to be so forward as to venture even the least critique on what is so magnanimously offered us here? If, however, such an impression may have arisen, then I beg you not to take any notice of it."

At meals, Stiassny sat at the end of the table: that is, next to or near me. He ate with a greed that had become

23

proverbial. "He eats like Stiassny" was said, for instance, about a horse that had been under the weather and refusing its fodder but was now finally starting to recuperate. Greatly as his excessive gusto repelled me, I could not help watching Stiassny from the corner of my eye. It afforded me a dark pleasure to see his noble, finely carved, sensitive, and overindulged profile wolfing down incredible amounts of all kinds of food, at times even compulsively, mechanically. My pleasure was the sort one receives from certain Mannerist paintings that along with beauty also show us its terrible reverse. Stiassny was far too sensitive not to feel my stealthy sidelong glances. He would turn to me when I least expected it, catch me off guard, and, offering his repulsiveness *en face* to my scrutiny, strike me with a smile of perfidious complicity, as though recognizing in me a confederate of similar vice. But he was generously content to establish this without showing that, even on a level of equal lowness, there is a hierarchical difference between the sovereign perpetrator and the subaltern wisher who is a sinner merely in thought. Yet his colorless eyes remained so expressionless that he seemed to be striving to conceal any advantage of his person—the aura of his intellect, enormous knowledge, and superiority—over the lowbrows he was forced to live among, his presumable vulnerability, and perhaps even his kindness and need for love; to camouflage them behind the mask of undisguised evil.

Naturally, such a look bewildered me. I would be disquieted for days, flung out of the saddle of my self-assurance, in which I sat—by no means a descendant of Count Sàndor—none too securely anyhow. Stiassny seemed to know this, and sometimes I thought he was trying to embarrass me permanently. Ever since I had come into my relatives' home—or rather, ever since he had to watch me entering into a growing intimacy and familiarity there, a familiarity that was more and more taken for granted ("Like an epiphany," he said with a smile, baring his ruined teeth)—he treated me with a civility that was too exaggerated not to convey an impression of sheer irony to even the most impartial observer. "Lo and behold, the heir apparent!" he would say, rising ceremoniously, whenever I came into the room, and waiting until I took my place before he sat down again, leaning forward as though waiting assiduously to hear what I had to say. Such behavior was bound to confuse me as much as his always addressing me with "*Sie*," the polite form, even though Aunt Sophie rebuked him about this several times. Finally, Uncle Hubi could endure it no longer, and when he exclaimed, "You sound like a bunch of shop assistants!" Stiassny stopped. But then he switched to apostrophizing me in a respectful and impersonal tone —of course, no less ironic—with a general "one": "One looks like a painting by Philipp Otto Runge this morning! Need I bother asking whether one has slept well?"

I had no idea who Philipp Otto Runge was, but I could grasp the malice in the reference, even if it was just the malice of Stiassny's knowing how incapable I was of puzzling it out. He was equally aware of how strictly I had been trained to display attentive cordiality toward adults. It was impossible for me not to answer or instantly parry his civility with even more eager civility. It thus came to out-and-out contests of amenities, which occasionally assumed grotesque forms—for instance, the classic situation of a door at which each of us wanted to let the other pass first. Ultimately, Uncle Hubi or Aunt Sophie had to terminate our rivalry with an irritated "Would you please cut out your ceremonies! It's like blackcock-mating season!"

The first time Stiassny saw me in my makeshift student getup, his pale eyes sparkled with amusement, but then instantly faded. He bowed servilely: "Oh, I see! One is reliving the prime of life of our venerable uncle, our mutual generous host. This is lovely—an act of true piety! The reenactment of collective high spirits—this is ethical in the finest sense. Passing on the banner from generation to generation—one feels German! Of course, with innate generosity, one will overlook the fact that the venerable Herr

Uncle's mother was Hungarian and Frau Aunt Sophie, a cousin of one's mother—if I am not mistaken—has as much Irish as Rumanian blood in her veins; nay, on one's father's side, one would have to wend one's way to Sicily to bare the roots of our Germanhood. But then who am I to bring up such things! We are all of mixed blood, we Austrians, especially we so-called German Austrians: children of an imperium of diverse peoples, races, religions. If, that legendary imperium having disappeared, we did not still, comically enough, feel Austrian, then we would have to own up to being American . . . but we lack political insight for that. . . . Such is life, alas; thinking is often replaced by moods. They are more durable, they are livelier in withstanding time, and, in fact, the more irrational they are, the better. For instance, the German yearning, the yearning for the Reich, the sunken Roman Empire of the German Nation, of Charlemagne, or Karl the Great, as he is known in German, the empire over which Emperor Barbarossa fell asleep so profoundly in the Kyffhäuser mountains that his beard grew through the stone tabletop he leaned on . . . to restore this Reich, to reunite it afresh, to revive it in all its mystical power and glory . . . yes indeed! That was what German-speaking youth wanted a century ago, and it is still their dream and longing, no matter where or what they may be today, this German-speaking, German-thinking, German-feeling youth—on the Rhein, from the days of Armin the Cheruskan and his Roman adversaries, perhaps of largely Nubian and Libyan blood; or in the territories east of the Elbe and of course especially in the nuclear states of Bismarck's new edition of the Reich, mainly of Prussian and Finnish and Wendish blood; not to mention in the lands along the Nibelungen Danube, so close to one's heart, of Slovenian and Bohemian blood. . . . No matter: it feels German, this German youth, Imperial German, Greater German, *nicht wahr?* Wistfully they dream of themselves under the grand rolling of the black, red, and golden flag—that most youthful of all flags, the black of death and

26

the red of foaming blood and the gold of blissfully dreamt promise. . . . Verily, I confess myself deeply moved: who am I that I may live to witness such things! A young German, still wet behind the ears, if I may be permitted to express it thus, not yet a stripling, but still a lad—and already he is gaily garbed in the costume of the Wars of Liberation, of the epigones of the *Sturm und Drang*, of the constantly redreamed and ever-abortive German Revolution! I sense a German yearning here, in the mother country of Rumanian voivodes, between the Prut and the Seret rivers, surrounded by Rumanians, Ruthenians, Poles, and Galician Jews. And one is proudly heedless of any possibility that one might look ridiculous in a disguise suggesting Puss in Boots—how beautiful, too, this fidelity to the folk wealth of German fairy tales! . . . No, no, one need not be ashamed; one is right in every respect. Even this Kingdom of Rumania in which one lives today is still a slip and a shoot of the Great Reich—after all, this realm is ruled by a monarch from the House of Hohenzollern-Sigmaringen, a German prince. . . . Permit me to utter my unqualified admiration for such a candid expression of belief, one that sweeps aside any petty qualms of political tact! Nothing strikes me as more solemnly German than the steadfastness of this attempt, here of all places, to maintain the proper tone against Herr Uncle's eardrum-killing deviations while one roars *Lieder* to Frau Aunt's nimble-fingered piano-playing! 'Oh, Ancient and Fraternal Splendor'! 'The God Who Let Such Iron Grow'! Surely one is pierced by the same holy thrills that must have throbbed in the hearts of those who first sang those songs, those young Germans three or four generations ago, who in the songs recognized one another as brethren, and recognized the nation in the community of brethren, and saw in the nation the promise of freedom. . . . But, certainly, one also senses in these songs the pain and bitterness, the gloomy defiance and yearning, that afflict all emotionally exuberant youth. One recognizes oneself, presumably; one sees oneself in the spring tempests of this mood; one is probably uneasy with the sense that the burgeoning florescence could perish all too easily under a new frost. One also senses the martyrdom, the gallows humor in one's realization of frailty, the revolt in the defiant 'Nevertheless!' and the shriek of despair. . . . Yes, indeed, that is what it is, over and over: youth infects youth, and experiences itself as disease, as both foaming life and suffering; it sings its experience out into the world and foments the same rebellion in kindred souls. Everywhere and over and over, the yearning for the uniting, soul-uplifting, liberating flag. . . . If one were to be so kind as to visit me in the wretched chamber assigned as my abode thanks to the noble-mindedness of our host and hostess, then I would take the liberty of producing a small object from my modest collection: nothing more than a tiny piece of clay, baked and glazed a turquoise color—albeit several thousand years old, from the earliest days of Egypt. This ordinary thing has the shape of a T-square: one long and one very short side—a *tau*, as we know, of course. . . . Well, to make a long story short, it is the hieroglyph for the notion of god—the first abstract depiction ever of divinity. . . . And originally, it was nothing more than the likeness of a pole with a whisk of straw tied to it and moving in the wind—the first flag, as it were. . . ."

I sensed rather than grasped the perfidy in this speech. Still, the reference to being wet behind the ears and above all the image of Puss in Boots stuck in my mind, festered. I am certain it was Stiassny's allusion to my ludicrous bedizenment that aroused me.

One bright day, wearing my getup, plus the doddering rubber boots, with the fox major's cap on my head, I strolled from the safe preserve of the tower and the house, the garden and the courtyard, through the gates, and out into the village. I knew I would at least cause a stir; and though I did not exactly reckon with open hostilities, I was ready for them Of course, I had not dared to spirit one of Uncle Hubi's sabers off the wall and buckle it on, even though this weapon really belonged to the fraternity arms. But I had my dachshund Max along, my slingshot, and a good handful of lead pellets in my pocket. As expected, after the first dozen paces, I was encircled by a host of curious Jewish children, which increased into a larger and larger, more and more tumultuous swarm as more children came running.

I walked on, my head high, and started up the road to the marketplace. I did not have to show my scorn of the urchins, who danced around me, howling gaily; I ignored them just as when I sat in the coach, next to Uncle Hubi or Aunt Sophie or both of them, and the urchins scattered before the horses' hooves, and certainly when they fled from the Daimler and then ran around it in the yellow cloud of dust, trying to cling to the trunks strapped on in back.

In front of Dr. Goldmann's bizarrely turreted and merloned villa, someone blocked my path. He was the same age as I, if a bit smaller and thinner; while better dressed and evidently better bred than the others, he was as unmistakably Jewish. His ruddy, downy face, enfurred by wiry copper curls, was spotted with freckles. He looked like a young ram staring closely into a blazing fire. ("The sun," Stiassny said later, "it is the sun that the children of the Tribe of Levi contemplate!") But even more unforgettable than the stamp of this face, the look of a downright smug self-assurance lodged in my mind.

"What is it? Purim?" he asked, blinking when I stopped short in front of him in order—as I imagined—to stare him down and out of my way. I knew that Purim was some kind of Jewish Mardi Gras, with colorful masks and things. I found his question insolent but considered it beneath my corps dignity to reply. Totally unabashed, he raised his hand and touched the foxtail around my cap: "What are you? A Hasidic rabbi?"

Now I had to show him who I was: I struck his hand away. And as though the others were only waiting for a signal, they promptly attacked me on all sides. In a flash, my lovely cap was torn from my head, soon shredded to rags in a turmoil of lifted hands and a general howl of triumph. I could feel the sleeves of my mining jacket separate from the seams beneath the epaulets; a few blows struck me, but I hit back sharply and nastily, taking a more careful and ruthless aim than the chaotic and basically playful assault should have aroused. What made me feel so wretched was the ignominious failure of my dachshund Max. In lieu of defending me, of furiously snapping out around me like a Molossian dog, he withdrew behind me with a whine, and a good portion of the kicks and punches that were meant for me struck him. But to my utmost surprise, the red-headed boy threw himself protectively over the dog, even though my first punch had smashed into the middle of his face. "C'mon, you thugs!" he yelled in a mixture of German and Yiddish. "The dog didn' do nothin' to you!"

The turmoil stopped almost at once. Then a resounding clap drove the gang apart. Haller, the blacksmith, was coming from the brewery on his way home for lunch. When he merely struck his horny hands together, it sounded like gunshots. The street was instantly empty. Haller gave me an encouraging nod and went on. Only the red-headed boy remained. He had my dachshund in his arm. Max tenderly wagged his tail, trying to lick the boy's face. "Just look at the cute little puppy!" said the boy, scratching Max's creased forehead.

I was about to say, "He's a miserable coward!" But I did not care to denigrate my dog in front of the Jewish scamp. I said, "He's still too young to be fierce."

"Because he didn't wanna face odds of ten to one?" asked the red-headed boy. "He'd have to be as dumb as a goy—as you, maybe." He curled his upper lip, and his tongue tested the solidity of his front teeth. He looked even more fire-dazzled than before. "I think you knocked a tooth loose," he said. "If it falls out, you'll have to pay for a new one in gold. They don't grow back twice!"

"Put the dog down," I said. "He's not supposed to become a lapdog."

He gently placed the dachshund on the ground, but Max jumped up again, demanding to be petted some more. The boy fondled Max's head. "Well, what *is* he supposed to become?"

"A hunting dog."

"To hunt what? Butterflies?"

"Sure, butterflies," I said. "I could show you what he's already caught." I was thinking of the glass-covered case in the tower with the collection of extraordinarily beautiful tropical butterflies.

"Why don't you?" he asked. "Are you afraid I'll bring lice into your home? I am the son of Dr. Goldmann." He pointed at the neo-Gothic villa. "You can come to my house even if your butterfly hunter has fleas."

This was the start of a friendship that unfortunately was not to last very long; but it made that summer, in which so much happened, unforgettable in many ways.

First, I had to decide whether I should take the liberty of bringing Dr. Goldmann's son into my relatives' house. The problem was not so much that he was Jewish, but rather the social gap that separated Uncle Hubi and Aunt Sophie from the other residents of the village. I had particularly sensed their distinct reserve toward Dr. Goldmann. Normally, landowners were on friendly terms with the local physician: Uncle Hubi and Aunt Sophie did send their servants and employees to consult Dr. Goldmann about more serious illnesses, but in lighter cases, they tried to get along without him. Aunt Sophie treated these lighter cases herself, with advice from the local apothecary, a Pole, by whom she set great store. But Aunt Sophie and Uncle Hubi would not let Dr. Goldmann tend themselves, and their ironical way of presenting his house as a curiosity to new visitors indicated that there was some special reason for keeping their distance.

Whatever this reason might be or have been, I could tell myself that my kinfolk would have long since entered into social intercourse with Dr. Goldmann had they attached any importance to it. As for using my own discretion to interfere with such abeyant relationships, I knew the social structure of our provincial world was too delicate for that.

For example, I had once heard Stiassny say something that I took literally and no doubt more seriously than he might have meant it: another guest had remarked that Uncle Hubi, who had after all attended a university and finished his studies (albeit without gaining a degree), ought to be considered an academic; to which Stiassny had said, "It is part of the national tragedy of the Germans that their elite is divided into so-called academics and so-called intellectuals." It was clear that these were two hostile camps. Uncle Hubi had confirmed this himself when, flying into a passion at Stiassny, he exclaimed, "What annoys me most about these intellectuals is that they never come right out and say what they mean. It's like the artillery: they never aim directly at what they want to hit but instead aim somewhere else so that they'll hit the place they think they should. Just like Jews." And Aunt Sophie, as usual endorsing and interpreting what Uncle Hubert said, added (although Stiassny was her declared protégé), "Well, of course Hubi doesn't mean that all artillerists in the war were Jews, though if a Jew didn't find refuge in the medical service or the war office, he probably was in the artillery. But Hubi is right: you have to watch what Stiassny means when he carries on like that. And yet he's good-natured and also very poor."

In any event, the heroes and warriors of the tower, Uncle Hubi's good friends from the great hunting days, were indubitably of a different stripe. They had a respectful but decisive reserve even toward academics who were, they said, "professionally trained people such as physicians and lawyers and similar cerebral workers who are forced to live on the fruits of their thinking, not men who just playfully ventured into the boundless realms of knowledge," by which they meant amateurs like Uncle Hubi. And if someone was not only wildly different because an intellectual but on top of it also a Jew—and this was not rarely the case—then bridging the social gap was beyond all possibility. It was an established fact that Dr. Goldmann was a Jew and an intellectual. It even turned out that he maintained a lively intellectual exchange with Stiassny.

Nevertheless, I was bold enough to tell myself that the tower had been assigned to me as virtually unassailable digs, where I could entertain whomever I wished. So I told Dr. Goldmann's red-headed son that he could come and look at the butterfly collection. "By the way, what's your name?" I asked him.

He was called Wolf. My reaction to this name was mixed. On the one hand, I was glad that my new friend had a name that did not have to be embarrassing, like Moishe or Yossel. On the other hand, it did not strike me as quite proper for his name to be like that of a knight in a German heroic saga. He did, however, explain to me that Wolf was a rather common name among Orthodox Jews; his father's name was Bear. Bear Goldmann . . . I had to laugh. What was my name? my new friend Wolf asked. I had to admit that I was called Bubi. He began to giggle, as stupidly as the chambermaid Florica had giggled when she first saw me in my getup. "If you had a sister, would her name be Girlie?" Probably, I had to admit. "And your parents would be Manny and Wifey?" It took him a while to regain his composure.

He had a similar reaction to the tower when I proudly led him into it. "Why is this a tower?" he asked on the steps. And when we were upstairs: "This is a tower? Lemme show you a real tower." He pointed out the window, where the merloned roof of Dr. Goldmann's villa could be seen above the treetops. And, indeed, a beflagged turret loomed up. I had to admit to myself that I had often gazed at it, fretting at how much better the romanticism of that neo-Gothic house matched my German mood than the garret that had aroused it.

"Is your room in the tower?" I asked a bit apologetically.

"I'm gonna be dumb enough to shlep up the stairs?" Wolf retorted. "What do you think I am? A goy?"

It embittered me that he used the Yiddish word for "Gentile" to designate clumsy stupidity per se. I told myself it was probably normal usage in his world, and I was glad he felt relaxed enough with me to speak as though he were among his own. If he wanted to, he could speak proper German very well (he was attending school in Vienna), but he spoke it like something carefully rehearsed. He used his mixture of bad German with Yiddish and Polish—in a word, he "yiddled"—because this linguistic carelessness, rich in astute, colorful, and witty expressions, was more in keeping with his character, his swift, supple mind, and his unimpeachable self-confidence. I, for my part, had been trained in a rigorously correct speech, despite all the Austriacisms of my family, who among themselves spoke a kind of unbuttoned German; but they could also speak crystal-clear High German if they liked, and theirs did not sound rehearsed. I listened with amused attention to my new friend Wolf, gauging him linguistically.

He was almost bored when looking over the objects in my tower. True, his interest was briefly held by the case of butterflies, but I had anticipated a more explosive effect. He found the ivory skull anatomically wrong: his father had a genuine skeleton on which he could show me the mistakes. Coming to the ashtray with the modeled playing cards and cigarette butt, he shook his head, turning away with a shrug. In front of the Uhlan and Cossack skirmishes from Galicia he nodded. Even Count Sàndor's riding feats captured his attention only for a moment: "Was he a circus director?" he asked, moving on, without waiting for my answer.

He focused more thoroughly on Uncle Hubi's crossed sabers and "little keg." "Do you guys wear the little cap under the fox hats?" he wanted to know. No, I said, it was not like the *yarmulke*, the small black skullcap worn by Orthodox Jews under their hats (incidentally, for students who were not fox-majors, the hat was a colored cap with a visor, known as a "*couleur*"). The so-called "little keg" was worn as a sign of veteran fraternal dignity at festive drinking bouts. I became heated, flaunting the wealth of my newly acquired knowledge about the manners and mores of dueling clubs at German universities. I informed him that the new pledges were called "foxes" and they were under the care of the "fox-major"—the very brother who, as a sign of his dignity, could sport the headgear that reminded Wolf Goldmann of a rabbi's hat. And I launched into detail about the "beer commentary," the rigorously regulated ceremony of drinking, the so-called "boozing," an important educational procedure: after all, a man had to learn how to hold his quantum of liquor decently and without loss of bearing.

Wolf Goldmann listened to me with that grimace of a young ram staring into fire. "And you sing songs about the pretty blonde combing her hair over the Rhein rapids?"

Yes, indeed—he meant "The Lorelei." By the way, this was a poem by Heinrich Heine, who, as everyone knows, was a Jew, I added significantly. My words had no visible effect on him, and I was annoyed at my possibly making it seem that I was trying to get familiar with him in such a grossly goyish way.

"Is that why the G-clef is embroidered on the cap, because you guys sing?" he asked.

That was no G-clef, I told him, that was the so-called corps cipher. I unraveled the tangle of letters.

He nodded again. His blazing ram-face stayed earnest. "But the swords? If they're supposed to pierce, how come they have no points?"

I could inform him about that too: those were no swords, or sabers or épées, but light rapiers, used only in student duels. You didn't pierce with them, you fenced. Standing with legs astraddle, motionless, your body swathed to the ears in leather and cotton armor, one hand behind your back, you dueled with your other hand, likewise heavily swathed, lifting it over your head and aiming only at the opponent's skull and cheeks. If you struck in such a way that the rapier's edge cut into him, then the seconds interrupted the match and inspected the wound. The referee was asked to verify a "bloody" for either participant. When such "bloodies" were sewn up, their scars became the "cicatrices" which a German academic could be proud of. The duel consisted of fifteen rounds, each with a fixed number of exchanges. It was settled by the number of "bloodies," unless one "bloody" was so serious that the physician—the "barber-surgeon," as he was known in corps lingo—stopped the duel and declared the wounded party "disabled." It was not shameful to be "disabled." But woe to either of the duelers if, upon receiving a "bloody," he twitched even slightly or actually tried to withdraw—that is, evade the adversary's stroke with his head. If that happened, he was instantly suspended, put under "beer blackball" for the length of his suspension. He was not allowed to take part in any drinking session or wear the colors, namely the cap and the ribbon across his chest; and he was most certainly ostracized from the drinking bouts—all this until he had purged himself of his shame by fighting a new and more difficult match. But he was not granted such a chance for rehabilitation twice. If he chickened out a second time, then he was expelled. His erstwhile brothers cut him dead. He was no longer "qualified to give satisfaction."

To my surprise, Wolf Goldmann knew what that was. "They declared us Jews unsatisfactionable," he said.

I did not know what to reply. The issue of being qualified came up only if someone was challenged to a duel, I said evasively. Duels were mostly so-called "encounters" and not affairs of honor. They were tests of courage and toughness to determine a brother's grit. His decency was proved by the many scars he received.

Wolf Goldmann giggled: "Like Africans. But at least they carve pretty ornaments into their faces." Besides, I wasn't telling him anything very new, he said eventually. His father had belonged to a Jewish fraternity when he was a student—

36

one without the ridiculous rites of duels and beer commentaries, but organized for sheer self-defense. It seems that the Jewish students had been harassed so much by fraternity members that they too formed associations, responding to challenges with decisive combat readiness. Each of these Jewish fraternities featured one outstanding fencer who defended the assaulted honor of his brothers. And they did not fence with light rapiers against skulls and cheeks; they fought naked from the waist up with heavy sabers, and they were so nimble that these duels required true swordsmanship—a keen eye, quick wits, and agility. If a dueler was "disabled," then it was usually because of true inability. The nationalistic German fraternities preferred to avoid encounters with such master swordsmen. That was one of the reasons, said Wolf Goldmann with a grin, why Jews had been declared unsatisfactionable. His father had told him that. Dr. Goldmann himself had been featured as the best swordsman in his club.

"Are you going to learn how to fence too?" I asked.

"I'm not crazy," said Wolf Goldmann. "I need my hands for other things."

At that time, it was not yet apparent to me what he needed them for. In any event, he treated them with conspicuous care. The skills at which boys normally try to excel left him cold. I had presumed that he would not, like myself, attempt to emulate Count Sàndor on horseback; and indeed I hesitated to expect the stableboy to saddle a mount for a Jewish boy from the village. But Wolf showed no ambition in other respects: he did not climb trees, he made no effort to excel in throwing rocks, he did not idly whittle sticks, he did not shoot with a slingshot or a bow and arrow, he did not even whistle through his fingers. My dexterity in these disciplines (my talent with the slingshot had always impressed people) gave me no sense of superiority now; his indifference toward such matters was too great. In fact, I began to feel childish in front of him.

We established that we were of the same age, nearly to the

day. But his sophistication was so far ahead of my own that I had to admit reluctantly that while if I passed the ominous makeup examination in the autumn it might at best smooth the way to my becoming an academic, he indubitably was already a budding intellectual.

I continued to have qualms about bringing Wolf to my relatives' home, although I visited *his* home regularly. The treasures he had to show me there did not have the desired effect on me, either. He acted sulky for the first time. He was disappointed. But try as I might, I could not find anything homey in those dark, disorderly rooms filled with papers up to the ceilings. For all the *grand bourgeois* airs—the heavy black furniture, the plush upholstery, and the artfully draped and betasseled curtains of ribbed silk—there was something of the dubious and unventilated confinement of *petit bourgeois* homes. The furniture might have appealed to me (like all normal children, I tended toward bad taste), for these ornately carved wardrobes and sideboards, tables, and armchairs were in the old German style of the turn of the century, which did, after all, fit in with my leanings. Yet not only was the quality low, the wood stained, and the carving poor, but the pieces had been neglected, moldings were chipped, locks missing, and books, newspapers, and magazines were heaped upon every horizontal surface.

Wolf did tell me that extraordinarily valuable collector's items could be found in these piles. His grandfather's library, he said, had contained many first editions with personal dedications by the authors, some of which were now hard to come by. And his father had a priceless collection of documents on Jewish persecutions from the early Middle Ages to the most recent times. If anyone had the courage to take up this theme and write about it, said Wolf, he would find an inexhaustible and scientifically pure source here.

I did not like Dr. Goldmann. He had the same freckled flame-lit ram-head as his son, he was curt with me, and I was a bit afraid of his tremendous hands, which were spotted like salamander bellies and covered with lion-red hair. As for the memory of Grandfather Goldmann, I was biased. Uncle Hubi's gentle irony had had its effect.

It was owing to Stiassny that the grandfather had been mentioned at all. One day, I was surprised to run into Stiassny at the home of my friend Wolf Goldmann. Strangely enough, he acted as though he did not notice me. We—that is, Wolf and I—were about to cross the room leading to Dr. Goldmann's office. Since the doctor had usually been in the house when I was there, I had not yet viewed the skeleton that Wolf Goldmann had bragged to me about. We were going to see whether we could inspect it while Dr. Goldmann was out paying house calls. Stiassny stood in the room that led to the office. The room was a kind of library, if one could use that word in a house where every room was bursting with books. Stiassny was leaning over a couple of volumes on a table. He held a pencil in his teeth, his beautifully curved red lips curling into a smile I had never seen on him before—an utterly relaxed, slightly reflective, blissful smile. For the first time, I saw his face undisguised, and even his eyes did not have that veil of feigned blindness or at least sightlessness which they normally assumed when he lapsed into his repulsive role of "Who-am-I." And he really did not appear to see us now. He was totally absorbed in what he was reading and what he thought about it—or rather, was thinking—for his lips moved slightly as though repeating or framing a sentence; then he leaned again over the works on the table in front of him.

We automatically wheeled around and tiptoed out. "Is he here a lot?" I asked. He had been coming regularly for many years; he was practically more at home in Dr. Goldmann's than in my relatives' house. But I was certain that Aunt Sophie and Uncle Hubi scarcely knew about this or would not admit it. I did not expect that he would mention our encounter, especially since he had scarcely been aware of it.

I was all the more surprised when at the next meal he quite

demonstratively turned to me and said, again with the old blind gaze and ashen smile, "The development of our heir apparent is taking a delightful turn. One is abandoning one's defiant isolation. One is becoming sociable. Nay, even more: one is spanning bridges across social chasms, reestablishing relationships that were broken off or, regrettably, never taken up in the first place. This will not win applause in circles whose *Weltanschauung* and national sensibilities are shaped by the Kyffhäuser Association. Indeed, people sharing the convictions of the Schönerers and Wolffs might view it as an outright betrayal of the sacred cause of Aryan thinking. But then, who am I to point out that one thereby evinces all the more agreement with the ideas of Fichte and Jahn and other Church Fathers of the student fraternity movement: the ideas of the Scheidlers, Riemanns, Horns, and whatever their names may be, all the Armins and Germans, whose goal, in the mighty blaze of nationalism after the Wars of Liberation, was simply freedom and thus, needless to say, the emancipation of the Jews as well! Why, they too would have found it unendurable to have a Heine or Mendelssohn or Rachel Varnhagen in the ghetto, *nicht wahr? . . .*"

Aunt Sophie, who may have noticed Stiassny's unveiled malice against Uncle Hubi, came to her husband's aid as usual by employing the intellectual method of indirect allusion—or, to put it in artillery terms, an auxiliary target. "I don't think it's right of you to confuse the boy with things he can't possibly know," she said resolutely. "He's like us. He shouldn't have so much muddled stuff in his head, like you. The boy should keep acting on his unspoiled feelings; then everything will be all right."

The last sentence was both an encouragement for me and a tender admonition for Uncle Hubi not to let the sentimental remnants of his nationalistically inspired past move him to object to my friendship with young Goldmann, which, needless to say, was by now common knowledge in the house. But Uncle Hubi, accustomed to far heftier allusions to the extravagances of his formative years, would not be jolted so easily out of his bright-eyed, bushy-tailed good mood, especially since, after all, most of his mockers ultimately agreed with him when it came to anti-Semitism. He gleefully said, "Oh, if old Goldmann had lived to see this—too funny, really too funny!"

This launched a conversation to which everyone at the table had something to contribute because the topic was local events and the old local gossip, a conversation that explained my relatives' aloofness from Wolf's family but that also quite extraordinarily complicated my image of Germanhood.

"Old Goldmann," grandfather of my friend Wolf and father of the physician Dr. Bear Goldmann, came from Galicia, in what had once been Russia. Tradition had it that he was the black sheep among the offspring of one of the erudite and extremely God-fearing rebbes who had their courts there. "Administrators of justice in all moral and religious issues," said Stiassny, "akin to the Holy Sheikh of Sufism, who, incomprehensibly, is studied by so many religious scholars and blue-stockinged countesses seeking the experience of God—indeed studied far more intensively than these troubadours of God, who are much closer to us and more germane to our own thinking and feeling."

Old Goldmann did not seem to have mustered the proper esteem for the rebbes' faithful ardor and visionary rapture. He had not observed the ancient custom of following in the footsteps of his father, who stood in the odor of sanctity; instead, he rebelliously declared himself a freethinker and moved to Germany, where, highly musical himself, he had been entranced to the point of ecstasy by Richard Wagner's music. On the side, he made a fortune (piquantly enough, in slaughterhouses), with which fortune ("Like many of his people—far more than anyone would care to presume or willingly admit," said Stiassny) he had helped to subsidize Bismarck's founding of the Reich. "Being both self-sacrificing and profit-making, I dare say," Uncle Hubi threw in, and he was seconded by Aunt Sophie: "Well, Hubi's right in this point. If there's one thing the Jews know how to do it's make money!"

There was uncertainty about when old Goldmann had come to the village to settle down at cattle-dealing, in an agriculturally prosperous region, and to build his "ridiculous show-off villa." Stiassny claimed he had come only when, in stormy allegiance to Nietzsche, he defected from Wagner; disillusioned by Bismarckian autocratism, he had turned his back on Germany. But this was contradicted by the flagrantly pro-German style of his house, a style which, appearing in a Habsburg crownland and introduced by a Jew, was bound to look rather curious. It *was* certain, in any event, that this had not met with the approval of Uncle Hubi's father, an ultraconservative Old Austrian who was almost religiously faithful to Kaiser Franz Josef and who, in the aura of his monarch's divine right, played the role of a patriarch here, outstripping Bismarck's autocratism by many laps. A Jew carrying on like a German nationalist must have struck the Old Austrian as an absurd blend of two incompatible, albeit equally repulsive, antitheses, a monstrosity so provoking that it would be best to ignore it altogether, simply to deny it out of the world so as not to be challenged by it. "Poor Papa did have his grief with me over that," Uncle Hubi had to confess, shamefacedly—although once again he got instant protective help from Aunt Sophie, who said, "But you were very young at that time, Hubi—just when was it?! Around 1889, 1890, or so, before we even met. You could hardly expect to do anything sensible at that time. Why, you'd just turned eighteen, since you're going on fifty-eight today."

Despite certain references made by my father, I had, in those days, only very nebulous ideas about Nietzsche, Bismarck's founding of the Reich and his antiliberal tendencies, and the repugnance felt by ultramontane Old Austrians toward German nationalists. Still, I realized there was an odd to-and-fro of pros and cons here, a bizarre exchangeability of contrasting attitudes and positions, with the hostilities becoming sharpest whenever one side took over dogmas from the other. Old Goldmann must have experienced this too closely for comfort. He had sent his son, Wolf's father, to Vienna and Prague to study what he himself had been unable to study thoroughly: the humanities, which, in his opinion, led to the spiritual liberation of a man and thereby to the freedom of all mankind. This son, so favored by destiny, had come back a dry-as-dust physician. The only other thing he had brought home from those old and venerable universities was a hate-filled distaste for his father's gushy Teutomania. He proclaimed himself a Zionist, a stubborn advocate of a Jewish national state in the Promised Land; and, to support this enthusiasm, he began to collect documents about the persecutions of Jews. All this to the bitter sorrow of old Goldmann, who had ardently striven all his life for the complete assimilation of the Jews in an enlightened world of liberty, equality, and fraternity. In the name of humanity, therefore, he wanted them to withdraw from all political, national, or religious fanaticism. This withdrawal, he felt, must be the goal of those especially who for two thousand years had been the victims of such fanaticism.

Stiassny became so animated that he completely dropped his usual disgusting servility, showing the best traits of his character. His face aglow with beauty, he proceeded with his explanation of the progressive views which old Goldmann, repelled by the iron-devouring nationalism of Kaiser Wilhelm's Reich, had wanted to bring into this heartland of ethnic and religious diversity. Goldmann had hoped to find fertile soil for his civilizing gospel here, in the atmosphere of an old imperial administration whose aim and goal should have been to keep a variety of creeds, languages, national characters, and ethnological habits in peaceful togetherness. But when Stiassny added that one might in fact try to understand the Bismarckian romanticism of Goldmann's mansion in these terms, he relapsed into his ironical "But-who-am-I." With faded eyes and the smile of a man who has eaten ashes, he explained that Goldmann's house could not be regarded purely and simply as an expression of Jewish presumption, the insolence of a go-getter who had grown rich much too quickly and by devious means. It was not the arrogance of a Jewish upstart, he insisted, using newly acquired wealth to don the robes of patrician respectability. No, indeed; those turrets and balconies, those pennons and weathercocks, actually expressed a yearning for universal chivalrous justice, which the people who might have passed it on from generation to generation had long since traded in for flat-footed bourgeois philistinism.

In his freshly ventilated good mood, Uncle Hubert was immune to this jibe too. Modest by nature, he never put himself forward in conversation even if he had something to say; on the contrary, he had to be prodded by Aunt Sophie with a "Well, Hubi, why don't you tell us what you think!" But once he began to talk, he did so with a dry humor that testified to his acute powers of observation and was far more effective than Stiassny's curling, abstract arabesques. And this time too, Uncle Hubert's sense of humor had its effect.

In a few terse sentences, he evoked the celebration that had taken place in the village in 1893, on the occasion of the forty-fifth anniversary of Kaiser Franz Josef's accession to the throne; he described the comical events that were bound to occur in a popular festival officially arranged in an East European Gotham: the confusion during the parade of the volunteer firemen, with the token Jew, his helmet sliding down over his crooked nose and his trousers over his knees; the dreadfully off key band; the mindless speech given by the sweaty mayor in a borderland German that distorted everything; the Alliance of Maidens dressed in white, eliciting ribald remarks from the boys; and so on and so forth. Uncle Hubi's father, being, as it were, the local deputy of His Apostolic Majesty, was showered with tributes, and, imbued with the responsible dignity of this vicariate, he likewise doled out honors. Having just accomplished the chore of bestowing a medal, he was about to betake himself to the town hall, followed by the clergy and the notabilities, past school classes and associations—when old Goldmann blocked his path. I pictured the scene in which Wolf Goldmann had blocked my path the day I had ventured out on my abortive excursion in fraternity gear: I imagined the same fiery ram-face and the same unimpeachable self-confidence. He was no longer brand-new in the village, old Goldmann. His bepennoned red-brick castello had been adorning the townscape for some time now. He himself, however, because of his eccentric *Weltanschauung*, had not even made contact with the Jewish community, much less any of the other religious, ethnic, or social grouplets. Now, he felt, the moment had come for him to break out of this isolation. After all, they *were* celebrating the forty-five-year reign of a patriarch of nations, under whose broad-minded fatherliness any race, nation, and religion, of any spirit and character, had found protection.

Uncle Hubi could not stifle a titter when recollecting this historic encounter. "Well, I can still see Papa peering at the Jew with his fat woman behind him, and the Jew sticking out his hand and saying, 'Excuse me, Herr Baron, but may I introduce myself on this solemn occasion: Goldmann's the name, Saul Goldmann. The Herr Baron may perhaps not have overlooked the fact that I settled here some years ago, and here in this community, to which I desire to belong in every way, I have erected my house. . . .' Now he yiddled a bit—not a lot, mind you, but just enough, something you can't get rid of altogether if you come from darkest Galicia. And when he said 'house,' it sounded like 'trousers,' and Papa, well, he turned around to the mayor and asked him, 'What did he erect in his trousers?' And then on he went, leaving the Jew standing there with his woman and his dumb face and his hat on his chest and his crooked legs and the pointed, turned-up clodhoppers . . ."

As usual, Aunt Sophie confirmed this tableau: "Well, that's very true, he was no beauty, really, old Goldmann, with his carroty hair, even if he'd made millions like

Rothschild. Yes, Hubi's quite right. His wife wasn't much better either, and at least twice as fat."

So far, I had formed no notion whatsoever of the women in the Goldmann home. Mention of old Goldmann's wife, my friend Wolf's grandmother, was the first time I realized that females must indeed have existed there. I vaguely recalled seeing a photograph among the scores heaped on the Goldmanns' piano; but it had not occurred to me that this could be Wolf's mother. A few days later, when Aunt Sophie extracted a letter to Stiassny from the morning mail and asked me to bring it up to his room, I saw the same portrait in a silver frame on Stiassny's desk. It was a regular face, almost too long, framed by a severe pageboy bob, with the expressive lips and soulful gaze that were typical in the era of the waning *Jugendstil*. Before it dawned on me that this was the same face I had seen on the piano at the Goldmanns', I had assumed it was an actress admired by Stiassny. Now, she began to interest me. "Who's that?" I asked Wolf about the photograph in his home at the next opportunity. "My birth-giver," he said without the least sign of emotion.

I was not sure I had correctly understood him. "You mean your mother?"

"Who else? A second father?"

"Is she dead?" I asked, a bit unsteadily.

"God forbid! Why should she be dead?"

"I've never seen her here."

"Divorced, of course. She lives in Vienna. Head ceramicist of the Wiener Werkstätten there."

"Stiassny must have admired her. He has her picture on his desk."

"Yes," said Wolf casually. "I think he was one of her lovers. The most famous was Peter Altenberg."

I did not know who Peter Altenberg was; in any case, I was shocked by the way my friend spoke about his mother.

"Do you ever see her?" I asked.

"When I'm in Vienna," he said imperturbably, then

turning fidgety in his way. "Anyway, you have to go now. I've got to work."

This was not the first time that he abruptly terminated our time together with the same explanation—usually, so it appeared to me, when some naïveté on my part enervated him. I could hardly ignore these moments—and this was why I did not ask what work he had to do. It could hardly be homework now, during vacation; nor, I felt, was it likely that he had a makeup examination ahead of him, as I did. What little he let on about his school in Vienna suggested that it was a thoroughly modern institution with a curriculum far too intimidating for me to ask about, but easy for him to keep up with. Anyway, I knew it was useless to hold him back when he claimed he had to work. I had quickly given up trying, and I ultimately profited from his firmness by going back to the tower out of sheer boredom and sitting down to my schoolwork, with my dachshund Max, highly satisfied, at my feet.

Sometimes, of course, I did not much care to spend any more time with Wolf Goldmann. His smug self-assurance hurt my feelings; and he was so relentlessly prosaic that he often seemed trivial. For example, that someone could talk so scornfully about his own mother as the mistress of a man who was not his father (and not just one but several such men!) repelled me—like Stiassny's ashen smile, which normally prefaced a remark that destroyed an illusion I had unthinkingly cherished. And although at the same time I was fascinated, this kind of attitude went against my grain, compelling me to question everything I had believed in. Now I resolved to do nothing to abolish the gap placed between me and young Goldmann by the fact that he had never been allowed into my uncle's home. Nonetheless, this situation changed quite unexpectedly, and of its own accord.

One of the few things with which I might have impressed my blasé friend was Uncle Hubi's Daimler—a car that was bound to quicken the pulse of any boy. Its paint-and-shining-chrome perfection, the clarity of its angles and proportions, its momentous solidity on the heavy, elephant-colored rubber tires, were undeniably erotic, something quite missing from today's assembly-line products. But Wolf Goldmann, seemingly unmoved, said, "What's so great about a car? My father could buy one too, if he felt like it. But that would be pretty crazy with the roads we've got here." He was not so wrong; the car usually stood in the locked section of the coach house, and we used the carriages far more often. Seldom did Uncle Hubert and Aunt Sophie drive the car to Czernowitz, much less to Bucharest. Still, Wolf could not deny that he too felt the sensual pull of the vehicle; it was a symbol of distinction and wealth, and, like a winged steed or flying carpet in a fairy tale, it granted power over space and time.

Geib, the butler, who functioned as the chauffeur for drives to the city, did not like us climbing around the Daimler, turning the wheel, and beeping the balloon horn, which in those days was attached to the outside; and he was reluctant to hand us the key to the locked part of the carriage house. He and Haller, the blacksmith, tinkered incessantly with the engine and the body of the car, which sparkled like new and functioned as though it had rolled out from the factory only yesterday on its maiden trip: Uncle Hubi insisted on its being kept in this condition. But I had discovered that the wall separating the garage from the coach house gave on to the hayloft, and from a skylight up there you could at least peer into the garage. Thus, if we did not feel like asking Geib for the key, we would clamber up to the hayloft over the stalls, creep along until we got to the skylight, stretch out in front of it, and have a good view down at the Daimler, whose technical features and merits we discussed at length. The horn on the car door bothered Wolf; he found it antiquated. And so for fun I took my slingshot and aimed at the rubber balloon; the sharp impact of the lead pellet made the copper horn beep short and loud. Geib, who happened to be nearby, quickly unlocked the garage door, came in, and carefully examined the entire automobile, more and more perplexed and puzzled as to who had honked.

This turned into a game, which entertained us as much as the slapstick scenes from Buster Keaton or Harold Lloyd comedies, which were all the rage then. If we knew that Geib or Haller was in the vicinity, I would shoot at the balloon, the honk inevitably summoned one or the other, and he would unlock the garage and comb every nook and cranny for the mysterious force that made the horn beep. Meanwhile, we lay well concealed behind the skylight, trying to choke back our mirth. When the fruitless investigation was abandoned and the garage locked up again, I would take another shot and the mystification would begin anew.

Once, though, Haller found one of my lead pellets, which he was familiar with because I cast them in his smithy. He put it in his pocket, and for a while we held back on our joke, waiting rather anxiously for the sequel. But nothing happened, and we resumed our mischief. I became so audacious, especially with old Geib, that I would shoot at the horn a second time the instant he turned away from the car, so that the blare at his back made him whirl around, as though the car were about to start by itself, honking at him to get out of the way.

Old Geib's naïveté was an inexhaustible source of amusement for us. Haller had probably forgotten to tell him about his discovery, or else he was waiting a bit maliciously to see whether Geib could figure out the weird goings-on. But Geib kept on being misled by us, as though he were hanging puppetlike on the strings of our despotism. It was incomprehensible that he did not notice the pellets bouncing around —whether because of the resounding shriek of the horn or an excessive zeal to expose the mystery I cannot say. He tried to outwit the self-activating horn, deliberately turning his back on it to wait, listening paralyzed, with rolling eyes, until the next shriek, then whirling around half triumphantly, and again seeing nothing but the empty Daimler. Slowly he brought his ear to the radiator hood and the upholstery, auscultating them with bated breath, finally crawling under the chassis, only to come writhing out as though stung by a tarantula, because, needless to say, I had shot at the horn again. Eventually, I felt almost sorry for the poor man. Lost in thought, he stood with dangling arms and then stormed out of the garage cursing, locking the door whether or not the horn tooted again.

Naturally, this game could not go on forever. One day, as Geib stood brooding, half turned away from the car, I shook my head wordlessly, refusing to take aim even though Wolf Goldmann poked me in the ribs, egging me on. I must admit that I made little effort to stop him when he finally took the slingshot from my hand, picked up one of the pellets which I had placed in front of me, inserted it into the loop, drew the powerful elastic taut, and shot.

I assumed he would not hit the target. But he was so wide of the mark that the pellet struck the middle of the windshield. The glass shattered in a narrow cobweb of cracks around a core of gravelly splinters.

Now, it was almost impossible for Geib not to discover us at our skylight. Even though we tried to scramble away behind the barn wall, he quickly spotted us and shouted and it was useless to hide. Shamefaced, we climbed down the ladder he had put up to get to us. "I'd like to tell Uncle Hubert myself that it was me," I said to him—less out of generosity than because I knew it would make our iniquity more forgivable if I were the wrongdoer rather than the Jewish boy from the village. "I'm sorry," I said to Geib. "I didn't mean to break anything."

But I had reckoned without Wolf. "What are you?" he snapped. "My guardian? Are you totally *meshuggeh*?" His ram-face was as red and twisted as if he were holding it very close to a strong fire. "Get a load of the goyish heroism! What's the big deal, a piece of glass! My father'll pay for it."

"You just explain that to his lordship!" said Geib, and took his arm.

"Hands off or I'll scream till the whole village comes

running!" said Wolf Goldmann. "You think I won't go on my own? I'm scared maybe? *Oy gevalt!*" He swiftly took the lead, heading straight for my relatives' house.

In the salon, where Geib had us wait, Wolf broke into giggles again: "The horns!" He pointed at the hunting trophies on the wall. "If I were you people, I wouldn't hang them up so publicly."

I did not understand what he meant. I did not know the figurative meaning of horns or what he was alluding to. But I felt as if I were seeing them all for the first time: the menacingly lowered horns and antlers of doe and stag and chamois all around us, the stuffed wood grouse with fanned-out tails, and the shiny razors of wild boar. Never before had I sensed the barbarity that dragged such Stone Age flaunting of power and ability into the twentieth century. At the time, of course, this was more a feeling than a thought I could verbalize. Nor did I have any chance to reflect upon it, for my friend Wolf had discovered Aunt Sophie's grand piano, and he emitted an appreciative whistle through his teeth. "A genuine Bösendorfer! What's it doing here?"

He opened the lid and struck one or two chords; then, without turning around, he pulled the piano stool over with his foot, sat down, and began to play—with a virtuosity that took my breath away.

Uncle Hubert apparently was not at home, and Geib had got hold of Aunt Sophie to call us wrongdoers to account. She entered, halted in the middle of the room, waited until the *Wunderkind* Goldmann had finished playing, then walked toward him, and said, "You do that very well. How long have you been playing and whom are you studying with?" She used an old-fashioned form of "you" which was generally reserved for inferiors.

Wolf Goldmann did not even go to the trouble of turning his head toward her. "Chopin always makes an impression on laymen," he said over his shoulder. "At the moment, I'm working on Brahms."

He struck a few measures, but paused, closed the lid, swung around on the revolving stool, and looked freely into Aunt Sophie's eyes: "I smashed the windshield on your car."

"I know," said Aunt Sophie. "But first, stand up and say good day properly; then we can go on with our conversation."

"Formalities," said Wolf with a theatrical sigh, but he did get to his feet. And to my amazement, Aunt Sophie laughed and said, "You will have to learn them all the same. And now, answer my questions. How long have you been playing and whom are you studying with?"

I was subsequently to make the acquaintance of a new feeling I had never known before: jealousy born of envy. It was ugly, it inspired all sorts of nasty thoughts and wishes, and, if it did not piercingly drive me to self-torment, it left me with an empty soul which was again invaded by that hazy and urgent yearning: *skushno*.

Aunt Sophie developed a true passion for young Goldmann. He was in the house every day; no sooner had we finished our second breakfast than he was sitting at the grand piano in the salon, and he practiced all morning, during which time everyone—aside from myself—was busy elsewhere. At midday, he vanished but was back again in the early afternoon, and he played until Aunt Sophie had finished her daily rounds. Then, when she had changed for the evening and appeared in the salon with the glowing face of a woman happy in love, on went the stormy tumult of the notes. Occasionally she would intervene to demonstrate an interpretation of her own, but mostly she would drop her hands and say, "Of course, I'm completely out of practice!" It sounded pious, as if she were illuminated by the promise that this boy had outdistanced her in order to achieve far greater things than she could ever have done. Almost blushing, with the happy self-renunciation of a lover, she added, "I only wanted to show you how I'd heard Liszt play this when I was a girl."

It was obvious even to me, a thirteen-year-old, that all the wishes, dreams, and hopes of her youth, buried for a lifetime, had gained new, tangible, blood-warm life in this red-haired boy. And when Uncle Hubi's eyes met mine or mine his, they clearly mirrored his regret at losing the familial unity and intimacy of our stirring national song soirées—losing them to something with a loftier status than our heartfelt musical bungling but which left us out entirely. Beyond this, however, we were bound by manly agreement not to interfere with Aunt Sophie, indeed, to strengthen and assist her and perhaps at some point protect her from herself. And at such times, of course, we could read in the other's gaze physical disgust at the Jewish brat, who had managed "insidiously" (as the ironical Stiassny was to put it), "by utilizing the blandishments of Aryan tonal art," to throw off balance this exemplary, warmhearted, prudent woman who stood so solidly in life.

It was almost uncanny to sense Stiassny watching me, to sense all he seemed to know about my feelings—and not just Stiassny, either, but just about everyone in the house, with the old butler Geib in the lead, except for Aunt Sophie, who was blind to everything. Bizarre scenes, whose tension was virtually woven from the resonance of the events, kept everyone fascinated, yet not the two oblivious protagonists at the center, Aunt Sophie and Wolf Goldmann, "the lovers."

Occasionally, for example, intense practice of a single passage would drag on even though Geib had long since announced dinner, and he would stand at the door to the dining room while Uncle Hubi tactfully inserted little coughs in the pauses during the tempest of sound, or ultimately almost whined, "Sophie, dinner's been ready for almost half an hour." But his efforts were in vain. All of us, even Stiassny, were under something like a spell, which weighted down our movements and gave each look so much meaning that no one dared glance at anyone else.

The mood would intensify until Aunt Sophie finally observed that it was enough for today; then she would turn to Geib and say impatiently, "Isn't dinner ready yet?" And when Geib answered that it was probably being warmed up for the second time, she would rejoin, "Set a place for young Goldmann!"

Uncle Hubi ventured to ask casually one evening, "Wouldn't it be easier if he just moved right in?" Predictably, he was supported by Aunt Sophie, though a bit absentmindedly and mechanically: "Well, that's quite true, it would be simpler. Why, Hubi's absolutely correct!" And we all stood and waited to see Aunt Sophie placing her arm around Wolf Goldmann's frail shoulders and leading him into the dining room, while we, lowering our heads under the stag antlers along the walls, followed the woman and the boy, intensely aware of the symbolism and its justified ludicrousness.

Stiassny, of course, was in his element. His colorless eyes watched Geib pushing the chair under Aunt Sophie and promptly coming over to show me the same attention. Then, while serving, Geib saw to it that Aunt Sophie did not fill the plate for Wolf, who was sitting next to her—"I'll serve him myself; it's easier!"—which would have left me waiting at the lower end of the table. Instead, Geib made sure to serve all the others, and myself, with special care and a discreet nod to the juiciest piece, until it was finally the "little Jew"'s turn. Stiassny's beautiful lips then parted in his most ashen smile: "May I offer my congratulations. The loyal vassals have not all defected as yet. The ferment of decomposition has not yet eaten its way through." He laughed, and Uncle Hubi shushed him, blurting out, "Stiassny, I find that rather distasteful!"

The old intimacy of kinfolk between Uncle Hubi and myself now grew into a friendship—the lucid and autumnally rich friendship of a boy and an old man, the kind that is cleansed of the passions between people of the same age and entirely given to perceptive kindness and unconditional trust. He took me on outings—inspections in the brewery and the nurseries—and the invitations were ostentatiously proffered whenever Aunt Sophie commented that it was our duty to do everything in our power to enable a genius like young Goldmann to have the best possible training. She declared that she agreed completely with his father, Dr. Goldmann, that it would be a crime to put the boy wonder, who was ready to perform, before an audience now; they should do all they could to foster his personal maturation as well as the development of his virtuoso abilities. To be sure, she did not go so far as to make contact with Dr. Goldmann himself, but used Stiassny to inform the father of her views, aims, and decisions regarding young Goldmann.

Aunt Sophie's designs for educating a genius, which were occasionally communicated to us, too, with poignant eagerness, would prompt Uncle Hubi to turn to me pointedly and ask, "Are you coming out to the farm with me? I have to check something about the sheep. I think they're driving them regularly into the new preserve by the river." And then, quite uncharacteristically, he would address Aunt Sophie tangentially, so to speak, as she sat at the breakfast table, wrapped in thought and spreading honey on her roll. "I don't think we'll be back for lunch," he said. "We'll eat out with the steward Stiassny will most likely say that we need have no illusions about the gap that we'll be leaving—*nicht wahr*, Stiassny?"

I loved riding out to the farm, and not only because it was conducive to my training as Count Sàndor's emulator. I would listen attentively to all of Uncle Hubi's tips and pointers, which he would illustrate by anecdotes; having spent his life on horseback, and being an old cavalry officer, he had made riding an ideology, the metaphor of a way of life, and despite his pyknic constitution, he was an excellent horseman. But beyond all this, I was very satisfied when I said to myself that the sight of the two of us riding through the village must have made an impact on the street urchins, the boys who had been about to humiliate me when Haller, the blacksmith, saved me from them as from a swarm of flies. Now they had to be convinced of the power behind me, which someday I myself would represent and embody.

For it was more and more obvious that Uncle Hubi intended to make me his successor. He began systematically to integrate me into the circle of his chores, duties, and activities. And, needless to say, it was once again Stiassny who could not help putting this situation into words.

"I have recently seen a little color in one's cheeks, which has caused me some worry about one's honorable state of health," he said. "Could this possibly come from one's now growing seriously into one's role of heir apparent? I mean, it appears no longer as a fiction, as a carefully considered possibility and hallucination, but instead has finally found the concrete relationship of function. One is learning one's future métier, *nicht wahr?* One is being confirmed in one's task, albeit for the moment only by holding the horses of one's predecessor in the chain of inherited duties, and whisking away the flies from those selfsame horses with a leafy twig, while Herr Uncle has his hours of chitchat with the steward about the situation and how to improve it. But still and all, one *is* present, one *does* listen, one is initiated and instructed. Why, that *must* strengthen one's self-esteem, mustn't it? Or am I mistaken? But then who am I to know of such matters? Still, the groom will one day be a cavalier and landowner, just as the squire becomes a full-fledged knight. Perhaps one no longer feels so utterly rejected and excluded from the loftier status that attaches our honorable hostess to young Goldmann. One is strengthened by the notion of becoming something definite, however different from and less spectacular than what one's more gifted friend is through his piano-playing. One must admit, of course, that what *he* is doing is quite extraordinary. But this very perfection, *nicht wahr*, this ruthless perfection that mercilessly excludes and degrades whatever is not equally consummate, making anything of middle rank a blasphemy—this very perfection has something cold and hard-hearted about it, something relentlessly and repulsively self-righteous. People talk so much about the demonic nature of the artist—yet that which strikes us as demonic is nothing else than this repulsiveness, the unconditional and absolute, together with the profound attraction exerted upon us by perfection. If I am expressing myself not altogether intelligibly (after all, as we know, I am considered a muddled orator in this house): that which one is to become and perhaps is already becoming, thanks to our Herr Uncle's kindhearted intention, namely a good, solid husbandman, is certainly not of the same rank as an artist; but, by way of compensation, it is more human, more outgoing, more universal. One becomes something that previous generations have been—nothing out of the ordinary, to be sure, but with a self-conception and a self-confidence that are painfully lacking in the artist. Whereas one need only be what one is, upright and modest, he, the artist, is committed to self-realization at every instant. He must act in order to be what he is, and by thus acting he challenges and tests himself anew, risking his existence. His life is an incessant gamble—and most especially when, as one's Frau Aunt maintains, he is a budding genius, an extraordinary individual; but, alas, he is these things in a wild isolation, which makes him an outsider to society. In contrast, it must be very agreeable—nay, downright inspiring—to know that one is unproblematically one of many similar beings in a safe, tried-and-true species, in the simple, unimpeachable existence of a farmer and—with a correspondingly venerable and traditional prosperity—an aristocrat."

These words sounded comforting and eased my mind, since it was beyond me to figure out the provocation that Stiassny, with his wonted perfidy, must have inserted. For a while, I more calmly accepted Wolf Goldmann's greater claim to my aunt's attention and—I had reason to fear—affection. I forced myself to act toward him with that chivalrous generosity which guards the aristocrat against the ignominy of being resented; and I acted as though our friendship were not the least bit changed or even strained. Once, when I asked him to interrupt his morning practice briefly to come and see a nest of young owlets in the hayloft above the stables, he snapped: "Go tell your grandmother about your stupid owlets!" But when, with unassailable aristocratic equanimity, I rejoined that he had not practiced around the clock in earlier days, he said, "You just don't know what it means, playing your Bösendorfer instead of the old crate at home!" (To my surprise, he used a clear and proper German before relapsing into his sloppily impudent yiddling.) "Maybe you can see it this way: it's like getting off that old gray nag biting the dust out there, and then mounting one of the fiery mustangs from your cowboy-and-Indian stories. Ya see? You goyim have to have everything translated into zoology before you understand it. Like your uncle, when he explains your master brewer's psychology in terms of a horse that's been ridden to death. You goyim know more about animals than people."

I could have hit him, I was so indignant. Showered with blessings by Aunt Sophie and taken into the house like her own child, he was still disdainfully labeling us "goyim," undisguisedly expressing how stupid and clumsy he considered us all. He noticed my response and he gave me a brazen grin: "Your aunt would like it if I became one of you, right? She's given me Rilke to read: 'Riding, riding, riding, through the day, through the night . . .' I should live so long. *I'm* reading Krafft-Ebing. Now, he could help you. He might explain what your uncle really wants when he keeps riding out with you, beyond the farm and deeper and deeper into the forest."

Wolf himself eventually explained it to me. Not only was Uncle Hubert suspected of homosexuality, but people had ideas about him and his friends, the rough hunting buddies who moved into the tower during the winter, those "last heroes and warriors" of a free, virile, wind- and-weather-beaten world of peril and daring. It was generally accepted that his friendships were relationships of homoerotic love,

58

and my friendly, good-natured, apple-cheeked kinsman was the laughingstock of the town, which viewed his well-rounded behind as the very symbol of sexual deviance. What about his model marriage with Aunt Sophie? Was I really so naïve as I seemed? exclaimed Wolf; didn't I know what to make of Stiassny's presence in the house for all these decades? What else was Aunt Sophie's spiteful refusal to have anything to do with his father, Dr. Goldmann, but an act of revenge? There was an ever-festering memory that the doctor's wife, my friend Wolf's mother, had had an affair with Stiassny. "You goyim always try to act like you ain't got no *potz* and your women ain't got no cunt between their legs," said Wolf.

I cannot describe the profound repugnance I felt during the next few weeks, not only toward Wolf Goldmann but toward just about everyone. Not even Haller, the blacksmith, was excluded, ever since Wolf had told me that Dr. Goldmann had once sewn up a serious injury on Haller's penis, a wound obviously made by human teeth and hardly by a woman inept in such amorous practices but, rather, in a passionate action by a man upon the member of the disciple of Hephaestus and the German descendant of Wieland. I almost threw up the next time I went into the smithy to cast lead pellets for my slingshot. Holding out his callused palm with the pellets he had found in the garage, Haller winked and asked, "What do I get for keeping my mouth shut the other day?" Wolf Goldmann had explained that sexual perverts regard boys our age as downright tidbits.

I was homesick. I missed my mother. Her sickly, high-strung sentimentality might be disquieting; but her feelings were probably deeper and steadier than those of her older and more robust cousin, who, however, was obviously no less rapturous, no less susceptible. Although repelled by the thought, I told myself that an encounter between my mother and Stiassny would have led to an incomparably more passionate and more poetic relationship than—if I were willing to believe Wolf Goldmann—the one between

Stiassny and Aunt Sophie. Nonetheless, everything in me rebelled against the idea that my mother could lie in Stiassny's arms and that I could speak about her and her lover as unabashedly as Wolf did. Now my hotheaded father's somber passion for hunting became the escapism of an absolutely pure and noble man who preferred the loneliness of the raw universe of mountains to the filth of the lowlands. I myself wanted to withdraw from the world's dubious hustle and bustle. I spent a lot of time in the tower, working on the syllabus for my makeup examination.

For the sake of old friendship, which was going to end anyhow the day we went to different schools, I once more followed Wolf Goldmann to his home. His father was out for the day, making calls in nearby villages, so we had all the time we wanted to look at his office undisturbed. Finally I had a chance to have a good look at the famous skeleton: it struck me as sinister because its bones were so shiny I couldn't believe they had ever been hidden in a human body. But even more I was fascinated by an electrostatic machine, which was meant for nervous ailments. As Wolf explained, the patient was made to hold two metal rods in his hands. They were connected with the electric current, which could be regulated from low to very high voltage, giving him either a gentle tingling and prickling or a powerful shock.

Wolf wanted me to try it, but I was too cowardly to grasp the rods. "What's wrong?" he asked derisively. "The goyish hero isn't big enough for a little tickling?" He took the two metal rods into his hands and nodded at me to switch on the machine. "Push the little button forward—but slow!"

Later on, I was unable to tell what had driven me to push the switch not slowly but with a brutal thrust up to the highest degree. But at the moment, in any case, the effect was comical: Wolf reared up, twisted convulsively, kicked his legs without really managing to move them, and his red hair stood on end like a scarecrow's. What delighted me most of all was his pleading look when he held out his hands with the metal rods, trying to get me to liberate them. All his smug self-confidence was gone and his ram-face was now the face of a sacrificial lamb—the face of the slaughterhouse cattle his grandfather had grown rich on.

Despite later accusations, I do not believe I hesitated long before pushing the switch back so that he could drop the rods. In any event, when I released him, he was on his knees, holding out the hands from which the metal grips had fallen, and piteously crying, "My hands! My hands!"

The summer was waning, while I was virtually suspended in my relatives' home—or, in the parlance of the dueling fraternities, I was "under beer blackball." That is to say: I lived in a generally shared awareness of having committed a transgression of which I most likely could not exonerate myself, no matter how hard I dueled. True, Uncle Hubi resolutely took my side, treating my delinquency as a bagatelle—which it was, when all was said and done, for after a few weeks Wolf Goldmann's precious pianist-hands were as agile as ever. But Wolf's insinuations about my uncle's secret motives for his friendliness toward me made me suspicious, no matter how hard I tried not to think of them. Involuntarily I withdrew from Uncle Hubi, too. Aunt Sophie treated me with an even, cool matter-of-factness. She did not mourn her dream; she let everyone know that it had simply been a dream and she had awoken from it. For, needless to say, Wolf Goldmann no longer came to the house. His father treated his hands very carefully with special massages and baths, and then sent him back to his mother earlier than scheduled. Nor did Wolf come to say good-bye to Aunt Sophie, much less to me.

I would have liked to ask Stiassny for news of the Goldmann house. He was presumably the only one still in contact with the doctor. But I made a point of not bringing up this delicate topic. I feared lest my parents might learn about my failures here too, among my loving and tolerant kinfolk; and oddly enough, I imagined that Stiassny was merely waiting for the right moment to tell them. I no longer saw him as baiting me with those ironically exaggerated courtesies, those repulsive homages full of dark allusions to my penitent's role. Instead of responding to them sedulously and in confusion, as in the past, I was as matter-of-fact and cool to him as I could learn from Aunt Sophie's example. Stiassny commented on my altered conduct, whispering into my ear, "Bravo! Now one is even developing character. Keep up the good work! Personality, after all, is nearly always the result of seizing the bull by the horns."

Naturally, I also avoided the smithy. My slingshot hung in the tower from a hook on the rifle stand; I did no more shooting with it, or with a bow and arrow. I resumed my protracted scouting in the countryside, accompanied by Max, who agreed with me about everything; we were reunited as a twosome. I did not resent him for his disloyal love for Wolf Goldmann, who, after all, had been my friend. It did smart a bit, to be sure, that Max's love had been so tempestuous; but I forgave him because he was young.

I was, however, resolved to make Max really tough and fierce. Character was the result of seizing the bull by the horns. I was convinced that a reckless dog would have to develop the virtue of unconditional loyalty to his master.

In a corner of the yard, under huge dark acacias, an old and now almost unused bowling green was decaying. A small kiosk of aged, rotting wood, the so-called gazebo, contained equipment for all sorts of lawn games: baskets and quoits, croquet mallets and badminton nets. The place was a paradise for countless stray cats, who had their kittens there, played with each other, and dozed in the shade. As they did in the mangy groves outside Dr. Goldmann's villa, the cats had multiplied here into a true plague; they stank to high heaven and sang all night long. I would always sic Max on them when I passed, and he stormed, intrepid, into their midst; they would climb up to the gazebo roof or into the acacias or over the fence and away to the village. Now I devised an installation to train Max for more earnest encounters. Taking a long, narrow crate which had once housed mallets, I buried it in such a way that it led into the earth like a slanting adit—an artificial foxhole, only with a pipe ending in a cul-de-sac. I removed the one wall of the narrow side to form the entrance hole. It was not all that difficult to capture one of the felines and put her in—then I added my dachshund Max.

The result was lamentable. There was a very brief and blustery racket under the earth; then Max shot yowling out of the hole, whimpering as he licked his scratched-up nose; and neither imperious commands nor friendly coaxing could get him to go back inside. Furiously, I stuck my arm all the way in to pull out the cat and have her continue fighting with Max in the open. I clutched something moving, hairy, and warm, but simultaneously I felt a violent pain in my hand. The cat had sunk her teeth between my thumb and forefinger. Unable to fling her off, I closed my hand as tight as I could and dragged her out of the foxhole. Her teeth were too deep in my hand for me to shake her away, so I just closed my hand all the more tightly; now she was kicking all four legs against my lower arm, baring her sharp claws. My shirt was shredded as quickly as my flesh.

To my misfortune, Florica, the Rumanian chambermaid, happened along at that moment. Catching sight of me smeared with blood and with the cat on my hand, she began to shriek at the top of her lungs. Now my bad conscience made me panic. I did not want everyone in the house to see this misdeed as well. The cook was already dashing into the courtyard; Katharina, the housekeeper, came running up; and Haller, alarmed by Florica's yells, raced over from the smithy. I did the stupidest thing I could. With the cat on my hand, I ran through the gates into the village. There, on the road, by the camomile-covered edge of the ditch, I knelt down on the cat's chest. Now she had to let go. I felt her ribs cracking; her fangs opened wide; I pulled out my hand. But when I got to my feet, I was surrounded by a swarm of yowling street urchins.

My arm was in a bad state. The cat had not exactly been clean, and an infection was very likely; I certainly had to get a tetanus shot without delay. That, at least, was Aunt Sophie's opinion, uttered authoritatively against the prattle of all the people around me—the Jewish urchins, nearly all the house servants and farm workers, and the tenants of the houses near the courtyard gates. They stood around me, full of hostility.

I was dragged off to Dr. Goldmann.

Dr. Goldmann may have already been told of the circumstances of my injury by the incredibly swift system of information typical of a small provincial town; sternly he declared he would not treat me. In stating this to Aunt Sophie, who confronted him for the first time, he was so gruff and insulting that later on, even those witnesses who fundamentally approved of his conduct had to admit that his vehemence had been excessive and unprofessional.

Alas, the affair was not without repercussions, although they were not grave so far as I was concerned. First, I was taken to the apothecary, who cleansed, disinfected, and bandaged my mangled arm as best he could. Next, I had the satisfaction of seeing Geib get the Daimler out of the garage just for me and drive me off in a kind of somber triumphal procession, followed by my old enemies the street urchins, as well as the not exactly friendly or sympathetic gazes of the adult inhabitants of the village. Upon reaching Czernowitz, I received medical care plus much tenderness from my mother. Instead of going back to my kinfolk, I stayed in the city until it was time for me to return to Vienna for the makeup examination, which, incidentally, I passed with flying colors thanks to my studying during my "beer blackball" period. I took all these things for granted, like the passing of my childhood in the scarcely perceived course of days.

For Aunt Sophie and Uncle Hubi, however, certainly for Dr. Goldmann, and presumably also for my friend Wolf, indeed even for Stiassny, the incident caused far-reaching changes. It may well have been Stiassny who brought up the absurd idea that Uncle Hubi ought to challenge Dr. Goldmann to a duel because of his unconscionable behavior toward Aunt Sophie; in fact, my uncle was supposedly obliged to do so both as a member of a dueling fraternity and as a former officer in the Austro-Hungarian Army. But whether Stiassny suggested it or not made no difference. Uncle Hubi refused; and his refusal was supported by my father, who claimed it was a downright impertinence, expecting someone to duel with a Jew. In the end, my father drove out with a specially chosen dog whip in order to "catch the filthy Jewboy in the middle of the street and teach him what'll happen to him if it crosses his mind to get cheeky." Luckily things did not go that far.

It seems out of the question that Uncle Hubi's refusal was due to a certain shyness regarding Dr. Goldmann's fencing ability, since the insult was serious enough to challenge Dr. Goldmann to pistols, which my uncle could certainly handle more effectively. Still, the rumors about his backing down circulated so stubbornly that the case was brought before a court of honor in Uncle Hubi's fraternity at Tübingen. The court would not accept the argument that as a Jew, Dr. Goldmann was not worthy to duel with. Although an intellectual, he was indubitably an academic as well, and consequently had some claim to defend his honor with a weapon. Uncle Hubi, until then a highly honored alumnus, was declared guilty of cowardice by the court of honor and "expelled," and in the most humiliating form to boot: namely "c.i."—*cum infamia*. It nearly broke his heart. Most of his old hunting buddies deserted him.

Aunt Sophie changed. Her blunt, crusty, warmhearted realism became sharp, occasionally gross. Instead of endorsing every statement of Uncle Hubi's, as she had done all her life, she now frequently contradicted him; and her "Well, Hubi's perfectly right again" was gradually transformed into an equivalent stereotype: "Well, naturally, that's one of Hubi's typical idiocies again."

I learned all this from hearsay, for I was never to see them again. I spent the entire school year in Austria, traveled during the vacations, and, above all, went more and more eagerly with my father on his hunting trips. Aunt Sophie died while I was preparing for my final school examinations; I could not even manage to get to her funeral. A few months later, Uncle Hubi also died. The estate passed to one of his distant relatives. I never went there again.

Sometimes, when I was in Vienna, I thought of tracking down Wolf Goldmann. It would certainly have been possible to find him through his mother—who, as I knew, was head ceramicist at the Wiener Werkstätten—or at the Academy of Music, which he must have been attending. But I did not look for him, partly out of laziness and partly because of a rather heavily burdened conscience. Although Dr. Goldmann had triumphed as a man of honor over poor Uncle Hubi, his refusal to give me medical treatment stood him in ill stead. The medical commission excluded him from its ranks, his license was revoked, and supposedly the district attorney wanted to look into the matter. Dr. Goldmann moved out of the village in which his father had "erected his house" as in a land of promise. Deserted and unsellable, the bepennoned red-brick villa soon went to ruin.

The only person from whom I had any sign of life was Stiassny. He moved from my relatives' home—I never knew where he went—but shortly after he left, at the Christmastide following the events I have narrated here, I received a package from him. When I unwrapped it, out came two small busts made of wood and ivory, which I had always beheld with as much fascination as disgust whenever I went into his room. The busts were a male and a female head from the Rococo period, both with wigs, very pretty and dainty and lifelike. But they were sliced in half, and while you saw their charming profiles and fresh cheeks on one side, you could peer at the anatomy of the skull on the other side, with bones, muscles, veins, and even the cerebral convolutions.

My parents felt this was no Christmas gift for a boy my age; the two busts were taken away from me, vanishing somewhere, never to be seen again. In regard to Stiassny, too, the only thing left was a memory, and memories are all I have retained of that faraway time.

Youth

When I saw her, two things happened to me. First, an impulse to hide gripped me; the vehemence of my movement was such that I could conceal it only by acting as though something across the street had suddenly caught my attention. At the same time, I felt the erection in the tautness of my trousers.

The second struck me as more peculiar than the first. At nineteen, one lives in the utter idolatry, therefore the extreme superstition, of sex. Monstrously exaggerated tales about sexual feats, which we listen to greedily, determine our expectations. The disappointments are correspondingly great. My reactions to the mere sight of a woman were not usually so obvious as this. Needless to say, I was worried.

I was afflicted by awareness of my inadequacy. I desired any even halfway attractive woman, whether alive or in a photograph; promptly, in my imagination, I saw her before me naked and myself on top of her. Every female whom I passed, whether a child who was barely a girl or a matron ripened almost to decay, I immediately saw as a partner for an imaginary sexual act. Of course, reality was woefully in arrears. In ninety-nine cases out of a hundred I was totally paralyzed by shyness. Therefore, even if a woman was willing, I affected a cold indifference that would have seemed rude. Fortunately, in most cases she saw through it; then her knowing smile pained me like a whiplash.

Now and then I did go to bed with someone. The points I chalked up to confirm my virility were probably not much under the average of any boy my age. But I knew every time that the point had been scored dishonestly. It was not that I, the he-man, had conquered the woman but, rather, that she had picked me. It was not that some irresistible stud quality on my part succeeded over and over again but, rather, that my little cock would once again fall into a trap.

It acted, accordingly, disturbed. Once, I was even prompted to consult my doctor. He gave me a pill. "Does this mean I need potency pills at the age of nineteen?" I asked in dismay. He laughed: "It's a tranquilizer; you're too excited. Have sexual relations a bit more regularly."

I made every effort to do so. But the successes were always quick defeats because they were not so overwhelming as my overexcited imagination demanded: thus I was left with doubts and anxieties; and, indeed, such striking counter-evidence as the spontaneous erection in my trousers when the girl was wheeled past gave me serious reasons for brooding.

She was certainly a beautiful girl—lamentably beautiful: a doll's face with pearly teeth behind red lips, and large, wonderfully soulful eyes. The heart-shaped face was embedded in a wealth of brown, crisply vigorous curls—by forty, or even thirty, she would probably be having difficulties with a touch of a mustache. Her breasts were outlined clear and firm in her light blouse, and her waist was slender; the hips were obviously quite sumptuous. Anything farther down was now swathed in a blanket and placed lifelessly on the footrest between the whirring spoke wheels of the wheelchair. Well, one could ignore the lower part—a surrealistic something of human limbs, no doubt—but the body above was all the more female; her eyes confirmed this, simply shouted it to the world. It was a heart-wrenchingly

69

ingenuous, disarmed look, the look of a woman tested by adversity—yes indeed, the look of a wounded hind, as the poets say. One involuntarily held aloof. But there was also humor and merriment and alert intelligence in her look, the strength of *joie de vivre*, and her look had struck me squarely, calling me to account . . . Oh, God, was I base!

I was base because I turned away. However, not without an equally total response to her look, if only for a split second. But what did *that* mean? After all, such interhuman data transmission eludes measurement. If I had gazed longer and more soulfully into her eyes, it would have been embarrassing; I could scarcely have expressed myself more distinctly if my fly buttons had popped in her face. My entire soul must have been offered in my look, a readiness to love her, to unite with her forever, to make her my wife on the spot, and to spend a fulfilled life wallowing every night on her beautiful torso and wheeling her about every day, proud and happy to keep all pity away from us.

How could I explain to her that it was not the sight of her wretched condition that made me turn away but a cluster of ignominious motives that concerned only myself? I wanted to run after her and tell her this, more than anything. She was obviously of good background, well bred, loved, cared for. Her clothes, the quality of the light blanket that was wrapped around the woefulness of her withered legs, the solid wheelchair purring along on white rubber tires, chromium-glittering spokes, and ball-bearing hubs, the person pushing the wheelchair—all these testified to a prosperous family, to high rank and class. But these were the things I feared most. I would gladly have told her why: I regarded myself as déclassé. It was that which made me sensitive—and, perhaps even more, my shame at feeling this way.

Needless to say, I knew I had lost her for good. I could not turn around, retrace my steps, and speak to her or her attendant on a pretext, or follow them to find out where she lived and then try to become acquainted somehow—I was too craven, too timid, too well trained in reticence, too thin-blooded, too sluggish. But it was pleasant, indeed soothing, to imagine myself telling her about what afflicted me—telling her all about myself and my fall from grace, my great ambitions, my disappointments, the world I came from, my childhood, my home and parents, the homesick years at boarding school, the time wasted at the University of Vienna, the two or three experiences that seemed crucial to me: in short, my life story, oppressively uneventful and then again turbulent and for me exciting. I would tell her these things in one of those passionate confessions that young lovers exchange to prove to each other that they have put an end to a life of confusion and are beginning a new life, one of bliss, virtue, and clarity in each other's arms.

Actually, I was in Bucharest as a refugee or even an exile. I felt alternately like one and then the other. What had really cast me away here was defiance. At least, that was the best interpretation I could come up with. I had been at the point of being inducted into the army; I had dropped out of school—not for that reason, of course; I did not want to go back to school after the army; I wanted to pursue my dominant passion, which at the time (if we leave out for a moment the constant preoccupation with love) was drawing and painting. I was determined to become a world-famous painter. This had inevitably led to a conflict with my parents, whose views and goals were unyieldingly conventional—and in those days, that meant far more than it does today. Certainly they had to admit I had a talent for drawing and painting, but I lacked training, and even if belatedly I had got some, my father would not have changed his mind. Granted, drawing and painting were welcome pastimes; like a gift for occasional poetry, they could become valued social virtues. Portraitists like Laszlo or, long ago, Ferdinand von Raissky, landscapists like Rudolf von Alt and even Max Liebermann (albeit a Jew), were highly respected, as were, needless to say, geniuses like Botticelli, Raphael, Adolf von Menzel. But these were giants; and did my untutored gift assure my achieving such a rank? My father dreamed of having his unfulfilled ambitions come true in me: if not the obvious goal of forest management, then zoology or simply biology, the science of the future.

At nineteen, life is a drama threatening to become a tragedy every fifteen minutes. The conflicts at home were unbearable. I disowned my parents, charged them with living in the past, with refusing to learn anything from the catastrophe of 1918, and I declared my independence from their notions of order and their values. I packed my belongings and moved from the provincial confinement of the Bukovina to the national metropolis: the Bucharest of 1933.

And here I was, doing everything but drawing and painting, and my dream of stamping my genius on the century was visibly fading. At nineteen, I had to regard myself as a failure. Even worse: I had gone in a direction that would probably exclude me forever from the world into which I was born and which had been presented to me as the only one fit for a human being to live in. I was an outcast. It had begun with my obsession with sex, or rather, the myth of sex.

My very first steps in Bucharest guided my destiny. I did not have any real plan, merely the aim, the wish, to stand on my own two feet—on the unconditional premise, of course, that I would do so through what had been so hurtfully doubted: my artistic gifts. I felt as vehement an urge to prove them as to demonstrate my virility. Yet I was so staunchly convinced of my artistic talents that for the time being, I wasted no thoughts on when, where, and in what manner I might apply them. The other thing was more pressing: to prove to myself that I could take, spellbind, hold, desert, and throw away women as I pleased. Wasn't the one as important as the other? Conquering women, conquering the world—wasn't it the same?

I tried not to count up how many months ago I had come to Bucharest. The day of my arrival was in any case fixed in my mind. I had brought some money with me, slipped to me by my mother, so I did not have to worry about food and lodging right away; I sent my baggage from the station to a hotel, and then, utterly carefree, I ambled out onto the street. The Calea Griviței received me with all the shabby enchantment of the old Balkans.

I was intoxicated. I saw, I felt, I smelled the nearby Orient. A dimension of the world that had previously been a fairyland became a tangible presence—filtered, to be sure, through a garbagey modernity in which all the dubious aspects of technocratic civilization came to the fore, decaying and degenerating, but nevertheless swirling with life, color, adventure. This was a world in which a man could still prove he was a man. Here, sheer strength was what counted—especially since cunning laid snares and set traps for it everywhere.

The Calea Griviței teemed with loafers, passersby, street vendors at their heels, beggars, strollers, sheep, chickens, trodden dogs, whip-cracking coachmen, knots of peasants on rattling carts, wildly honking automobiles—and out of this swarm, a young Gypsy girl came toward me. She was straight out of a picture book: fiery eyes, glittering teeth, flashing silver coins, raven-wing blackness. A slender bent arm, from which the full sleeve of her blouse had slipped, supported a huge flat basket of corncobs on her shining head. Her skin was as golden as the corn in her basket. Gazing into every pair of passing eyes with an unabashed smile, she sonorously called, *"Papushoy!"* But no one bought any.

As she approached, she had to sidestep a ruffian who almost knocked her down. A movement of her hip, which made the flower cup of her skirts whirl, brought her past him. But this caused her left breast to slide out of her deeply cut blouse; touchingly girlish, with the uneven seam of the rosy areola, it bobbed full and bare for all to see.

She was not the least bit embarrassed. With a casual motion of her free hand, she adjusted her décolleté so that the breast slipped back in; then, still laughing with her white teeth, she called *"Papushoy!"* at me.

I stopped her. "How much is your corn?" My heart was beating in my throat.

"One leu a cob. Five cobs for four lei."

"How many do you have in your basket?"

"Seventy or eighty."

"I'll give you a hundred lei. But you have to come with me." I swallowed. "I have nothing to carry them in," I added awkwardly.

She had long since got my drift. "Let's go, my handsome young man!" she said merrily. "But you'll have to give me one pol more."

A pol was twenty lei, but I did not want to act too docile. I ignored her request and walked ahead wordlessly—besides, I was embarrassed by the attention our commerce had aroused. A couple of Jews were standing in front of a shop. She followed me, and I heard laughter behind me and a few dirty cracks.

I could not be wrong in assuming that here, by the station, there would be some dubious hotel for traveling salesmen where a room might be rented by the hour. The hotel was sleazier than I had imagined. The unshaven fellow between the rickety table and the switchboard did not even have a shirt on, just an undershirt; the trousers hung from a belt under his belly. He was unusually powerful; his tremendous lower arms were matted with black hair. He demanded payment in advance, three hundred lei. At that time, so many counterfeit hundred-lei pieces were in circulation that businessmen tested the coins by throwing them on a flat stone and deciding on their genuineness by the ring of the impact. I was surprised that he did not do so, since the stone lay before him on the table. But I gave it no further thought. Above his head, from a nail in the keyboard, hung a small, light-blue tin box stamped with a Star of David—the box was a *kupat kerem kayemet*, for contributions to build the Promised Land of Israel. It was typical for such a seamy hotel of ill repute to be in Jewish hands.

Just as we were about to climb the stairway—or, rather, the ladderlike steps—to the rooms upstairs, the man behind the table snapped at the Gypsy girl: "The basket of corn stays here."

"Let him have it," I said to the girl. "If he doesn't want to eat the stuff because it's not kosher, he can sell it—for pig feed."

I experienced all this in a kind of trance. This was not my first visit with some female to a bedbug-infested room, but this time it corresponded in every way to my notion of domineering virility and swift, casual adventure. The more disreputable the surroundings, the more authentic the adventure seemed.

I did not even look the room over; I pulled the door shut behind us and locked it.

The Gypsy girl stood before me. Her mute, sarcastically challenging laugh hinted that if I approached her, she would leap aside at the last moment and start a hatefully teasing game of tag, such as coy girls launch in order both to delay and to provoke the brutality of the sex act. But she stayed where she was, never stirring, nor changing her sarcastic look; all she did, when I was close to her, was to hold out her hollow palm. I put in a hundred lei piece. She remained motionless. I placed a twenty-lei coin upon it and then a second one. Quick as a flash, she pulled back her hand and spirited the money away.

She had not averted her eyes; as I stripped the blouse from her shoulders, she kept smiling and gazing into my eyes as if she knew I was doomed to fail. And for one instant, I was spellbound by her naked breasts, overpowered by a reality more precious than all daydreams. This was it: those breasts—two sturdy handfuls, warm, silky-smooth breasts, scented with almond milk and tipped by rose buds, which contracted, hard and wrinkled, when I touched them, these witnesses to a blissful thrill coursing through her body into the darkness of the womb; the crunchy-black funnel caught the thrill, leading it to the moist grottoes charily wedged between the thighs, which she now gently opened. . . . That was what I saw, most clearly and most excitingly, in my erotic fantasies; that was what tightened my throat in anticipation of delight; that was what sank sweetly, heavy with tenderness, into the pit of my stomach: the epitome of the feminine, the purest image of the essence of woman, that eternally alien, laughing, always elusive essence, which always slips out of reach, the creature whom I feared, scorned, and had to love, to my torment, to my damnation. Entering a woman's womb was already something abstract, it made her image vanish, it snuffed her out: I was being received not by her but rather by the universe, the huge, dark hollow of the cosmos, swallowing me, snuffing me out too. But her breasts were life, blood-warm, living Being, sensory fact, reality . . .

When I raised my hands to take hold of her, there was a knock on the door. Startled, I pulled up the girl's blouse, walked over, and opened. The man from downstairs stood in the doorway, holding out a coin: "This hundred-lei piece is phony."

While he peered over my shoulder into the room, I fished another coin out of my pocket, gave it to him, and shut the door. The Gypsy girl was still standing there, mutely laughing. "C'mon!" I said, leading her to the ghastliness of sweat-yellowed linen, rachitic pillows, and a feltlike horse blanket—our wedding bed. She lay on her back without the least resistance. That too confused me. All the myths of vigorous malehood surrounded me like totem poles. All my fears and self-doubts fluttered around me in alarm and fanned out. I ordered myself not to listen to myself, for God's sake, not to hear whether I would be able to respond to her readiness with my own. Slowly, I slipped one hand under her skirt and felt for her breast with the other. There was a second knock at the door. Once again, it was the fellow from downstairs; this time, decidedly insolent: "This hundred-lei piece is phony too!"

I gave him another one. "I do not wish to be disturbed any more," I said, and instantly heard how ridiculously out of place this luxury-hotel formula sounded, not to mention the arrogant sharpness in my tone. He dawdled; he peered into the room and at the Gypsy girl lying on the bed, her skirt up to her groin and her breasts exposed. I slammed the door in his face, then ostentatiously turned the key in the lock twice and went back to my untouched beauty.

This time I kissed her, and she returned the kiss knowledgeably. With an unparalleled burst of happiness, I felt her putting her arm around me, drawing me over, grabbing my hair with one hand to hold my head and press it harder against her mouth. Her mouth was soft and sweet; I wanted to close my eyes to feel her lips more intimately, but I saw that her eyes were open; they seemed to be sparkling sarcastically, and I wanted to see her overwhelmed by pleasure and closing her eyes. There was a knock.

Now I was ready to ignore it, but the fellow was soon banging furiously against the door, and the girl in my arms laughed and said, "You're really a sucker. Can't you see he's passing all his phony coins off on you?"

I could not let her believe I was a greenhorn, to be taken in by just anybody. I went and opened the door.

The guy held out his hand with a hundred-lei piece. "Is this one counterfeit too?" I asked hostilely. I saw the heavy muscles on his arms and shoulders.

"What else?" he snapped back, bringing his hand up.

"*Du-te'n pizda mâti, jidanule!*"—a popular Rumanian curse that could be heard all the time, which made it no less nasty: "Get into your mother's cunt, you filthy kike!"

I had expected him to hit me, so his punch did not strike me squarely, but the force was so great that my ears hummed. It also knocked me to one side, so that my return punch barely grazed him—and I could not manage a second one; his fists were hailing down on me. Under a flood of curses, he beat me out of the room and into the corridor.

I do not know how I got down the steps to the lobby, but I waited for him below. I had grabbed the flat stone on which he tested coins and I hurled it into his face with all the strength I could muster. But even though he roared with pain and blindness, he kept on punching, beating me out into the street, where I started to run, just to save my bare life. I did not care if a swarm of street urchins were howling after me or a gang of men perhaps following them to catch me because I had knocked his eye out, or if someone was holding him back to prevent him from dashing after me and killing me.

I ran until I felt halfway safe. There was a stitch in my side, and I was bleeding. Trembling in fury and humiliation, with a roaring skull and aching teeth, ribs and ears, I trudged toward the center of Bucharest. I was ready to continue the fight with anyone who came along and in whose eyes I would read amazement and then prompt understanding: to think that this well-dressed young man, who doesn't fit in with this disreputable neighborhood, could be walking around in broad daylight with a ripped-up shirt and blood-smeared jacket, his face all scratched and swollen—he must be coming from a very shady adventure that turned out badly for him.

But I would have my revenge. I would buy a pistol in the next gun shop, go back, and shoot the fellow down like a mangy dog. I knew, of course, that I would not do this, but I felt good imagining it. It soothed the burning of my humiliation, the indignation of my wounded ego, to picture him twisting under my lashing shots, sinking down, and dying on the ground like a cur. I would shoot him in his belly, heedless of the consequences. Perhaps his Jewish brethren would form a mob and lynch me, and the Rumanians around the Calea Griviţei would finally be fed up with the riffraff that sucked their blood, would rise up against them and murder them all, a pogrom would erupt throughout the land. . . . I felt good picturing it: the howling wives and children, the old crones with dangling breasts, wringing their hands and shrieking *"Vai!"* when the soldiers skewered their sons on bayonets. . . . Or it could even be just the Gypsy girl's tribe who came in the night to beat the man black and blue. She had probably fallen in love with me, she had kissed me and run her fingers through my hair, she must have been as disappointed as I was by the sudden disruption of our amorous idyll. . . . Besides, the stone I had hurled into his kisser, his bestial roar—I hoped I had knocked out an eye, or his teeth—showed that I had at least smashed his nose. . . .

It did me good to think such thoughts, and to recall the details of the Gypsy girl's kiss again, her hand in my hair, her adorable, precious breasts. . . . And this promptly unleashed my impotent rage again and my thirst for vengeance, the bitter humiliation of being thrashed by a Jew and not chastising him for the insolent way he had gawked at my girl's exposed breasts, the disappointment, the distress that I had not kissed, not caressed these precious, adorable breasts, that I had not been able to chew them up in the unconsciousness of lust, that her sweet reality had become a lost phantom, a vision among so many other, similar visions.

The evening of that first day in Bucharest, I was covered with swellings and discolorations. Nevertheless, after more or less putting myself in order at my hotel, I picked up one of the prostitutes on Calea Victoriei. She was anything but beautiful; her face was hard, her hair was dyed a strawy blond, her speech was vulgar, and her voice was unspeakably common. When we entered her (frightfully expensive) room, she did not even want to undress; instead, she pulled up her skirt, pushed her panties down to her knees, cursed me for not being Johnny-on-the-spot, milked me impatiently, and then lay under me like a corpse. Luckily, I came almost immediately, after tormentingly pushing my way in, only half stiff. . . .

And the Gypsy girl's breasts, which I forced myself to think of during the act, moved ever further away into the tantalizing kingdom of wishful thinking. I almost vomited.

Three days later, panic-stricken, I was leafing through the telephone book, looking for a specialist in skin and venereal diseases. In those days, two anxieties gave every amorous encounter a touch of imminent catastrophe and just deserts for sinning. The lesser anxiety concerned impregnation; and now the greater anxiety was brandishing its scourge over me. It was all the more ominous because I was stricken by a mysterious complaint with symptoms that no warning adviser had ever depicted to me.

The clap, I had been taught, could be recognized by a purulent discharge: "The first day, it burns. The second, it drips. The third, it runs." Syphilis, on the other hand, had a different primary stage: crater-shaped, raspberry-colored, hard and insensitive symptoms; but they appeared only after several weeks; you could hardly ever be certain about whom you'd got it from and whom you might pass it on to. If you had a soft chancre, then something also hurt or swelled up; in case of doubt, it was the lymph gland or the head of the penis. In any event, it was not so bad as the other two stages, which were considered practically incurable. You could, of course, use Salvarsan to hold up the development of the second or third stage—the latter usually involved softening of the brain. But even with Salvarsan, traces of cerebral damage remained, as we had known at least since Nietzsche. And the spinal marrow was sometimes affected—everyone knew the bizarrely twitching, marionettelike walk, the occasional digressing sidesteps of elderly cavaliers who suffered from so-called tabes. This walk was a bit ridiculous, to be sure; but it was not without a certain elegance. And the clap, too, was actually something you kept all your life. Whenever you thought you had got a new dose, it was just the good old one you'd had originally. And what *I* had, this horrible multiplication of unbearably itching, reddish, yellow-crusted dots around the penis and on the thighs,

80

could only be some dreadful disease—a Balkan specialty, no
doubt, hence particularly malicious. And if not ultimately
mortal, perhaps, then at least with destructive consequences
at the level of my fly.

The physician I randomly picked and consulted was
named Dr. Maurer, even though he was a thoroughbred
Rumanian. "Where did you dig up these splendid specimens?" he asked after briefly inspecting my lower abdomen
and upper thighs. I was crawling with crablice.

At this moment I paused to evoke the past few months in
my memory. Supposing the girl in the wheelchair had really
become my beloved and had been willing to hear the
confession of my past. How, I wondered, could I have told
her about such base incidents and circumstances? In reality,
I could scarcely do so without embarrassing her or at least
arousing her amazement, perhaps even abhorrence. She had
looked protected and innocent, such as only a girl of good
background, especially in her ailing condition, could appear.
And yet she seemed intelligent and open-minded, and tested
by her suffering—yes indeed, by her own suffering. That
had to make her sympathetic toward something so bad, at
least so humiliating, embarrassing. When all was said and
done, this too was human.

In my imagination, she now played the part of the ideal
companion. Scarcely had I passed her on the street, just a
few paces, when I knew I could tell her anything, no matter
how dreadful. I considered her as my twin soul, from whom
I could hold back nothing. She was the good sister who
understood every danger in a man's life, and she was also,
incidentally, my beloved, her breasts at least as firm and well
shaped as those of the Gypsy girl—whiter, probably; purer,
more innocent. I would be able to respect her, even if I had
sex with her, voluptuously and thoroughly, despite her
crippled legs. And she would be grateful to me and would
long since forgive me for the distasteful adventures that the

man who now made her so happy had once been forced to endure.

But, after all, this was not really what I wanted to tell her; it was not the explanation for my turning away and going past her, though it did, of course, lead to it. The episode with the Gypsy girl was at the beginning of my plunge into shame, and I had to tell her how one thing had led to another. Out of context, the events took on distorted perspectives and erroneous proportions, and I wanted her to have the precise picture. It was *I* who was urging myself to communicate. I wanted to experience myself in her once again. She was the mirror I held up to myself, reflecting my image pure and full, not warped by the fragmentation that so distressed me when my agitated mind recollected events in emotional bits and pieces. A logical, indeed chronological, narration yielded a far more harmonious picture.

In any case, if I had not gone past her but spoken to her, got to know her, and taught her to love me, and if she had truly become my beloved and my sister, my sisterly confessor, then I would have to tell her about Dr. Maurer. For, indirectly, it was he who had brought me into circumstances more embarrassing than crabs or beatings—so embarrassing that the sight of a young girl of good family terrified and made me turn away, even though (or perhaps precisely *because*) I found her so attractive, despite her crippled legs, that I entered a state I usually only dreamed about.

It had begun with Dr. Maurer. This excellent specialist in skin, venereal, and other juvenile diseases noticed my relief when I learned I was afflicted merely by crabs and not by some previously unknown variety of genitoinfectious leprosy. Then he began gently to inquire where I came from and what I was doing in Bucharest; my bumps and bruises also interested him, both medically and humanly. He was fairly young, in his mid-thirties, though graying slightly, and had that virile gravity and solidity which always put me in an obedience relationship of adolescent to adult. But his questions were not avuncular, nor did he seem to judge what I said. I promptly told him everything he wanted to know and a little more, especially about my adamant intention of starving to death rather than betraying my vocation as a world-famous artist.

"I have a friend who runs the publicity office in a cosmetics firm," said Dr. Maurer. "I know he has trouble finding window decorators. I can't judge whether this has much to do with your art. But if you're interested, I'd be glad to recommend you to him."

It had nothing to do with the art of drawing and painting at all. When I presented myself as an applicant at the address he gave me, I found myself trying out for the position by constructing an agreeable pyramid of empty cold-cream jars with gaudy festoons of crêpe paper wound around them. The man to whom Dr. Maurer recommended me, my future boss and ruler of the publicity department of the Aphrodite Company, Inc., seemed to find utility in my clumsiness. He hired me. And that was what made the final schism within my soul.

My crippled beloved (if she *had* become my beloved) would certainly have been able to understand the dichotomy. On the one hand, I was puffed up with pride, a world conqueror who had taken his first step toward triumph. I was earning a salary—modest, but indisputably mine. In other words, I was independent; from now on, I could make my own decisions. Of course, what I was doing temporarily was in no way what I wanted to do, not even what I had imagined I might have to do, but I felt I had started out on the road toward that destination. The Aphrodite Company was one of those concerns that are now called "multinational." Even in those days, achievement could lead to promotion and quite possibly even a transfer to a more important country with better training possibilities or even to the central office. The latter employed world-famous commercial artists, including Cassandre, whose work I tremendously admired. Such first-rate people would discover my talent sooner or later and guide it to its true vocation. The huge advertising division of the central office, which supplied us with posters, packaging, and other publicity material, obviously had a dearth of men of my stamp. In short, the future lay before me. My triumph over those who had not believed in me was only a question of time. On the other hand, I gnashed my teeth under the humiliations I had to endure in the here and now.

The Aphrodite Company both distributed and manufactured many things: from laundry soap to shaving cream, from toothpaste to shampoo, pretty much anything that could serve cleanliness and beauty hygiene on a soapy basis. It was the task of the window decorator to bring all these items into the windows of the Bucharest drugstores and cosmetics shops and to display them, cyclically featuring one or the other article, as eye-catchingly and as temptingly as possible. In those days, the city of Bucharest had more than two hundred such places. A few elegant boutiques in the center, around the royal palace and the Calea Victoriei; several large places with a big turnover in the commercial sections around the Boulevard Elisabeta and the Lipscani; and the swarm of tiny shops in the farther peripheries and suburbs, making the area around the Calea Griviţei where I had suffered my misadventure seem metropolitan by comparison. This gradation determined my experiences, albeit in a reverse hierarchy.

My duties appeared simple. I set up a model decoration, as flexible as possible to fit into various types and sizes of display windows. Then, taking along the materials, I systematically traipsed from client to client of Aphrodite. Unfortunately, the shops also patronized other firms, competitors that used the same method to catch the consumer's eye. With all the offers of free displays, the shopkeepers were spoiled—indeed, fed up. I and the rival decorators took the doorknobs out of one another's hands. It came to out-and-out races between us as to who could arrive first at a potential victim and get the order.

This might have been fun, had it not been for the scorn with which we were treated. In the elegant downtown boutiques, my requests to beautify the windows with pyramids of cold-cream jars and garlands of crêpe paper were usually rejected with an arrogance that sent the blood rushing to my face each time. Back home, no Jewish ragpicker would have been dealt with so rudely. And if I entered such an establishment as a customer to purchase a bar of soap or a bottle of cologne, or, even more, if I escorted my mother, whose use of cosmetic articles was considerable, I was treated with melting eagerness. So the arrogance, in contrast, made my downfall all the more painful, and I was further embittered by the humiliating need to go on acting friendly and officious to the proprietors and their staff—all of whom disposed of a repulsive gamut of expressions from bootlicking to baseness.

In the large stores with the big turnover around the Boulevards Elisabeta and Lipscani, the rejections were no fewer but more businesslike. Here, however, now and again, if the competition had not outraced me, a store manager was willing to grant one corner of window to Aphrodite products, and that meant I had to get down to work on the spot. I despised this work, which I did clumsily. Erecting pyramids of toothpaste tubes, setting out bars of soap, adding an artistic touch to a spread of shampoo containers—these struck me as the classic occupation of shop assistants, and I suffered torments because to a certain extent I was on display myself; anyone passing in the street could see me doing this silly and hardly presentable work. I was tortured by the fear that some acquaintance of mine or my parents might come along and halt, to stare incredulously through the panes, watching me crawl around tacking coils of crêpe paper around soap boxes or garlanding them over cartons of detergent. With a small cluster of other rubbernecks gathering about him, the acquaintance might tap on the glass, and then, shaking his head and expressing astonishment with gestures and grimaces, he would let me know he was wondering what on earth I was doing here. Even if I had been willing to explain this merely unusual, perhaps, but still courageous step toward world renown as a draftsman and painter, I could not have concealed my shame.

Naturally, I was also ashamed of these feelings of inferiority, and that made the whole matter even worse. I had to ask myself, what was my pride made of that it could be injured so easily? I soon acknowledged that the sensibilities of a mama's boy with a highly dubious self-confidence caused me this anguish. After all, people were beginning to accept the notion that work was not necessarily shameful—something my family still found hard to fathom. Of course, it very much depended on what kind of work it was. Commerce per se was embarrassing, but if the trade was in weapons, hunting gear, or riding equipment, then it could pass. Likewise, commerce in luxury items like wine, caviar, and pâté de foie gras, taken up by many ex-officers, was excused when it occurred as a necessity brought on, alas, by the times; and it did not occasion any loss of fashionable friendships. But anything connected with selling in a store was below social acceptance. This was a privilege of the Jews, and no one cared to dispute their right—at least, no one with any self-respect. I had been brought up to behave as though I did not consider myself anyone special and yet secretly to have a very high opinion of what I was. Under no circumstances would it have occurred to me to put myself on the same level as Jews. Yet I was now being placed there by the kind of wares I helped to peddle. Soap, toothpaste, and shampoo—who else should hawk them if not a Jewish shop assistant? The awareness of my being a kind of hod carrier, an out-and-out menial, for mostly Jewish shopkeepers cut sharply into my richly prejudiced self-esteem.

And yet at the same time my prejudices angered me. I rebelled against the people who had ingrained them in me. The thought of what my father might say if he found out what I was doing here sent a hot feeling of shame through me which instantly turned to rage—but, alas, impotent rage. I knew I basically thought the way he did. I hung in the threads of my background and upbringing like a fly in a spiderweb.

How could I ever get rid of experiences like, for example, the following one: when I was fifteen, my father had taken me along on one of the big shoots that were the prestigious high spots of the hunters' season; only the very best guns took part. For me this was the climax of an exceptionally successful year. For once, I had studied well and passed my exams without the usual difficulties. I had therefore been allowed, in the summer, to join the local tennis club. My father didn't know that the club's newly chosen president was a Jew, a wealthy banker, elegant, soft-mannered, ambitious. He had accepted me as a young member with extreme politeness, as if it were an honor for the club as well as for him personally that I join. All summer he had shown me his friendliness. Now, upon our arrival at the meeting point for the first of the great winter shoots, he was the first person my father saw as we approached the group of hunters who had already arrived. My father stopped abruptly. "We must be mistaken," he said in a loud, purposeful voice. "I thought I had been invited to a shooting party, but obviously we have come to the stock exchange." He turned on his heels and went back to the car.

Before I could follow him, the banker came forward and held his hand out to me. "Good morning," he said with a kind smile. "What a pleasure to realize that we are hunting mates as well as tennis partners."

I hesitated for just a split second. I knew my father was expecting me to turn my back on the pretentious Jew and follow him. But the drill I had been given to behave politely with everybody, no matter who, was too strong. I took the banker's hand and shook it, mumbling a banal phrase of conventional politeness, then quickly followed my father. My father did not speak a word to me all the way home. The punishment he inflicted on me was the cruelest one: for the rest of the season I was not allowed to join him for a single shoot. My humiliation was the more effective as, at the same time, my studies deteriorated. I did not have the moral right to nourish rebellious feelings. I had shown that I lacked character in every way. I was a shame to my family, my class, and myself—not only because I had failed to behave as my father expected me to do; even more so because of my cowardice in not standing up for what I myself thought was right.

So here, years later in Bucharest, I waxed defiant. The sense of dishonor intensified; and with almost masochistic readiness, I exposed myself to the humiliations that my activity as a publicist for soap and toothpaste afforded to the squeamish.

To be sure, I didn't have much choice if I cared about keeping my job. Aphrodite was a company managed by Sudeten Germans and Transylvanian Saxons, and thus it cultivated a ponderous work discipline that resolutely opposed Balkan dawdling. I had a fixed daily itinerary of drugstores and cosmetics shops to drop in on at least, where I cordially offered a window decoration whether it was desired or not. I could not report too many failures. It was up to my persuasiveness, my cajolery, my charm—any method would do. And if I was rejected, the fault was mine. There were no excuses. Nor was there any chance of claiming I had decorated a window when that was not the case. The job was verified by the salesmen, who made the rounds with their offers.

Thus, I was, so to speak, among commercial travelers—if my father had only known! And yet my artistic abilities (on which, of course, insultingly minor demands were made) were not all that was called upon. I was expected to have diabolical diplomatic skills, an irresistible manner, a flattering yet compelling way of getting what I was after. In short, my bosses needed something kittenish that would inveigle every boutique proprietor or manager to place his window at my disposal without further delay, allowing me to remove the competing wares and replace them with the alluring commodities of the Aphrodite Company. Such conduct was the very opposite of what I was gifted in or had been made capable of by my upbringing. I had been taught restraint and discretion, not "dash." I had so little dash that I was actually unable to find a simple way out of my dilemma by turning my back on the Aphrodite Company. I stayed with my job not out of ambition or defiance—"I'll show them!"—but rather because of drilled-in cowardice, an unconditional obedience that was typical of my class and based on something that had been hammered into me since childhood: self-contempt. The girl in the wheelchair would be bound to understand this. In a certain sense we were both cripples: she physically, I spiritually. If I claimed I did not have what it took to be a successful shop assistant, I was merely evading the secret knowledge that I had even less of what it took for something better. I lacked clarity, solidity, and authority.

I had no opinion about whether or not I might expect my imaginary beloved to understand what had been done to me by my training in unquestioning respect for fixed rules and institutions. Not only did this obeisance make me shiver about whether I could fill my assigned quota; it also exposed me openly to the pecking order at the Aphrodite Company. Try not to as I might, I shuddered at a frown from the publicity chief when I handed him my lacunary decoration list. If the head of sales said something appreciative about my display of cold-cream jars, I was no less delighted than any other wage earner would have been in similar circumstances, even though socially I regarded such a wage earner as a petty philistine. My response was all the more intense since most of my superiors, or rather the higher-ups, were much older men—that is, "adults," toward whom I, a young pipsqueak, was accustomed to behaving in a zealously complaisant and officious way.

Then again, there were moments when I pictured how pridefully I would gaze back at this difficult beginning time, once I had made my breakthrough. The big boss from the central office abroad would arrive, see one of my bath-soap decorations, and exclaim, "Who has done this? Why, this shows an extraordinary artistic talent! What is this man doing here? Send him out for further training at once—the company will pay. Why, this boy is a genius. We probably don't even have the right to keep him. He belongs to the world. It will be more useful to our firm if we show that we realize our obligation to mankind than if we selfishly think of our own advantage."

I knew such fantasies were pipe dreams, as remote from any reality as the likelihood that my getting punched on the Calea Griviţei would unleash a pogrom to wipe out all the Jews in Rumania. Still, I felt deeply that it would have to come somehow or other, that it *would* come just as I imagined. For a few days, I would hold my head higher than I had before—until some Jewboy kicked me out of a shop, and all my wild hopes suffocated in rage and shame.

Thus I lived in a constant interplay between humiliation and impotent rebellion, between the craziest faith in auspicious promise and dreadful doubts about myself and everything I was doing. Occasionally I was struck by the dreadful thought that all these experiences assaulting me and arousing such contradictory sensations were characteristic and normal only to those for whom I had been taught since childhood to feel contempt: Jews. That was probably why they were so unstable and jittery. After all, wholesaling and retailing were pretty much the only turf that was granted them. Traditionally involved in the so-called business world, they were assigned this livelihood—an existence disfigured by the compulsive notion of success, by competition against the ups and downs of the economy. Their hereditary milieu was the world of open possibilities, in which a man could just as easily become a Midas as get stuck in the lowliest form of donkey work. In the discrepancy between reward and performance, between pushy supply and manipulated demand, it was no wonder that their feelings were torn as incessantly as mine. I now understood their restlessness, their anxieties, their messianic expectations, the abrupt change from immeasurable arrogance to shamefaced self-debasement. I even understood the source of their often presumptuous insolence and repulsive bootlicking. I began apologizing to them for my previous contempt. Still, I hardly found it edifying to comprehend their behavior in terms of my own emotions. My ego thus received its final rude setback.

A growing awareness of how shaky my ego must always have been sometimes led to bright moments. I began to realize how much I had been lying to myself when I pretended I was doing something contrary to my taste, self-esteem, and social orientation solely because it might help me reach my real goal. Quite the opposite: I knew that my work was in fact estranging me from my vocation; and this was quite all right. With every day I lost at the Aphrodite Company, the dreams of my future as a world-famous painter grew thinner and thinner, but I also felt the same measure of relief. I was making excuses to give up all my ambitious goals of times gone by. What made me stick to my guns was no longer the hope that a stage of transition would grow into the fulfillment of grand wishes. Instead, an oddly fatalistic persistence kept me suspended, as it were, while my life drifted toward a different destination, as yet unknown. Clenching my teeth, I went through the weekly rotation of decorating as many shop windows in Bucharest as possible with the products of the Aphrodite Company, Inc.

In the swarm of tiny shops on the outskirts of the city, my successes required less effort. The Mahalàs were sleazy, filthy, poverty-stricken, but life-swirling suburbs, which attracted me even though, or because, the milieu was similar to that of the Calea Griviței, where I had had my inglorious adventure. Here, in the slums, the situation was clear-cut. A decorator was allowed to beautify the window if he cleaned off the dirt that had made the glass opaque. You had only to steal a march on the competition; then you could clean the panes and lay out your goods.

At first, in order to convince myself that my activity was necessary, I tried to put something like a work ethos into the business of displaying toothpaste tubes. So, I was angered by the vile utilitarianism of these slum drugstores. But I soon got used to being welcomed with exuberant friendliness and treated to a cup of strong black coffee. After which, I was allowed to spend a few hours sweeping away dead flies from the display-window boxes, wiping away finger-thick dust, and cleaning the panes—to prepare for the actual decorating. Depending on whether lavender soap or lemon soap was to be displayed, the window was lined with lilac or yellow crêpe paper, each thumbtack meticulously camouflaged with a crêpe rosette and thus made part of the adornment. Next came the artistic construction of the powerfully fragrant products in a bed of artificial umbels, with individual items in packages of three or six. This edifice was encircled by a bold loop—an arc of Aphrodite products, from the shaving cream of the well-groomed gentleman to the toothpaste for the entire family to the soap flakes for the ladies' fine lingerie. I was soon quite hardened to what happened next, after my completion of this work of art and dismissal amid renewed protestations of friendship: no sooner was I out in the street again than the display window filled up with nail files, douches, jars of leeches, packages of condoms, and, even worse, goods from our competitors.

I appreciated the chats, the coffee, and the friendly, if sanctimonious, reception. I began liking these slum shopkeepers: careworn, arduously crawling through their petty existences, shrewdly callous or sagely resigned. We became friends. It was, if you will, my first real encounter with life—that is to say, the life of other people, of other species of human beings: a discovery of the world, often no less mysterious or wondrous than in childhood. I began combing through the Mahalàs of Bucharest with the same lust for adventure with which I had once combed through the garden of my childhood days. I peered with the same curiosity into the lives of these other species; I listened with the same devotion to the essence of the unknown. As a child, I had found I could not but be amazed at my life, and so again now: experiences lodged in me as "mood motifs," and only after the mood had taken shape did they become clear images and recollections. The pitiable ugliness, the wretchedness, the meanness and brutality, of which I saw such a profusion in the slums of this Balkan metropolis, lost their repulsive immediacy, and were ordered into a complex picture, whose patterns and colors had no value per se but achieved real significance only in counterpoint with the rest.

The factory of the Aphrodite Company was also located on the outskirts of the city, where the Calea Moşilor turned into a highway; broad and dusty, mournfully lined with poplars, it ran out into the vast countryside whose horizon melted far away into the haze of the Danube plain. The neighborhood around the factory, a settlement from the Turkish period, had coalesced with the exuberantly growing city. Every week, a horse market took place in a huge, empty square surrounded by two-storied houses made of either wooden boards or, back then already, characterless cement cubes. But over the flat rooftops loomed the notched, melon-shaped dome of an old *hamam*, the local steam bath; and the carvings on the hoary wood, the faded pink, ultramarine, and pistachio-green of the paint, the ancient motifs of tulips, cypresses, and pomegranate blossoms stamped into the plaster, contained all the poetry of the Orient.

I did not see all this with the eyes of an archaeologist of his own lifetime, ever watchful for the "unspoiled world" of the past. I was utterly ingenuous in absorbing the anachronisms, the contrasts and contradictions, as a unity and a presentness. Everything was integrated as a matter of course into a picture of my world which I virtually inhaled, while in my imagination I dwelled in a future world of immeasurable promise that seemed to lie ahead of me.

In the morning, I steered my already antediluvian Model-T Ford with its cargo of publicity material out of the factory gates. Halting, I was checked and at last politely given the go-ahead by a giant Bessarabian watchman who guarded the plant as if it were a seraglio. I then turned into the street to begin my daily calvary through the stations of nicely graduated humiliations in the elegant boutiques on the Boulevard Bratianu, on to the comfort of the down-to-earth humanity in the parti-colored stores in Văcăreşti, which carried not only cattle salt and copybooks but also laundry soap. My first stop was Mr. Garabetian's bazaar.

Mr. Garabetian was an Armenian of great embonpoint and charm. Day in, day out, from dawn to dusk, he sat like a Buddha, immobile, in front of his store: a chain of artfully carved apricot pits gliding playfully through his dark fingers tipped with rosy nails; the heavy lids half shut over the shiny almond-shaped eyes, which were like black olives preserved in oil; and a pea-shaped, aubergine-colored growth on the violet lower lip, under the Charlie Chaplin mustache.

His store was spacious and inexhaustible. Like a real bazaar, it was laid out as a honeycomb of adjacent stalls, each containing a different commodity. Canopies were drawn over the sidewalk, above piles of sheepskins and sharp, dry cheeses, cooking utensils and cans of kerosene, sacks of cornmeal and boxes of American chewing gum, down pillows and hemp ropes. You could just as easily buy a whipcord here as a portable gramophone, donkey-meat sausages, pastrami, and Moldau wine as well as nonprescription remedies from aspirin to vermicide; and according to need and commercial consideration, you could purchase a pack of sewing needles or dispatch a load of Anatolian hazelnuts to London. Mr. Garabetian had several dozen employees, whom he supervised from a stool at an octagonal sidewalk-table inlaid with mother-of-pearl arabesques. He sat there, heedless of the yells of sheepherders, who drove their flocks past him, or the chirping of the sparrows that tussled over chaff in the horse manure on the roadway, undisturbed by the heavy clouds of dust trailing every passing motor vehicle. Using a folded gazette, whose news he had unflappably registered early in the morning, Mr. Garabetian indolently fanned away the flies from his pickle-shaped nose, smoked Macedonian cigarettes, and drank innumerable cups of Turkish coffee.

Although naturally he carried every kind of cosmetic article, I had no professional dealings with him. After all, there was no display window to decorate. The wares lay open all the way into the street. Any shopper, even a window-shopper, could pass in and out of the convoluted stalls unimpeded, like the birds in the crown of a gigantic old elm tree that shaded all this. And Mr. Garabetian probably cared as little whether his goods were displayed agreeably as whether their quality was convincing. Anyone interested in checking them could pick them up, weigh them, smell them, determine their solidity, their ripeness, and then either purchase or put them back. It made no difference whatsoever to Mr. Garabetian. He did reveal his Armenian preference for pink by the arrangement of silks, mineral pigments, roasted pistachios, and *rahat lukum*. But that was as far as his aesthetic sensibility went; any attempt to use a picture of a jubilant bathing beauty to inveigle a buyer into purchasing a shampoo would have struck him as ludicrous. Nevertheless, we had got humanly closer.

It all started with my greeting him. I had begun doing so spontaneously because I was incapable of pretending not to know a person whom I passed several times a day. Thus, I had nodded at him with a smile, and he had responded with Oriental expressiveness. For a while, things went no further than this mimetic exchange of friendliness, in which Mr. Garabetian was always the more generous. I waved and smiled at him; and he clutched his chest with a gesture of surprised—nay, startled—and joyful recognition. His smile radiated dazzling white from the darknesses of his mustache, lips, and lip growth; then, scarcely hindered by his enormous belly, he leaned forward with closed eyes, casting out his arm and hand in a vast, flat curve, solemnly affirming unconditional submission.

At some point or other, we exchanged a word or two, and he permitted himself to offer me a cup of coffee. Although three times as old as I and no doubt aware of what a low rank I had among the Sudeten German and Transylvanian Saxon gentlemen in the hierarchy of the Aphrodite Company, Mr. Garabetian treated me as a person commanding respect; and, needless to say, I reciprocated his cordiality. He seemed to like this very much. The invitations to coffee were repeated, and eventually I got into the habit of dropping in on him. When the office was closed for the day, and I was done with my rounds as well as with the ensuing paperwork and the preparations for the next morning, I would go over to the bazaar. The gradually waning daylight would be growing thinner and clearer, while the turquoise sky was taking a step into the universe and igniting at its edges. At Mr. Garabetian's side, I would sip mocha; the coffee grounds in the tiny cups curdled into Japanese ink-brush drawings, while the two of us waited to catch the twinkle of the first star and soon after that the blinking of the pale street lamps in the descending twilight.

We were fairly monosyllabic at such times, like truly close friends. But perhaps the thing binding us in silence was chiefly our disparate solitudes: the afflicted loneliness of youth and the mellow loneliness of imminent old age. Once, he introduced me to his son, whom I had long known by sight. Garabetian junior was a few years older than I and a rather striking person: he was the beau not only of this suburban neighborhood but presumably of very different, far more fashionable districts of Bucharest. Even in the daytime, his hair, black as patent leather, seemed to reflect the neon frames of the nightclubs he frequented. Tall, slender-hipped, in dandyishly long, sharp-shouldered jackets, baggy trousers, and black-and-white shoes, he moved elastically on inch-thick rubber soles. He drove a Chrysler convertible and was always accompanied by breathtakingly beautiful, high-bosomed, cherry-eyed girls, such as I knew at most from the front pages of the yellow press.

I complimented Mr. Garabetian on such a proud offspring. He scornfully waved this off with his folded newspaper. After a while he said, "You come from a home in which it is not customary to do any sort of work—don't ask how I know; I can tell. Nevertheless, you don't consider yourself too good for it."

I held my tongue guiltily. Had I confessed my shameful scruples to Mr. Garabetian, his indolent eyes would have gone all agape.

"He," Mr. Garabetian continued, with a scornful snort through his nostrils and with his chin motioning in the direction in which his son had vanished, "he won't have anything to do with his father's work, much less any work of his own. Did you notice how hurriedly he said good-bye? He knows who you are, of course, and he's too embarrassed to admit he's my son."

I wanted to object, but Mr. Garabetian anticipated me, waving off my objection. "I see him twice a month. On the first, like today, when he comes for his allowance, and on the fifteenth, when he comes for an advance on next month's allowance."

I could not reply to this either, unless I told Mr. Garabetian that until recently, my wish to go home to my parents had been equally cyclical and prompted by the same motives.

Mr. Garabetian took a sip of coffee, lit a new cigarette, and inhaled the smoke, deeply filling his lungs as though trying to free his mind of wearisome thoughts and switch into a more philosophical gear. "What can you do," he said. "That's the way he is, that's how he's made—or rather, that's how *I* made him. When I was a child, I was poor as a churchmouse. I wanted him to be spared that. What he *has* been spared is being considerate, being a decent person. I've spared him that and the ability to think about things in general. All he's got on his mind, if anything, is women."

It was unsuitable, I felt, to add to Mr. Garabetian's paternal grief with the disabusing news that he was nurturing illusions about me in this respect too. If anyone in the world had only women on his mind, it was I.

But, alas, I had them only on my mind—that was what I wanted to tell my siren in the wheelchair. She was to know everything about me, even things I barely admitted to myself. I was filled with great tenderness for her as I pictured myself sitting close to her poor, blanket-wrapped legs, holding her hands warmly in my own, and explaining with a guilty smile that I was schizophrenically split. I ran around convinced that I was a lothario and an irresistible seducer, or at least acting as though I were, and I believed that other people believed I was too. But if ever I did get a chance at seduction, fear of my own clumsiness turned me into an oaf. But not just this fear, I wanted to tell her. Also a sense of the ideal. She had to believe me. Certainly, I was always on the make, as they put it; I wanted to omit nothing, miss none of the erotic possibilities—usually imaginary, alas—offered me at every step. But I did not want to give my heart away below my rank—my *moral* rank, of course. That was something she had to know.

In any event, I had diminished my chances as a lover through another passion. I had told my parents only very vaguely what I was up to in Bucharest, and I had not revealed anything about my job and my—albeit modest— salary; as a result, my mother kept on sending me money. I accepted it without a thought, assuming that spiritual well-being is at least as important as physical well-being, and I applied the cash to my old and ardent passion for horses. Every morning at five, I was at the riding track and in the stables around Shossea Khisseleff and Shossea Jianu, where the thoroughbreds gathered for early workouts in the courtyards of old caravanserais. Being light and having a good hand, I almost regularly got a mount. At seven, I was at the Aphrodite Company, changing from the life of a riding-enthused gentleman to that of a window cleaner, loading up my Model T with publicity material. All day long, I worked—if one can apply the term "work" to enriching junk-shop windows with packages of soap. In the evening, after drinking my coffee with Mr. Garabetian, I ate my *grătar*—grilled meat—in some small surburban restaurant and went to bed, dog-tired—I did not know how. I had little opportunity to meet people of my own age, nor did I seek them out. For months, Mr. Garabetian was the only person I conversed with, beyond chitchat with my clients and a few banalities exchanged with colleagues at work.

Naturally, there was the occasional erotic encounter; the girl in the wheelchair ought to know this too. A waitress in a restaurant where I sometimes ate my modest dinner would not be taken in by my superior airs; she dragged me up to her room. I owed a proud night to her experience, but there was no repeat. She might do for a casual adventure, but an out-and-out relationship with a waitress was, I felt, beneath my dignity—by which I meant, to my disgrace, my social dignity. There was a pretty salesgirl in a boutique in Cotroceni, a remote area where a residential district had grown around the palace of the Queen Mother Maria. I knew this salesgirl had a crush on me, and accordingly I treated her badly. One day, I asked her out to the movies, then to supper. She refused to come to my room; she was scared of God knows what, perhaps only of getting home late. So we finally did it on the park bench where we had been necking and squeezing each other for hours. The discomfort and constant fear of being discovered by a park watchman or late stroller made it so horrible that when I saw her again, on the occasion of a decoration change from Velvet soapflakes to mint toothpaste in the windows of the boutique she worked in, I acted as if nothing had ever gone on between us.

For a couple of weeks, I was even in love, or at least fascinated—the focus of my attention being the extraordinary horsewomanship of the daughter of a trainer who now and again let me ride one of his horses. She was an impish creature with a pug face and tow-blond, curly hair; but to see what she did with a horse when she mounted it gave me such sensual pleasure that it turned into desire. She would have come to my room without further ado and would probably have soon installed herself there: a convenient long-term affair. But I carefully kept my early-morning role as a gentleman rider separate from my daytime role as a window decorator for the Aphrodite Company, and I revealed nothing of the circumstances under which I changed costumes from one role to the other to either my work colleagues or my riding colleagues. Even if I had been willing by some chance to let someone in the cosmetics world know where and how I lived, I refused to allow anyone in the riding world to find out anything about what I did for a living. Thus, she and I got together on bales of straw in the fodder room; the pungent odor of the girl's body, especially her very wet vagina, prevailed so victoriously against the mare and cat urine that I felt almost sick. It was because of her that I consulted Dr. Maurer again, this time to get a prescription for potency pills, because, for a while, I was incapable of any repetition. Instead of potency pills, Dr. Maurer repeated his prescription for a tranquilizer. When I called upon the sharp-glanded horsewoman once again, I found I had long since been replaced by an English jockey.

Meanwhile, my imagination blazed away. If just once I could call one of them my own—one of those long-legged, high-bosomed creatures with curls tumbling luxuriously on their shoulders, the kind of woman that Mr. Garabetian's son drove around in his Chrysler! If just once I could sway with one of them, nestling body to body in a dancing-bar to the rhythms of nostalgic blues, feel her breasts, her lap pressed snugly against my thighs, my lips in her hair. When the bittersweet voices of the saxophones had died out, I would wander with her somnambulistically into the starry night, hand in hand, lead her to my bed, strip her clothes off piece by piece while she threw her head back, cover her bare body with my kisses while she moaned, unite with her tenderly yet mightily, almost drunkenly. . . .

I did not envy young Mr. Garabetian for his beauties. I merely took them as the basis of departure for my dreams, although, of course, I realized what kind of shady tarts and floozies they were. The imagination is flexible, as we know; my fantasy beloved, as I saw her, was physically as exciting as those others, and also much sweeter, softer, finer, better bred—less vulgar, to be blunt. She was a lady from head to toe, and she had a wonderful soul. Needless to say, she was an excellent horsewoman and she loved country life —horses, sheep, dogs. In a word, she was perfect. All too frequently, her image inserted itself between me and the real women, who could not hold a candle to her but who were willing to make at least the erotic part of my wishful thinking come true.

She, of course, the girl in the wheelchair, fitted my ideal image almost perfectly, even though there would probably be a hitch in regard to country life. She could have as many dogs and sheep as she liked, but there would probably be no question of her riding. The rest was exactly what I wished for, especially her breasts: I thought of them with inexhaustible delight; I pictured them vividly in my mind. Nor was there any doubt as to the depth of her soul; her gaze had revealed it to me fully. I wanted her to know that I treasured this soul of hers far more than the charms of her body, which, maimed in the lower extremities, was probably all the more manageable above the waist.

Despite my fiery thoughts about sensory joys, I cared more about her mind, her empathy, her education, her good breeding, her ladylike qualities—everything I awaited from a lifetime partner. That was what I desired more than anything: to have someone I could love constantly, all my life. That was what had spirited the hard-on when I saw her: the delight, the divine joy of encountering a human being whom I could love all my life because her soul was congenial with mine and her rank equal to mine.

And that was why I had to tell her about my true fall from grace, about how I had betrayed her by giving my heart away. Betrayed not only her, but my ability to love, betrayed them shamefully below my dignity: with a widow, an aging widow, and a Jewess, to boot. Whether I could ever regain the purity of my feeling, and thereby of my dignity, depended on her forgiveness.

It was not all that long before, a few weeks at the most. My itinerary included the cosmetics stores of Văcăreşti, Bucharest's Jewish quarter. A nearby district was called Crucea de Piatră—the Stone Cross. The one-story petit bourgeois houses, with gabled ends facing the street and narrow longitudinal courtyards in between, were all brothels. These courtyards teemed with girls; they swarmed through the streets in an eternal, plundering Mardi Gras, which—odd as it may sound—fitted in with one of the mood elements of my childhood. For this carnival made something obvious: the fundamental erotics in Surrealism, whose origin, I thought, could be traced back to some fanciful artists of the *Jugendstil*. There were mouths with black lipstick, and green eyelids under powdered rococo periwigs, such as I knew from illustrations in some of my mother's books; thin, supple riding crops and fans, corsets and tutus; one girl had a toreador jacket on and was naked underneath down to her pirate boots; another wore wide Turkish pantaloons of transparent muslin with her bushy pubic hair sticking through; another had enormous breasts dangling naked out of a tangle of necklaces that constricted her body like shackles—Beardsley characters. Still another was entwined in a black feather boa like a serpent; her skinny naked body, which stilted along on towering high heels through the throng of musketeers, veil dancers, sailors, dragonflies, looked as if it had been drawn by Beyros. Sphinxes lay in the windows, corseted trunks like that of the "trunk lady" in sideshows, putto heads with gigantic ostrich plumes, flowing Mary Magdalene hair, fiery red wigs around pre-Raphaelitic angel faces, rachitic adolescents, matrons, crones, fatties. . . .

I spent as much time here as I could. At first, when I was still feverishly longing to become a world-famous artist, I would go there to draw. I saw myself as a new Pascin. But my efforts got me into hot water. When the girls realized what I was up to, they alerted a couple of goons, who made it clear to me, short and plain, that their charges were plying an earnest trade and did not wish to be viewed as curiosities and committed to paper. I speedily packed up my drawing pad and watercolor box.

Strangely enough, however, my urge for self-expression with a pencil and a brush waned. My dream of world fame as an artist was suffering from consumption; the drawing pad and the paint box remained untouched for longer and longer periods. It was as if the world I was discovering day by day were too vivid, life too immediate, too powerful, for me to capture it. I first had to shape myself according to this world. I was too confused, too self-tormented, far too self-absorbed, to be a mirror of things; I had to take things in, stow them away, store them up, let them take effect and mellow before I could hand them on. I went through a time of looking, of observing, or storing, of not doing.

Here, too, in the red-light district, I did nothing but look. As the most favorable vantage point, I picked a table outside a small tavern at an intersection; sitting there over a black coffee and a glass of *raki*, I could gape in all four directions of the compass. Diagonally across, in one of the courtyards where the erotic carnival was frolicking, two lemon saplings in green tubs flanked a plaster column with a teasing amoretto; in front of the column stood a crib, and in the crib lay something like a Mardi Gras queen, the madam of the house: an excessively fat dwarf in a wide, transparent directoire gown and a black-velvet ribbon around the sweaty throat, which was wedged between the double chin and the bosom, and a second velvet ribbon knotted around the forehead under the severe, ballerina hairdo. With her cheeks painted peony red and the doll-like gaze of eyes in coal-black circles, she looked highly artificial. I did not need my pad; I sketched her into my memory—or rather, into my soul— along with the fat cat wearing a brass bell on a blood-red velvet ribbon around her neck. The dwarf queen leisurely stroked the feline, like a black panther in her lap, while an old crone renewed the water in a glass every fifteen minutes. After inserting a spoonful of jam from a jar into her tiny, cherry mouth, the dwarf would very delicately take a few sips from the glass, elongating her little finger, which sparkled with the diamonds of countless rings.

One day, the afternoon light was growing dimmer and finally became abstractly transparent; I suddenly realized I had sat there too long. It was late, and I had not filled my quota. I had just enough time left to beautify a single display with fresh crêpe paper and soap bars, and the window I chose was the one closest by. Unfortunately, the proprietress was the most difficult.

Normally, it was pleasant working in Văcăreşti. The usually Jewish shopkeepers were kind and mellow people so long as the two-thousand-year-old panic did not flare up, which made them hysterically vehement, and they never gave me much trouble when I arrived with my motley jumble. But this one woman, the owner of a store called Parfumeria Flora, had always been a ticklish case in the itinerary of the decoration campaign.

She was all on her own—a widow, it was said—and in the trade, even among the salesmen, she had a bad reputation for being harsh and disagreeable. This was not, incidentally, the only reason why she was talked about so much; she had a solid place in the salesmen's erotic gossip. No sooner did her name come up in a discussion at the Aphrodite Company than several voices evoked her with the husky undertones of desire: the embodiment of the raven-haired Jewess, whose succulent ripeness contrasted sexily with her coldness. Probably only the oldest representatives knew her real name; she was generally called the Black Widow. And it was also generally felt that sinning in her company may have been good business, for her shop was doing well and she seemed to have money on the side. Unfortunately, they said, she was a block of ice, and you could freeze off practically any part of yourself.

The Black Widow treated me with an insulting arrogance that was not outdone by the owners of the elegant boutiques around the Hotel Athenée-Palace. But while I had gradually developed a thick skin against their insolence, *her* impertinence here, in the humble Jewish district, around the whorehouses of Crucca de Piatră, made me livid. This time, too, she received me like a bothersome *shnorrer*. And had it not been too late to drive to other drugstores and try my luck there, I would have wordlessly turned my back and gone my way. But then, perhaps out of sheer weariness, she abruptly, albeit still very ungraciously, condescended to allow me to remove a dusty arrangement made by our bitterest rival (world famous for their lanolin cream) and to replace it with one of our artworks publicizing lily-of-the-valley soap.

The day was now swiftly drawing to its end. Along with the twilight, something tormentingly uncertain descended into the world. I was struck—I can still feel it today—by a mournfulness, as though I were utterly orphaned. Like an abrupt pain, I felt homesickness: for home, for the Bukovina, where I had loved this hour just before darkness so much that I had always run out of the house and into the countryside, into that abstract, lilac-colored light. Its lower part would be awhirl with flitting bats and smoky with the dust of darkness, while the night wind wafted the fragrance of hay from distant meadows into my face; and before me the enormous source of night, where, toward Galicia, the flat earth fanned out to melt cosmically into the heavens. I had always been bewildered by the forlornness of the settlements in this landscape under this deeply nocturnal sky, the frailty of the blinking lights, those poor man's stars behind the battered sheet-metal blinds. The light bulbs ruthlessly exposed the stark walls and crooked eaves of the sad little petit bourgeois houses, pulled them out of the swelling and thickening darkness, deprived them of mystery and thrust them into reality, while the surrounding world subsided into the dramatics of creation myths. Few things touched my heart so keenly as the desperate intimacy of a window shining golden yellow in the hard, bluish, whitewashed wall of a Jewish shack at the entrance of such a village.

Now, here, the eternal carnival of the red-light streets in Văcăreşti was still churning away; it kept going on all the more spookily, just a few blocks away, under the radiant street lamps—I still had the tumult at the bottom of my eyes. And now the same forlornness as outside, in the flat land, was descending upon the Jewish district all around me. The city and its hurly-burly, the evening swarm of people into the streets and avenues, the strings of light, the tumbles of light, the cascades of light overhead—all these things were meaningless; they were only a haunted world, a carnival of the bereft and desperate, lost under the enormous sky that was giving birth to the night.

I felt and thought all this while doing my job with an anger turned against myself. I had only barely cleaned the display window—it was still filthy—and now I was putting together the publicity material for Aphrodite, no doubt deploying more awkwardness than artistry. I was furious at this woman, this Jew, this huckster of notions; forlorn and bereft in her stony widowhood, she belonged in one of those Galician shtetls. Her arrogance, too, would have been more appropriate there than here. I owed it to my own stupidity that I was doing such low donkey's work for someone like her and being treated like a peddler.

Scornfully imitating an artist who steps away from his easel to check his masterpiece, I backed off after setting up the last carton of soap—and suddenly blacked out. When I came to an instant later, I found myself in darkness between sacks of coal and oil drums. I had failed to notice an open cellar trapdoor behind me, and my artist's step had led me into the void and plunged me into the depths.

I was quickly on my feet again, checking as a matter of course that nothing was broken and that my fall had not been too hard. And then I looked up. A ladder had softened the impact, and I scrambled up the rungs. Arriving at the top, I still felt a bit numb, but just for a moment. I needed only to make sure that my clothes had not been messed up.

I was absolutely amazed to find the Black Widow in a panic bustling around me, touching me, feeling me up, knocking the dust off my jacket and stammering unintelligibly as though she were the one who had tumbled into the cellar and not I. Laughing, I calmed her down. A minor, trivial accident, a clumsy action on my part, at the very moment when I had been thinking what a stupid person I was—funny, wasn't it—she didn't have to worry; nothing had really happened. . . .

But she was beside herself with fear and terror. She was probably afraid of being sued for negligence—I couldn't think of any other reason for her being in such a state. It was well known that the Rumanian authorities were not exactly merciful with Jews who got on the wrong side of the law; normally, the mere mention of the police was enough to make a Jew's face turn gray. What if I had broken something, for instance my back, and were still lying down there, dead? Or if, although uninjured, I thought of bringing charges against her? They always expected some calamity, these Jews.

Still, her excitement was peculiar. She babbled away and

kept feeling me up to see if any part of me was harmed. Finally, she found a smudge on my jacket and demanded that I take it off so that she could clean it instantly. Then she thought of more important necessities, and, even though I staunchly protested and tried in every way to calm her down, she forced me into a back room, where I had to stretch out on a sofa. She ran off—to get a glass of water or a cognac or even smelling salts.

I must have suffered at least a minor shock, or perhaps I had drunk too much raki and black coffee on an empty stomach earlier in the afternoon. In those days, I ate next to nothing, in order to keep my weight down; I was investing as many lunacies in the dream of becoming a riding champion as I had in the old one of becoming a great artist. Be that as it may—by the time the Black Widow returned, I must have dropped off into a temporary stupor, for I was just coming to when I felt her stroking my cheek; she seemed almost unconscious with fear, kneeling by the sofa, holding my head, her fingers in my hair, caressing me and stammering, "My little boy! My darling! My baby!"

When I put my arms around her, I did it almost instinctively; I had no choice: there was such ardent motherliness in her face, such total identification of her existence with mine, her essence with mine, that it pulled me into her. She was no longer a near stranger whom I barely knew by sight, a notoriously inhibited woman, a pathologically callous person who, just a few minutes before, had made her contempt for me crystal clear (which had been so insolent, downright provocative, when one thought of who and what she really was, with her dumpy Jewish shop next to the hooker district of Văcăreşti). No, at the moment she was the human embodiment of feminine goodness and warmth, the materialization of pure understanding, such as only women can produce, because they alone are capable of giving birth to another human being, creating another human creature through their bodies, flesh of their flesh, blood of their blood, spirit of their spirit. That was why she was the great absolver, the mother of mankind, the cosmic birth-giver, the womb of all life, in which the tormented living creature found its way from its loneliness into being one with the other. . . .

When I put my arms around her to draw her to me, her eyes widened in horror, as though she had beheld the depth and core of all evil. She made an involuntary movement to repel me. But then I witnessed a surprising change; I could only guess at what it was: the marvelous fulfillment of a dream she would never have expected to come true, the sudden transformation of an age-old fear into joy. . . . In any case, it was very beautiful: her dramatic face, the "Andalusian face," as I was to call it later in tender moments, was flooded with happiness more blissful than all desire— and so powerful that it tore a moan out of her.

I know that this change in her face was what made me love her. Subsequently, I did all I could to conjure it up, over and over again, this melting of harshness, nastiness, anxiety, banality, this lovely fading of the bad signs of life under the intensely happy surge of erupting love. I succeeded—at least for a while—in recharging my love in hers. For even though I loved her—and often so passionately that the thought of her was like a punch in my solar plexus; sometimes indeed quite simply, relaxed and happy and always with sincere gratitude for her love—I was tormented by the sense that through her I was deceiving "love" itself: the love I wanted to hold in readiness for the girl whom I could love all my life.

It is mortifying to admit, but she in no way matched my image of this ideal beloved, and I fought a losing battle against this wishful-thinking affliction. The ideal had been stamped into me so early and so thoroughly that I could not rid myself of it. I felt like someone who makes a daily resolution to stop smoking and then greedily reaches for the first cigarette every morning.

Yet I had to tell myself that this ideal of a curly-blond, long-legged horsewoman surrounded by playful grey-hounds, a woman with whom I intended to spend my life in a whirlwind of Grand Prix races, operas, masquerades, at ski lodges, seaside resorts, and on the upper decks of ocean liners—I had to own that this ideal was utterly banal and downright embarrassing, truly the clichéd dream image of every shop assistant. In contrast, my Black Widow—or rather, my Andalusian, as I now tenderly called her—was of a different caliber in every respect but one: she was, alas, a petit bourgeois Jewish woman and almost twice as old as I. Our liaison could remain, must remain, but an episode.

Yet her age—she was at least in her mid-thirties; I never found out exactly how old she was, nor did I ever ask her—her age bothered me much less than her being petit bourgeois. She was beautiful. Early on, I had learned the old cavalier saying that a woman's body ages later than her face. She didn't have to prove it. Despite its occasional harshness and sometimes cheapness, her face expressed duennalike dignity; it was smooth and taut and amazingly youthful, especially around the full, fleshy lips with the very lovely teeth, though not around the tragic, darkly embedded eyes. And her body was splendid. Naturally, she was a very ripe woman, but that was precisely what fired my passion; I did not have to consult Dr. Maurer for potency pills.

I felt I could ask the girl in the wheelchair to forgive me for such details if I actually got to the point of offering her my confession. Would she be discriminating enough to know just what I was talking about? Not, of course, a cynically perceived erotic experience: at nineteen, after all, one wants to make sure that everyone understands the moral purity and logical consistency of one's every action, feeling, or thought; whatever one does has to seem of the purest purpose and most honorable intention. No, this was no frivolous sexual encounter; it was sincere love—on my part, too, even though it lasted only a short time. And *that* precisely was the cause of the conflict: despite its genuine and spontaneous beginnings, this love was not intended for the woman it went to. It had, so to speak, dropped into her lap, a fruit that had long since ripened for someone else. It was originally meant for the personification of my *anima*, whom I finally met today: my siren in the wheelchair, of course.

True, the girl in the wheelchair did not correspond to the criteria of my *anima* in all particulars. You could not say that she had blond Jean Harlow hair; her attractive mop of fuzzy hair was an intense chestnut brown; the little face framed by the hair was perhaps a bit too chubby-cheeked and doll-like; and despite the obvious merits of her torso, any mention of the long-legged horsewoman's figure would have been downright tactless. But after all, the physical factor was not the decisive one. In regard to the physical, one becomes more experienced and more mature, and one adjusts one's ideals more flexibly to the insufficient realities. Everything else was all right, and that was the important thing: her proper birth, her careful breeding, the aura of her good background.

I would have been lying if I had not admitted that the aura of her lowly origins was what made my love for the Black Widow as rotten as if it were crawling with maggots—a gradual crumbling under minor irritations that gnawed in, bored in everywhere. It was not just the way she spoke—she could not, of course, deny she was Jewish. Her race was written in her features, in the very face that had overwhelmed me with its inundation of happiness; but not only that: she could also take on a different expression, which I loved, an owllike, archaically wise expression of primordial motherhood. At such times, she looked like an ancient goddess. . . . But her language, as I was saying: her singsong, the flattened vowels, the peculiar syntax of people who, although having known an idiom since childhood (in her case, Rumanian), remain alien to it, and then the Yiddish expressions interjected all over the place—these things betrayed her the instant she opened her mouth. And yet that was the least that irritated me. I had finally understood that it was quite possible for me to love a Jewess, not in spite of the eternal Jewish tragedy, the age-old Jewish sadness showing in her face, but because of it: to see that face

111

suddenly transformed by happiness—in fact, actually inundated with happiness—affected me deeply. But then I was equally affected by the "earth mother" look on that face when she was in a serious mood. Thus, experiencing so many astonishing things in myself, I accepted her Jewish features as part of her, just as I would have endured tattoos or brass disks grown into the lips, had it been possible for me to love a Central African native.

Besides, the specifically Jewish quality in Jews had never repelled me so much as the attempt—doomed from the start—to hush it up, cover it over, deny it. The yiddling of Jews, their jittery gesticulation, their disharmony, the incessant alternation of obsequiousness and presumptuousness, were inescapable and inalienable attributes of their Jewishness. If they acted as one expected them to act, so that one could recognize them at first glance, one was rather pleasantly touched. They were true to themselves—that was estimable. One related to Jews in the same way as an Englishman to foreigners: one assumed they would not act like us. If they did so nevertheless, it made them look suspicious. It seemed artificial. It was unsuitable. Like the Englishman confronted with a foreigner behaving in an assiduously British manner, we saw the so-called assimilated Jew as aping us.

Perhaps it would have been good if I had spoken about this frankly with my Black Widow. She surprised me sometimes with an intelligence and often with a knowledge I would not have attributed to her milieu. She most likely would have if not approved of it then at least understood that for us Gentiles ("goyim," as she would put it), the point at which our hair stood on end was when Jews revealed in their social pretentions their desire to belong to us. Not because we might have feared compromising ourselves by accepting them as our own but, rather, because the attempt was so feebly presumptuous. In so-called polite society, they were insufferable; they gave it an "as if" quality, thereby making it base. It was even worse when they tried to break into a class whose characteristics antagonized us anyway.

That was exactly what my Black Widow was doing. Even if I could have discussed it with her, I could not have made her see that my resistance was grounded not in arbitrary fictions but rather in a real difference in mentality, in psychic constitution, a difference that could not be bridged by the best will in the world.

As for the girl in the wheelchair, I expected her to be so genuinely of my breed that if I described these tortures, she would, like me, burst into laughter, the helpless, enervated laughter of surrender. Notwithstanding the tragic element (mainly for the poor Black Widow), it was grotesquely comical to see how my amorous paroxysms would be chilled by the cold spurts of some aesthetic affront—I say "aesthetic" because it really was a question of class aesthetics, the tremendous effect of which is often overlooked.

Once, for instance, the passion of our frantic discharges of love wrenched a noise of enthusiasm out of her that did not come from her throat. And my fiery Andalusian was almost driven to suicide by mortal fear, deep shame, a contrite sense of guilt—all of which shocked me much more than her innocent and spontaneous utterance of enthusiasm, which had the advantage that it could not be mendacious and which I instantly rewarded with a surge of tenderness. But no: she was so embarrassed that she raced out of the room, and for days thereafter met me with a bewildered hostility and injured mien, as though I were the one who had farted and not she.

It was certainly absurd, nay, downright scandalous, to think that this rare gift of destiny, this fortunate event—the love of a beautiful, vivacious, experienced, and emotionally mature woman for a young man still wet behind the ears, a love that could cast a blissful glow over the rest of his life—would have to be destroyed by such fiddle-faddle as her leaving the spoon standing in the coffee cup like a

113

pitchfork in a heap of manure, whereas "one" was accustomed to one's taking the spoon out and putting it on the saucer, or "one" did not vanish under the table with muffled apologies when one had to blow one's nose during a meal. But that was the way it was; I had to admit it. The toothpick that Mr. Garabetian, even while speaking, seldom removed from his mouth (and then mostly just to clean his ear) did not detract in the slightest from my affection and friendship for him. Yet my love for the beautiful Jewess, in whose face I saw all the sun-drenched passion of Andalusia (where, in gratitude for everything that the Jewish spirit had contributed to Western civilization by so grandiosely fusing Occident and Orient, the stakes had blazed), my love for the golden, happiness-flooded face of the beautiful sufferer, dissolving in a smile satiated with the mystery of mortal bliss, like the smile of *La Belle inconnue de la Seine*—my love was wiped out, chewed up, ground down by the way she dressed, the way she stuck out her little finger when she ate ice cream, the pretentiously pompous respectability with which she behaved toward her customers, with which she laced the splendor of her breasts and hips as firm as cannonballs in rubber armor, in order to be "ladylike," the way she did up her beautiful black hair like a pastry cook's masterpiece when she wanted to go to a restaurant with me, the way she would act "refined" when dealing with people to whom she felt superior, raising her eyebrows, shoulders, and voice, speaking through her nose, and taking on the bitter, hostilely cautious expression of people who have social pretentions beyond themselves, just barely far enough beyond themselves so that they never get further than that.

It did not help telling myself that she loved me with a terrifying passion and that this ought to be more valuable to me than good taste or the notion that she belonged to the finest society. For her, I must have been the fulfillment of a dream she had never dared to dream; with her passionate yet sober and distrustful nature, she would never have managed to believe that it could come true. It was obvious what was going on. If one viewed it in terms of Freudian depth psychology, which terms were specifically Jewish, after all, then one could reel the whole thing off like a grade-school homily: I was the son who had been denied to her, and simultaneously a most fiery lover, whose caresses were no doubt enhanced by the notion of sinful incest.

I mocked Freudianism. Was there anything like a Jocasta complex, I was tempted to ask, which, lying dormant within her, had disturbed her relationship to others? If so, she could now abreact it to her heart's content. Here I was, her pet, her doll, her baby—so why did she care about the rest? There was no one who mattered to her in the slightest. Her immediate family had died out, she said; the others were scattered somewhere in Bessarabia, she did not know exactly where, nor did she care. Thus it was all the more incomprehensible to see how she worried about what her neighbors thought of her. She was a shrewd, prudent, hardheaded businesswoman, but her accumulation of money was leading to nothing, as she desperately admitted; it had long since become an end in itself, a compulsion, egged on by a cold unfulfillment and presumably also by that anxiety never totally overcome, rooted deep in her race and permeating her entire being. The tenderness she showered me with was all the more poignant since it erupted out of her contrary to her nature and to all her habits; sometimes I had the impression that when she resisted it, she did so as a mere reflex. But when passion did burst through her inhibitions, then she was plunged into a kind of golden intoxication, a happy delirium which radiated from her like a monstrance. She became beautiful merely by looking at me.

To be sure, this was not the case from the outset. After that initial daze, when we had plunged into each other's arms on the sofa in the back room of the Parfumeria Flora, we went through alternations of being overwhelmed and dismayed, feeling shame and guilt, reservation and temptation, attempts to break away, irresolution, affected yielding and renewed scruples—all the emotive ups and downs that decent burghers use in their love affairs to make their own lives interesting and other people's lives difficult. During this phase, the noble sentiments with which I tried to quell my anti-Semitic feelings were put to the acid test. Weren't these exaggerated dramatics typically Jewish? I would have liked to discuss it with Mr. Garabetian, whose judicious and unsentimental views had a calming effect on my own exaltations. How could a woman with the sensual riches of my Andalusian act in a way you would expect of a Sacré-Coeur schoolgirl losing her innocence? Unless, together with all the burdens encumbering her much-afflicted race, she was also cursed with irredeemable philistinism. And that this was true, alas, was borne out—certainly not alone, but at least most eloquently—by the apartment in which I underwent the toil and trouble of putting down her resistance, which kept flaring up.

The apartment consisted of three rooms behind the sofa room, which lay next to the sales space of the shop. The three rooms were appointed with assembly-line furnishings in exaggeratedly fashionable Art Deco style, or rather a Balkanese version thereof, in which the futurist element joined forces with the ornamentation of carved shepherds' crooks: dining table and chairs, complete bedroom set, parlor furniture with a mirrored cabinet—everything displayed as smartly and sprucely as at the department store where all this splendor had been purchased. With the help of crocheted doilies, tiny little vases with artificial-flower arrangements, and Pierrot and Bonzo dolls, the hand of the lady of the house had provided the warmth of a personal touch. All this was billeted in an almost rustically simple one-story house; and the back wing, facing the yard, had a wooden goat shed attached to it.

In such an ambience, I regarded it as a proud achievement to muster up sincere romantic feelings. That I ignored it, in the end, was probably due to another achievement: my courageously seeing the Black Widow as a Jew and wanting to love her even though she was Jewish—no, precisely *because* she was Jewish. This Jewishness, I thought, obviously involved that bad—or shall we say utterly different—taste which with its Oriental elements was something of its own, a bastardized European taste all right, but a taste that was as much a part of the Jews as their yiddling and their agitated hands. I had to accept it; I felt the same way about her initial philistine resistance to my courtship and her recurrent scruples. Could I tell whether or not some religious bias within her involuntarily rebelled against miscegenation with me, the goy? After all, everyone knew how extremely rigorous the Jewish hygienic regulations were.

Naturally, this resistance also excited me; her yielding excited me. I think I must have acted like a child begging its mother for repetitions of a favor, for instance a fairy tale retold over and over. For it was like a fairy tale, the changing of her face when she overcame her scruples and gave in to her passion. Everything I could insinuate onto the dark severity of the primordial owl-face or onto the golden brilliance that flooded it when she perished in desire—everything passed into mythology. I called her "Astarte" and "Gaia," even "Gaia Kurotrophos," the Child-Nourisher, and when she remarked, "The things that come from your *meshuggeneh* head, baby!" her smile seemed as sweet as the smile on the effigy of an archaic goddess.

These ecstasies were so intense that the plunges into sobriety were painful; and as our relationship got under way, I began to anticipate the descents with anxiety. Indeed, they multiplied as we got to know one another better. I would then hate the petit bourgeois Rumanian Jewess whose triviality ruined my raptures. Once, in the midst of the most passionate embrace, she rolled away from under me so violently that I was almost hurled out of bed. With a grimace, she grabbed a framed photograph from the Balkan-futuristic night table and concealed it in the drawer. "What the hell's got into you?" I asked furiously.

She was so upset that at first she could not even answer. Then, with tears starting out of her eyes, she managed to say through her teeth, "He was watching!"

"Who?!"

Again it took a while for me to get it out of her: "My husband."

"I thought he was dead!" I said heatedly. "I thought you Jews didn't believe in life after death. When it's over, it's over, right? That's why you people are so scared of death you start to shake the moment someone mentions it. And now, all of a sudden, some fellow is supposed to be watching from the beyond when his broad climbs into bed with another man, the sacred marriage bed! What was it like, anyway? Were you allowed to sleep in it with him? Or did you have to tease him and throw your marriage wig at him, and get permission to come to him only if he graciously held on to it instead of tossing it back?"

"Don't talk like that, baby," she pleaded. "You're all worked up; you don't know what you're saying."

I was beside myself. "If you feel you're cheating on him even though he's been dead for ten years, then maybe it would be better if I left. After all, it might occur to me that when I'm with you I'm cheating on someone who doesn't even exist."

"You don't understand, baby," she said, her face bathed in tears. "I love you. I love you more than myself. More than anything in the whole world."

"More than the dead?"

"The dead!" she said with an ineffably scornful shrug. "Who cares about the dead! You just don't understand, baby. Come, I'll show you how much I care about the dead! I'll burn the photo up. Look, I'll dump it in the garbage!" She took the photo from the night-table drawer.

"Let me look at it, at least," I said.

"What for? The dead are dead. Why awaken him?"

"Don't talk such rubbish! I want to know what the man you married looked like."

I took the photo from her hand. Her husband was in his fifties, dark-haired, graying, massive, with an intense look in his eyes that reminded me of someone I may have met earlier, but couldn't tell when or where; so I kept studying that face, until she took the photo away from me. "That's enough!" she said. "And now look what I'm gonna do with it. I want to keep the frame; it's still good. But the picture—just look how much I care about it!" She took the picture out of the frame and ripped it up into little pieces. Her expression was so wild that it frightened me. The scene was stamped vividly in my mind, almost as an archetype, and I haven't been able to think of it since without horror: the naked woman with the bushy pubic hair at her groin, standing in front of her equally naked boyish lover and tearing her dead husband's picture to shreds.

Gradually, I learned the story of her marriage—that is to say, I got it out of her bit by bit. There had been no great intimacy between them —hatred, if anything, rather than love. He was a very strange man, with no head for business, which he pursued merely to earn money. In the end, he had left the shop entirely in her hands, while devoting every available moment to his two passions—or, if you will, his two vices: Jewish philosophy and women. Of course, my Andalusian added, they both amounted to the same thing for him, the ultimate philosophical problem.

I failed to understand. In what way?

Well, she said with a heavy sigh, it touched upon the crucial problem of all Jewish philosophy, namely—as much as she understood it—the incompatibility, or rather the sought-for compatibility, of rational knowledge and divine inspiration. This brought up the question of free will, and that was his existential conflict. He was extraordinarily, almost uncannily attractive to women—one might as well say he was cursed, it was his doom. So irresistible was his magical effect that he became its victim, he was defenseless against the women he fascinated. She said that ultimately he shook his fists at heaven in blasphemous despair because of yet another woman—or rather because he had fallen victim yet another time to the fascination he exerted on women. It killed him in the end. Finally, one day, he had been found, his head slumped over his book, his mouth foaming.

Not to her uncontrollable grief, she had to admit. During the years of her marriage, she had gone through all the torments of hell. Upon saying this, she embraced me desperately, as though it were my job to save her from the memory of that life.

"What a fabulous fool," I observed.

"A fool, baby? How do you mean?" She had looked upon him as damned, she said. He knew he was possessed by an evil spirit. All he had to do was walk down the street, and some female was ready to give herself to him. And he had to take her; it was compulsive. She soon was forced to pity him; in the last years of their marriage, pity was all that bound her to him, pity plus respect for his earnest way of trying to deal with the problem philosophically.

"That's exactly why I said: what a fabulous fool!" I was grumpy. I felt challenged. "There's only one philosophical attitude toward that problem. Do you know the story of the man who had a gulash at Neugröschl's Restaurant, a famous place in Vienna?"

She peered at me with that mixture of timidity and resistance, devotion and distrust, which emphasized all her racial characteristics.

"Don't make that owlish face again," I said. "This is the story. One day in Vienna, a man eats gulash in Neugröschl's Restaurant, as he does every day. The instant he comes home, he makes his wife twice, his sister-in-law three times, and rapes the maid, and they only manage to capture him just as he is about to try it with his own daughter. The case is medically so interesting that a committee gets together, chaired by a world-famous professor. The family doctor reports that the man has not done anything unusual; he has merely been to Neugröschl's to have a gulash. 'What does the Herr Professor feel should be done?' they ask the great scholar, all eyes on him. 'I don't know what *you'll* be doing, gentlemen,' says the professor. 'But as for me, I'm going to Neugröschl's to eat a gulash.' "

She slapped me tenderly—a teasing motion contrasting bizarrely with her tragic expression. "You're being wicked, baby, honestly. I love you precisely because that's not you. You don't know how horrible it is to be afflicted by sex. At first, when I met him and was swept off my feet—" She hesitated, unwilling to frame it in words; then she shook her head and clutched me. "Ah, baby, that's why I love you, because with you it's different."

That made it all the worse for me. Now the thorn of jealousy was in me. I gave her no peace. What had been the secret of his attraction? Was he so potent, so powerful? Did he have such great endurance, such amorous skill? All the myths of sex reared their heads again in my imagination and plagued me with scoffing challenges to measure myself against the competition. I was very sorry that she had ripped up his photograph. From his face, I might have been able to glean something of the essence of his supernatural virility and learn what it came from. The face had reminded me of someone I knew, and I finally decided he looked like the man in the sleazy hotel on Calea Griviţei, the one who had cheated me and beaten me up when I tried to make love with the Gypsy girl there. This delusion entrenched itself firmly in my mind, and confused me.

This thug was not only an irresistible ladies' man, he was also a philosopher?! Scornfully I asked just what "Jewish philosophy" was, anyway. I instantly felt as if I had started a rockslide over my head. All my embarrassing ignorance became obvious. Not only had there been a specifically Jewish philosophy in Alexandria during pre-Christian times, reaching its initial high point in Philo Judaeus, but also in the early Middle Ages, Jewish philosophy had flourished under the aegis of the Arabs, mainly in Andalusia, with the Kalamists, the Jewish Neoplatonics, Aristotelians, and Anti-Rationalists. I was cascaded with names like Judah

121

Halevi, ibn-Daud, Maimonides, Gersonides—names I was hearing for the first time and did not know what to make of. I was chagrined about my defective education; I felt barbaric and presumptuous. She, however, my Andalusian, seemed to enjoy telling me about it all. She would assume her owl-face, the "eternal" face of a not just physical but spiritual motherhood. It was, indubitably, her love that inspired her to tell me about her forebears, as she would have told a child about them; nothing was further from her mind than to show me up in my ignorance. Nonetheless, a suspicion crept over me: obviously she had taken great interest in the spiritual potency of her deceased husband just as, in the beginning of their marriage, she had taken active part in his sexual potency, and I went so far in my self-torment as to suspect her of letting me know this in order to fire my performance in bed. Never before had my not very stable ego been so shaken.

Oddly, that did not diminish my love for her. On the contrary: so long as jealousy tortured me and the feeling of inadequacy humbled me, I was in bondage to her. But no sooner did I feel superior to her than my criticism of her began—shameful as this was, I had to admit it to myself, and thereby to the girl in the wheelchair. I was enraged by the idea that even my blond, long-legged *anima* might fall victim to the irresistible erotic attraction of this Jew.

What drove us apart in the end was even more shameful. The girl in the wheelchair would understand this. It began with my Andalusian's pride in me, her desire to flaunt me before the world, as though for her, a widow in the prime of life, I was a desirable catch and an enviable erotic property, in any case an achievement for which she could take embellishing credit. "You just want to show off with me," I rebelled. "If you had your way, you'd get all dolled up like a Yiddish mama on *shabbes* and promenade through town with me on your arm and bask in the delight of the passersby at your *boychik*, isn't that so?" She wanted to mold me according to her ideas; she smeared brilliantine in my hair and wanted me to wear certain suits—the very best, needless to say—and she gave me the most dreadful neckties.

I shuddered at the thought. I was horrified that the district representative of the Aphrodite Company would inevitably get wind of our affair. I could foresee the wave of gossip that would sweep through the Sudeten German and Transylvanian Saxon gentlemen in management. Although not quite able to suppress my pride at having succeeded in "melting the iceberg," I told her that it could have very disagreeable consequences for me professionally if anyone found out about our affair. Of course, it was hard to explain why, especially to her. Since we had begun seeing each other regularly, I had had a free hand at the Parfumeria Flora. Soon, the displays were showing nothing but Aphrodite products, different ones each week. If I did not decorate the window, because it struck me as too conspicuous, then she did it, as a favor for me, behind my back. "It would be simplest if you just stuck me between the toothpastes and the soaps. If possible with the legend 'Not so good in bed as my late husband, but still . . .' Only that wouldn't be what Aphrodite is aiming for," I said venomously. "After all, they're paying me to publicize their products, not to have their products publicize me."

Only later on, after we broke up, did it sometimes cross my mind that there was something that might have helped me understand her vanity better, namely an element of defiance in her pride. No doubt her neighbors, all Jewish, did not fail to perceive what our regular get-togethers were about. Once, an elderly man had spoken to me: smiling into the evening, as it were, very amiably, very kindly, with discreetly closed eyes, he had asked me whether I did not care to come to prayers now and again, and I had replied, more gruffly than intended, that I was not Jewish. This must have got around. Ridiculous as the prejudice against the admissibility of our relationship might seem to me in an enlightened world, chances were that the bias existed. I ought to have been touched by the courage with which she stood by me.

But the very opposite was the case. When she suggested our dining in one of Bucharest's large, well-frequented downtown restaurants, I suspected her of using me for an attempt at social climbing. "That's all phony," I tried to explain to her. "All the people you see there are nothing but philistines trying to put on the dog. The truly elegant people eat at home or in a few exclusive places like the Capşa, not in a dump like that."

She looked at me blankly. "Do you want to eat in the Capşa, baby? Even if it's more expensive, that's all right."

Yet I had been doing my best to show her something of my world—or at least that tiny bit of it which I took part in during the riding half of my double life. For I was still riding every morning, and indeed spent more and more of my free time in the stables and at the track. But her encounter with the fashionable milieu of the turf ended catastrophically. "That's supposed to be fun?" she wailed. "Me, a hardworking woman, I'm supposed to get up at four in the morning and watch someone plopping onto a wild horse and galloping off like he's crazy or something? Baby, please, you're gonna break your neck! Just look at how skinny you are, all because you won't eat anything to keep fit for such a stupid, boring thing. And that stench in those stables—it can't be healthy. How can anyone feel normal that way? No wonder that old bag who talked to you for hours on end behaved so strangely with me. She didn't even shake hands. With all that horseshit in her lungs, she lost her good manners. What did you say she was? Lady-in-waiting to the queen? She can be the queen herself, for all I care. If she feels all right in the horse manure, well, let her. She must know what she gets out of it; she lets the stableboy grab her tushy whenever he lifts her up on her nag—I saw it with my very own eyes—yet she must be sixty-plus if she's a day. But you, baby, you don't need that stuff. If you like, I'll buy you a

124

little buggy; a horse you can get cheap. There's a market every Thursday out by your factory; you're sure to find something suitable, and we can put it right here in the back yard; I'll just give notice to the people keeping goats there now; well, and a little hay and oats—how much can that cost? And a little buggy won't ruin us either; we can go riding every Sunday on Shossea Khisseleff. What else do you want from the nags except to have fun? You don't wanna become like that *gonif* of a trainer who thinks he can milk those dumb rich people dry, and those fellows do the biggest business with those poor devils who bet away their last penny. . . ." She looked at me with tender solicitude. "You're no *shmegegge*, baby, are you? Why do you want it?" It took her weeks to calm down.

I had even less success trying to open her eyes to what excited me about the seamy life of the suburbs: my snobbish passions, such as the turf, were bad enough, but this was truly unintelligible to her. "What's so wonderful about the desperate face of a thief who's been caught stealing? His despair? Do you know what despair really is?" she asked, shaking her head. "Honestly, baby, I just don't understand you. First you go to pieces telling me about some dog that's been run over and his master can't stand seeing him suffer so he cries and kills him with a club. And then, when I ask you to come along to my neighbor's funeral, you tell me it's none of your business. First you tell me that I should throw away the stone I check the hundred-lei pieces with, because the riffraff bring so many phony coins into the shop, and that it's hardhearted because they've been fooled themselves, and vulgar, too, not suitable for me, you say. And then you want me, a decent woman, to go with you to Crucea de Piatră and look at the hookers. You can watch them baking bread there for hours, with the cockroaches strolling all over the dough, but when I rub in my mascara with a little spit, you hit the roof. Has anybody ever seen so much contradiction? If you knew the Mahalà as well as I did—always scared of someone sticking a knife into your ribs—you wouldn't say that life was more honest here than in the quarters where the rich people live. . . ."

I hated her when she talked such rubbish. I felt she was committing treason against herself. I could have beaten her for such petit bourgeois narrow-mindedness, for it snuffed out the face that made me love her whenever tenderness overwhelmed her.

But one day, even the sight of her happiness turned dull for me. We had gone out again one evening, for God's sake, just to the kind of place she loved: a garden restaurant. Blue, yellow, and red light bulbs in chestnut leaves, a Gypsy band playing, and a singer singing with eyebrows raised like circumflexes. She was wearing an unspeakably awful dress, a kind of elflike, innocent version of a Pierrot costume in white, with gigantic black polka dots and a silly ruff. All she needed to do was let her breasts hang out and don a gauze cap with two huge feelers to play a splendid black-and-white ladybug in the masquerade teeming around Crucea de Piatră. But no, she had had some hair stylist in Văcăreşti bake one of her horsehair cakes again, and she had stuck in a celluloid Spanish comb with rhinestones—it just about turned my stomach.

She was excited by the fashionable atmosphere around us. "Look over there," she said, "but don't be obvious about it. Isn't that a chic couple?"

I looked: it was young Garabetian in a white suit, razor-sharp shoulders, fist-sized knot in his tie, reflections in his Valentino hair, and accompanied by one of his enviably well designed high-class whores. He glanced over and smiled ironically as he murmured a few words to his lady, who burst out laughing; then he greeted me with a sarcastically exaggerated bow.

"Do you know him?" my black-and-white polka-dotted widow asked respectfully. I knew not only him but also the two men sitting a few tables farther on and watching us with equally great interest. It was the chief clerk and a department head from Aphrodite, with their Sudeten German spouses.

I had no desire to spoil her evening, but it was impossible for me to conceal my bad mood. While she chatted away, I poked around in my food, drinking too much wine too quickly and vehemently. Then she likewise fell silent. At first, the silence—hers timidly guilt-ridden, mine defiantly pouting—hung over us like a cloud that might drift past. But it expanded, entered us icily, eventually took full control; neither of us could break it. We left the restaurant as though we had just put a wreath on the grave of our love.

I drove her home in my Model T. When I saw her to her door, she unlocked it and went inside without a word but leaving the door open behind her. It would have meant breaking off totally if I had not followed her. For an instant, I wondered if I should let things reach that pass. But in defiance of my friend Garabetian's foppish son with his floozies, and of the clerks from Aphrodite and their fat-assed wives, I followed her into her house.

Inside, she received me in despair. "Forgive me, baby! I'll do anything you tell me to. From now on, we'll only go to places you like. Honestly, baby, I swear to you. But please, please, be nice again!"

She was more ecstatic than ever in my arms, and I caught myself observing her with almost scientific attention. I was on the alert for the change in her face, the increasing rapture, in which the boring mask of her ancestral tragedy dissolved to make room for the slight and mysterious smile of the *Inconnue de la Seine*, until passion broke open the lips and an eruption of happiness inundated her features. She drew out this moment now, keeping her eyes shut and letting her smile drift, filled with the inner happiness of the blind. And I had the crazy flash that if she opened her eyes, this blessed, soulful smile might take on a cunning aspect, like the Mona Lisa's, which, after all, were she to shut her eyes, would simply be a smile of voluptuous pleasure. A pang of wild jealousy cut through me at the thought of how basically

127

questionable this ennoblement of a woman's face was, how little really I had to do with it, and how much more convincing that ennoblement must have been when my Andalusian was spellbound by her husband's incredible erotic aura. That same instant, I felt, to my horror, that I was ejaculating—before the point that was the rule in our well-coordinated lovemaking, that is, before her face turned to its ultimate and most beautiful state.

If she was disappointed, she tried to conceal it. She showered me with tenderness. "Don't worry, baby, it was beautiful for me too, really; it makes me happy because it shows that you love me despite everything."

I was uncertain how to interpret this "despite everything." I linked it, insanely enough, to my delusion that I had seen through to the trivial and selfish character of her ecstasies, and I said to myself, If you only knew. . . . Most likely I could not have supplied this seemingly stunning evidence of my love had I not been assisted by the image of her pleasure in her husband's arms. . . .

With a sudden insight into what I was doing and thinking, into the kind of home movie I was screening for myself, and how I imagined I was thereby regulating my feelings and bringing them to climaxes I could not otherwise reach, a choking horror at myself overwhelmed me. I should have felt a still greater horror at the thought of our abysmal solitudes. Cosmic spaces separated us while we believed we loved each other.

I pretended to be asleep when she went on calming me, stroking me, and whispering, "My little boy! My darling! My baby!" I wished she would stop calling me "baby."

I had never gone along with her wish that I spend the night and wake up in her arms the next morning. Nor had I lost my fear of this typically Jewish luxury marriage bed with its profusion of down pillows in the Art Deco bedroom: it was a trap. Even the petit bourgeois house, in a district that was actually a ghetto, got on my nerves. It could just as easily have been a house in some shtetl under the evening sky toward Galicia. It had too much Chagallian poetry. In fact, I had avoided getting established in that house, preferring brief, passionate sex on the Biedermeier sofa in the shop's back room where we had first embraced. The fact that I had to be at the stables by five A.M. in order to get a mount had always been an effective excuse. This time, I did not even bother with my excuse. I left with no explanation after pretending to awake from my brief slumber.

But she kept her promise. The next time we went out to dine, we did it in *my* style.

I had always planned to take her to one of the countless little pubs at the outermost edge of Bucharest. This was where the market laborers ate their lunch and Gypsies fiddled in the evenings—not like the symphony-sized bands of operetta Gypsies who played in the supposedly chic city restaurants, but the genuine bands that you saw in the country: three or four men with a fiddle, a double bass, and shoulder-slung cymbals. And here we would not run into young Garabetian with his floozies or the Sudeten German and Transylvanian Saxon executives of Aphrodite and their wives.

Actually, I picked a tavern that old Garabetian had recommended. "It's a decent place," he had said. "I know the owner; he buys his garlic and peppers from me and he gets his meat from the butcher across the street. I've watched him there. In his place, you eat more simply than in the Capşa, but it's more nourishing and only one tenth the price."

The tavern, not much more than a whitewashed, sheet-metal-covered clay hut with an open hearth in the huge main room and a charcoal grill for roasting meat in front of the door, was located way beyond the horse market and the factory grounds of the Aphrodite Company. It stood at the end of Shossea Moşilor, which abandoned its suburban character here and turned into one of the poplar-lined exit roads from Bucharest, fading into the vast, melancholy countryside. The customers ate outdoors at rough wooden

129

tables and benches, under the towering foliage of gigantic old elms where orioles dwelled. From under the broad awning, quail in wooden cages were calling; they were long since accustomed to adjusting their ringing *pitt-palak* to the rhythm of the Gypsy fiddles. From the distant fields in the huge plain, their free brothers and sisters answered in amazement.

Since the tables under the awning were all densely crowded, we had to seat ourselves under the elms, even though I knew she found it unpleasant dining so close to the road, where a rattling truck left a five-mile wake of dust, a good portion of which settled upon us and our food. But I particularly enjoyed the view of the countryside from here. I relished the evening mood. Behind us the city pinned lights all over itself. Before us lay the plain, vaporizing in the rosy light of the waning day. In the haze, growing denser on the horizon, myriad frogs rang their changes in countless swampy ponds. Every sound—the frog croaks, the distant calling of the wild quail, the barking of a dog far, far away, the seemingly endless clatter of a farmer's wagon somewhere out there—every sound tried in vain to measure the immensity of the earth under the darkening sky. The tavernkeeper placed storm lamps on the tables.

I could hope only very timidly that my beloved would understand what I was feeling in this atmosphere. It would have been pointless to tell her how profoundly I felt the suspense in this encounter of two great solitudes—the encounter of two bleaknesses consuming one another: here the wasteland of the city with its encroaching horrors, its progress, which was decay, the mange of rust and mortar; and there the relentlessly misanthropic vastness and power of nature, against which no sky-storming walls, no denser and denser throngs of lost people, could grant permanent protection. . . .

My Jewess must have known this forlornness in the enormity of nature from her native shtetl. She was certainly familiar with the threat from the evening sky, its picture-postcard kitsch camouflaging all its disastrous forebodings. The gentle breeze that the sky sent us was sheer mockery; I quite understood how a woman from Galicia or Bessarabia might want to choose the city rather than sit in contemplation of that tragic beauty.

No, I could not ask her to understand why I preferred merciless nature, much less what pleasure I felt here, at the sight of the titanic struggle between the two wastelands. That view of beauty could only have inspired a painter of battles, not a defenseless Jewish widow who hid behind her mascara and her kitsch furniture. I tended to persuade myself that I was about to say farewell to my youth and its anacreontic poetry, and to exchange them for a more mature existence with a more refined poetic sensibility. But a secret unease warned me against the danger of delusion. I saw myself as old in my youth—at least a century older than this Jewish woman, whose race, despite two millennia of suffering, maintained unshakable faith in man's destiny as the child of God, while I looked down scientifically from cosmic distances at the planet and at myself and the likes of me, microscopic earthworms, tiny particles of an infestation that was soon to be swept away.

It annoyed me that she made no effort to conceal her discomfort. I imagined introducing her here to an audience of friends. I knew many of the people (almost all men) at the surrounding tables at least by sight: artisans and small tradesfolk from the area around the Aphrodite plant: the coal drayman, for instance, some of the horse dealers from the Thursday market, and the types that sat around in taverns there or watched the farces of Karaghios staged by itinerant comedians. I had not failed to notice the attention aroused by our entrance, for my lady friend's succulent ripeness had been generally acknowledged. In one of the faces turning to us, I had recognized Mr. Garabetian—the father, of course. I wanted to wave to him, but another head interposed itself, and I could not see him. We were sitting at an unfavorable angle, but still, I told myself, he was bound to see us, and I wanted her to make a good impression on him. "A decent business," I thought I could hear him say. "An attractive, mature woman and obviously not penniless. No floozy like the sort my boy runs around with."

But she was not relaxed. Now, granted, the bench was not exactly well carpentered or even particularly clean, but she perched on its edge as if that alone were already too great a concession to an environment which in no way matched her social standing and demands. The food, while primitive, was hearty and tasty, but she barely touched it, although she usually ate with gusto. Very delicately nauseated, she poked around in her salad to remove a bug that had dropped out of the elm tree; she barely sipped the wine; her responses to my—more and more artificial—expressions of well-being were chillingly monosyllabic.

At least, I thought to my relief, I had managed to prevent her from disguising herself as a *grande dame*. Her hair had a simple part and was combed back naturally, and she could have made a beautiful Gypsy with her fiery head and magnificent décolleté. But when I told her that and tried to slip a red carnation behind her ear (in my good mood, I had just bought the flower for my buttonhole), she struck my hand away, lapsed into offended silence, and then, when I kept urging her, finally squeezed out *sotto voce* that for her it was no compliment to be compared to a Gypsy.

"Not even an Andalusian Gypsy, for God's sake?" I asked.

"No, not even an Andalusian Gypsy. It's hard enough being Jewish," she concluded, with a hateful expression on her face that I had never seen.

At this point, I began to seethe. She hasn't successfully disguised herself as a mock lady, I told myself bitterly, and inwardly her effort is even less successful. And now, here she's forced to realize that it's all useless. Here everyone is quite simply what he is, I thought grimly. But not she. She's too "elegant" for her own good. If only she finally accepted herself, if only she finally admitted that she's a middle-aged Jewish shopkeeper, and that's all! . . .

To prevent the silence from growing between us again, something I had been fearing since the last evening we had gone out together, I heedlessly started to chatter. Frivolously I talked of my intention—postponed, to be sure, but not canceled—someday to devote myself to the fine arts. I explained what welcome subject matter could be found in popular scenes, once painting came of age and freed itself of the constraints of devotional martyrdoms and kingly portraits: just recall the Dutch painters and certain realists, whose master in Lombardy was *il Pinochetto*, Ceruti, or the most delightful of all, Jean-Siméon Chardin. . . .

I might just as well have been speaking Chinese. Her eyes were as blank as mine must have been when, *à propos* her deceased husband's studies, she told me of the importance of the addenda of the Saburaim and Geonim in Talmudic learning. Only she, when doing so, had worn her primordially maternal owl-face, full of kindness, a happiness-gilded smile always ready in the depths, while I went on angrily, tormenting myself. Finally she said, "What are you straining yourself for? Why don't we just stop talking for a while?"

Then I saw a sudden terror in her eyes, and trembling lips, and I turned to see what she was staring at. A troupe of *lautari* had come by, itinerant players and jugglers, and they were about to put on a show. They had a tame bear on a chain. He waddled upright on short, crooked clown-legs with in-turned paws, sported a Turkish fez on his thick skull, and wore a leather muzzle on his face. On one of his long-clawed paws a tambourine was tied, and the other paw banged clumsily against the tambourine's bell-jingling hide.

I knew these dancing bears; they had been the delight of my childhood. Most of them were trained to kiss the hand that tossed a few coins into the tambourine, and I could never forget the fearful, blissful tickle in the pit of my stomach the first time the muzzled jaws, one bite of which could have mashed my hand into a bloody pulp, sent the long lilac-colored tongue slithering out like a serpent to lick my fingers, while the bear's trainer raked in the coins from the tambourine with a magician's skill. I called out to the man who led the bear to bring him near me.

I had not reckoned with my lady friend's panic. She leaped up, incapable of uttering a sound, her eyes widening in mortal horror, her fingers clawing at her teeth. I found this terror so overexaggerated that I could not help laughing. Her behavior was too childish—after all, the bear was muzzled, and a powerful man was holding him on a thick chain. I felt I was about to lose my temper. I said, "C'mon, stop acting so silly; he only wants to kiss your hand nicely!" And I took her hand and tried to bring it to the bear's moist nose. But she resisted vigorously, and now I really did lose my temper and pulled her hand to the bear's nose. She whimpered like a child. Then, with a final desperate exertion, she wrenched her hand free. For an instant, I totally forgot myself and slapped her face.

It was like a stroke of black lightning. For one split second, the pain brought forth the look of her ecstasy. But instead of ending in transfiguration, it slowly changed to bedazzlement. She closed her eyes. When she opened them again, her face was lifeless; it revealed no intelligible expression. Yet it was marked; it bore an invisible sign, the blemish of something beyond comprehension whose overpowering reality must be accepted. No personal sorrow could mark a face in that way. What I saw was no longer a face; it was humanity facing the inevitable character of suffering beyond all notion of despair. I had seen this lack of expression in the face of a thief who had been caught in the act and then captured after a wild chase.

I must add here that all these reflections came retrospectively. At the moment, I had no time to think: someone had grabbed my shoulder and was pulling me around. I stood nose to nose with four or five of the men who had been sitting at the nearby tables. One of them, whom I knew from the factory, a carpenter with whom I had often joked around when we met, was clutching my shoulder and hissing into my face: "Take it easy, punk, if you don' wan' us to beatcha outta your jacket! In dis place, you don' hit a woman 'cause she's scared of a bear, unnerstan', you piss-elegant dude! In this place, ya don' force no body to play wit' wild animals. We'll teach you to act like a *boyar*!"

My urge to punch him, no matter how badly it would turn out, was paralyzed by amazement. These men, whom I had all liked, whom I had considered my friends, were standing around me as enemies. They had not just become hostile after my faux pas, which I regretted already. No: they had always been hostile to me; they had never considered me as one of their own, never taken me seriously. I had always been fundamentally different for them, someone of a different race. And they despised this different race to which I belonged, and I probably repelled them all the more for trying to ingratiate myself by acting like one of them. . . .

This reflection too I must have had only later on, even if I felt it fully at that moment. I had no chance to think, for Mr. Garabetian interceded. "Let's not have a riot here, fellows!" he said with a compelling authority in his indolent voice. He took me aside, and the circle of my opponents disbanded.

"If you hit a woman, it has to come from the heart," said Mr. Garabetian as he walked me to my Model T, signaling the tavernkeeper not to worry about my check. "Otherwise, you show them that you're afraid of them." And after a tiny pause: "We"—I knew he did not mean the community of slum dwellers but rather the members of a very advanced and fragile state of civilization, where he was probably quite lonely—"we do not hit. We stopped hitting long ago. . . ." It was up to me to glean from this humiliating rebuke that he rather regretted having spared the rod with his son or that other fathers had spared it with their sons.

The Black Widow was waiting mutely at the car. During the drive home, she said not a word. I held my tongue, too. There may have been a lot to say; perhaps something could have been made good again. But nothing could be restored to what it once had been.

When we came to her house, she got out, unlocked the door, and walked in. This time, she did not leave the door open, but pulled it to: without dramatics, without the arrogance of the offended lady, without any *éclat*, but firmly and definitively. I never saw her again. Through the district salesman, she informed the Aphrodite Company that she no longer wished to be inconvenienced by visits from the display-window decorators of the firm. This made little difference to me as I soon left the company anyway.

I could only be grateful for my departure from Aphrodite, for how would I have felt if I had encountered the girl in the wheelchair as I crept out of a drugstore window with a pile of soap boxes and shampoos under my arm? Now that I no longer had to fear being caught at such an embarrassing occupation, I looked back with some ironic aloofness to my anxieties in this respect; ultimately, my excursion into the world of shop assistants could be taken as good fun. Yet even now, at the sight of the girl in the wheelchair, I involuntarily whirled around as though trying to conceal myself; and this threw me back once again into the spiritual ordeals and the muddled conflicts of that time.

Something must have happened to me. Something basic in me had shifted, had broken and crumbled—and it was the ground under my feet. No longer did I feel I belonged to a caste enjoying authority by dint of universal respect. Rather, it was a caste that blemished me, as though I were Jewish. And no matter what I did, I could no more change my nature than a Jew could. The most painful humiliation of all was how I had been rebuffed by the men I had tried to ingratiate myself with. That would never happen again, I promised myself. It was worse than when a Jewish woman running a dumpy shop put on ladylike airs.

A lot of things that Mr. Garabetian had said whirled

through my mind. Was it really true? Was I afraid of women? The girl in the wheelchair—but she was a phantom: I had walked past her, turning away as if not really noticing her, as if my attention had been caught by something else. Then I was cowardly, too! Frightened in this, too! . . . She had probably not even noticed me; I could not have meant anything whatsoever to her, a passerby, a pedestrian among hundreds of other pedestrians. Any possibility of her becoming my mistress and ideal beloved was sheer fantasy. And yet I was answerable to her.

Very well, I had been charmed by her being so well taken care of, by the aura of the child from a good background. The mama's boy in me was homesick. That was all. No doubt, the sight of her passed so spectacularly into my gonads because of my involuntary notion that she, being crippled, could hardly defend herself if I attacked her. Jews, too, challenged you with defenselessness, especially Jewish women, and particularly Jewish widows. . . .

So perhaps Mr. Garabetian was right, and I would never tell him so, now that I did not drop in on him every day. But if he wasn't right, he wasn't wrong either: I did fear women. And whenever I might believe I did not need to fear a woman, then a shaft instantly grew in my trousers—and aimed into nothingness.

Löwinger's Rooming House

In 1957, for reasons and under circumstances I won't go into now, I stayed for a few days at a place called Spitzingsee, in upper Bavaria. As I had to spend the greater part of my time there waiting, I often went for walks. On one such excursion I discovered a place to hire boats at the lakeside.

I am not a dedicated oarsman; on the contrary, a traumatic experience in early adolescence put me off rowing forever, and I still tend to regard it as a vulgar and in no way exhilarating pastime.

The instigator of this aversion was a relative of mine, my senior by many years, a man who was recommended to me as a paragon in every sense. He was what one calls a *Feschak* in Vienna: an Uhlan squadron leader who had returned from the Great War safely and in one piece, he had adapted to civilian life easily and become a successful businessman, was handsome, elegant, a sports- and ladies' man. He used to spend his Sundays at a rowing club on the Danube, and since it was hoped that his company and the fresh air would influence my frail character and wan state of health beneficially, I was often encouraged to accompany him there. I transferred all my carefully nurtured hatred from him to the club he frequented.

It was rigorously exclusive; already at that date, 1927, one of the conditions for admission into the aquatic society was watertight proof of Aryan birth. The comradeship of its members was generally regarded as exemplary. These venerable gentlemen—one and all of an optimistic disposition—would climb into the single sculls, double, foursome, and eights, and heave up the river moving like metronomes all morning, then turn and shoot back down on the crest of the current in little more than a quarter hour. Under the showers, where they then sluiced away the sweat of their labors, I was to hear the remark that became the basis for my lifelong animosity against rowing.

I was scarcely thirteen and very shy. I hated the studied nonchalance with which these muscular men dropped their shirts and shorts and stepped naked into the showers. There they would stand, spitting and spluttering, their hair plastered over their faces, and, without the slightest abashment, mix yellow jets of urine into the clear white of the water, send farts reverberating around the tiled walls, and discuss "women."

A prominent subject was Josephine Baker, who was appearing at a Viennese theater at the time. Needless to say, I was head over heels in love with her, and I suffered torments as I listened to the detached professionalism with which her charms were discussed as though she were some favored racehorse. "Class," my dashing relative said, turning his face in a screwed-up grimace to the nozzle, soap suds oozing from his armpits and pubic hair, "that's what she's got, class, even though she's black. Better than a Jewess, though, all the same. I tell you, if I weren't in training . . ." And like an echo coming from the tiled walls a voice answered him: "Well, let us know if you succeed—it's only fair among friends and members of the same club."

Thirty years later, then, on the banks of the Spitzingsee, I felt not the slightest desire to hire a rowboat. Out of sheer boredom I exchanged a few words concerning the weather and the business prospects of the morrow, a Sunday, with the proprietress. The woman's odd accent arrested my attention.

"You're not a Bavarian," I said.

She shook her head.

"Yugoslav?" I ventured.

"No," she said, "you'll never guess."

Nevertheless I tried; the gulash of nationalities and accents in Central Europe is indeed quite confusing, but an attentive ear can generally localize them, and to my trained one it was clear that she came from some neck of my own woods.

"I'm from Bucharest," she finally admitted, and I delightedly addressed her in Rumanian. "But I'm not Rumanian," she added.

"What, then?"

She was Ukrainian.

Her evasiveness aroused my curiosity. "What did you do in Bucharest?" I wanted to know.

"I was an artiste," she replied with a coy mixture of demureness and twinkling eyes that put me on the scent of some nocturnally practiced art.

"A dancer?"

No, a singer, not of the operatic or *Lieder* kind, simply a singer in a Russian chorus.

I felt a thrill. "In a garden restaurant behind the Biserică Albă?"

She gazed at me in astonishment. "How did you know?"

Yes, that indeed was the question. By the grace of God alone, apparently, and it confused me even more than it did her, for I had never set foot in this restaurant, wasn't even sure on which street or passage behind the Biserică Albă it was situated. But I had heard the chorus, every night, a whole summer long.

It was a summer that according to my memory consisted solely of lavender-blue skies and unfulfilled longings; only a few isolated events and disjointed situations still hover in my mind; the one thing I remember distinctly is that it was insufferably hot; no dog showed its nose on the streets until sundown. I spent most of my days, certainly most of my evenings, under a canopy on the terrace of my tiny apartment, which was perched on the flat roof (today one might grandly refer to it as a penthouse) of one of the high-rise buildings that even at that early date and especially in the quarter around the Biserică Albă had shot up all over Bucharest. At that time my passion for horseracing had taken me by the scruff of the neck in the truest sense of the word: I'd been thrown, had dislocated three joints in my spine, and was obliged to wear a plaster cast around my neck and shoulders, like the unforgettable Erich von Stroheim in *La Grande Illusion*.

With this mishap my own illusions, which had also been sweeping, evaporated into the lavender-blue heavens: my intention, for instance, to transport steeplechase horses to Abyssinia, making a fortune with them in the flourishing colony of the Italian Empire, and then returning home to convince a certain young lady that her refusal to unite her life with mine had been a mistake.

I felt no need of company. I stayed at home, cooked my own meals; a half-crazed jockey who had lost his license ran my errands. I lay on a deck chair in the shade of my canopy and read, and when it got too dark, I laid my book aside and drifted back into the dreams which the paling void above my head had absorbed so effortlessly. And night after night, on the stroke of nine, the strains of abrasive-sweet young girls' voices singing *"Hayda troika,"* the prelude to an ensuing nonstop revue of banal Russian folk music, rose from one of the alleys below me.

More than once I crossed to the balustrade and looked over in the hope that in the deepening dusk the glow of light that certainly marked the spot would rise to me, too, for it was audibly clear that the singing was being done in the open air, and my knowledge of the gardens and bars amidst the towering walls of the stark *modernaki* buildings told me there would be garlands of colored light bulbs dangling over the tables between potted lemon trees; the orchestra dais too would be framed in a blaze of light, and a multicolored neon sign with the name of the place in Russian letters and a double-headed Imperial Eagle would decorate the entrance. In my mind I saw the chorus girls clearly before me: the stiff, puffed bells of their skirts, the sturdiness of their legs in red saffian boots sticking out beneath, their embroidered blouses and blank doll-like faces with lurid circles of carmine dabbed on their cheeks, their streaky hair beneath the gold-edged triangular bonnets that always reminded me of the all-seeing eye of God as depicted on icons—all these details remained imprinted in my memory because they had been merely imagined, images evoked by the melancholy of the songs. This dragging melancholy came not so much from the *shirokaya natura*, the weighty Russian soul, as from the robotlike monotony of the girls' singing; wafting aimlessly through the lofty echo chamber of those nights, the melodies became tokens of the emptiness of my days. Although I often thought of going down to find out whether everything was as I pictured it, this intention was also to remain unfulfilled. I was irresolute that summer, apathetic, not, I reassured myself, in the Oblomov sense, more in the nature of Dürer's *Melancholia* or the medieval drawing of Walther von der Vogelweide, sitting on a stone mulling over a finished chapter of life while vainly seeking the key to the next. Apart from which I knew I'd have to change lodgings in a few weeks' time.

This tiresome necessity was due to my own neglect; I knew from experience and acquaintances' repeated warnings that for some reason the Bucharesters were given to changing their dwelling places with astonishing regularity and that the dates of transmigration were fixed as irrevocably as the advent of spring or fall: in May, on St. George's Day, and in October, on St. Demetrius's. On those two days not a single van was to be had in the whole city; the streets were choked with carts and wagons precariously loaded with everything including the kitchen sink. I'd heard it said that neighbors on the same floor would rather swap flats than face another half year in the old one; those who did not have the foresight to get extension clauses in their leases past these dates were liable to be evicted without ceremony. It happened to me. With the dawn of St. Demetrius's Day, the new tenants stood puffing at my door, and I had no choice but to gather my few belongings and descend to the street. By luck I soon found lodgings at a place called Löwinger's Rooming House.

This establishment was run by a family consisting of Mr. and Mrs. Löwinger, his mother-in-law, and his sister-in-law. Mr. Löwinger, who looked like a prematurely aged rabbinic student, was a peace-loving gentleman pampered in every conceivable way by his womenfolk. By way of profession he sold lacquered pens—cheap, brightly colored wooden pens used mostly by schoolchildren; the colored lacquers on the shafts had a pleasant marbleized look but the disadvantage— or advantage, for Mr. Löwinger—of chipping and flaking easily, so that the pens frequently had to be renewed. Nevertheless, Mr. Löwinger's profit was slim enough. He also ran a line in carved imitation-ivory pens in whose holders lenses showed the Castel Sant'Angelo in Rome or the Eiffel Tower in Paris, tiny, but in minute detail, as though viewed through the wrong end of a telescope. But these more expensive items had nothing like the turnover of the wooden ones.

Mr. Löwinger augmented his income by gambling, play- ing games that demand intelligence rather than those that depend on Fortuna's smile. At chess, dominoes, and all advanced card games he was more than a match for most of the players who sat waiting to try their luck in the cafés, although, by his own admission, he was a dilettante compared to his father, who had lived on this source of income alone, never done a stroke of work in his life. One advantage he had had, Mr. Löwinger said ruefully, was that the cafés were full of suckers in those days.

Mr. Löwinger Junior was a mite of a man, a fact he himself never ceased to marvel at, since his father had stood at six feet four and weighed nigh on three hundred pounds. Minute again in comparison to her husband was Mrs. Löwinger, whereas her mother and sister were positively Amazonian; the old lady with iron-gray hair reminded one of a fairground crystal-ball gazer; the sister, Iolanthe, was similar in type, with Oriental features and pronounced physical charms. When I moved in, Mrs. Löwinger was four months pregnant. The long-term lodgers informed me that this was regularly the case with Mrs. Löwinger at intervals of five to six months, and that the next miscarriage was surely imminent. Only once had one of her pregnancies gone the distance, but the resulting infant had been so small and feeble that the lodgers had laid bets on its chances to survive. One coarse gentleman remarked that the only one to make a killing had been the infant itself; it had died within the hour.

This initial conversation characterized the general tone of Löwinger's Rooming House. With one exception, a lady of whom I shall relate in due course, the boarders were exclusively male: traveling salesmen, students living in Bucharest for the term, a starving Russian sculptor, a man with radical political views who'd started professional life as the rear end of a horse in a circus, a journalist down on his luck. Regularly and for months on end the house was peopled by the members of a wrestling troupe, the glorious gladiators of what they themselves called "Luptele Greco-Romane."

Largely on their account the meals served at Löwinger's were gargantuan. The Löwingers were Hungarian Jews who came from the region of Temeshvar, where Hungarian, Rumanian, Austrian, and Jewish culinary arts mingled in happy harmony. Both the mother-in-law and Iolanthe cooked exquisitely. The whole community ate at a single *table d'hôte*, all except the Russian sculptor, that is; he was too poor to participate and preferred to starve in his garret alone. When the wrestlers were present, extra portions of noodles and other pasta were added to the already sumptuous dishes, since with men like Haarmin Vichtonen, the Finnish world

champion, and Costa Popowitsch, his Bulgarian counterpart, or the Nameless One with the Black Mask, who always
mysteriously and decisively made his appearance toward the
end of the tournaments, it was not merely a matter of
keeping up the muscle tone but of keeping up their weight as
well; the very walls quaked when they entered the room.
Outside the ring they were mild as lambs, at times quite
timorous. Duday Ferencz—whose task it was as Hungarian
world champion to play the savage Philistine in Rumania
with no regard for fair play and so incense the Rumanian
spectators to outbursts of scorn and hatred (in Hungary this
lot fell to Radu Protopopescu, a Rumanian)—Duday Ferencz once complained that the public had stormed the box
office and made off with the night's take. In answer to our
question as to why they, the mightiest men in the world,
hadn't intervened, they looked at one another wide-eyed and
said simply, "But that might have led to violence."

The wrestlers traveled a lot between their sojourns at
Löwinger's Rooming House and had a tale or two to tell; the
mealtimes grew longer by the day. The students, whose
families apparently feared their offspring would come to
grief on their meager allowances in the big city, were
bombarded with packages from home, from the contents of
which the boys readily distributed what they were incapable
of eating themselves. Rumania was a rich land in those days;
sausage and ham, pastries and pies, flowed into the house in
vast quantities. When the point came where the mere
mention of food turned our stomachs, someone would
invariably have the brainstorm: "Cherkunof's starving!"
meaning the poverty-stricken Russian sculptor upstairs.

Cherkunof was a rather unpleasant man who hardly ever
deigned to show himself: some maintained this was because
he had no shirt to his name, and indeed, if one did happen to
run into him on the landing, he would clutch his threadbare
jacket over his naked breast and mutter something that might
as well have been an apology as a request to go to hell; even
the Löwingers, who hadn't received a penny in rent from

him for years and allowed him to stay on out of sheer brotherly love, did everything they could to avoid him. Iolanthe had made attempts to draw him into the family circle but had been sent packing, although one vitriolic tongue at the dining-room table implied that Cherkunof's reaction had been prompted not so much by the victuals she'd offered him as by the libidinous favors she'd expected in return: poor Iolanthe was no spring chicken, and she badly wanted a man. Be that as it may; after weeks of solitary confinement, during which he might well have died and been well into the process of decomposition for all the other Löwinger inhabitants could have cared, Cherkunof would suddenly find himself confronted with a string of well-wishers bearing whole salamis, liverwursts, apple strudel, and chocolate cake. Again, and perhaps understandably, his response was anything but thankful. With livid, hate-filled eyes he would stare first at the untimely offerings, then at their bearers, among whom, to top it all off, the rear end of the horse was prancing—a man whom Cherkunof as a White Russian loathed with all his being because of the man's Bolshevik convictions.

"You vont to poison me?" he shouted. "Vell? You vont to poison me! See vat I think of your offers! So to your offers!" He spat, and went on spitting on the slabs of bacon and poppy-seed buns until the foiled benefactors beat a hasty retreat, laughing their heads off.

It was my first experience of such a milieu, which only served to heighten my enjoyment of it. After the splendid isolation of my "penthouse" near the Biserică Albă and the Russian restaurant I never saw, I delighted in adapting myself to a community, however motley. Not that I felt so out of place; with my plaster-of-Paris collar, my bizarre professional ambitions and brief past among jockeys, trainers, stableboys, and frisky fillies, I fitted in quite naturally to this freak sideshow and did my best to blend in.

As is often the case when men of none too delicate upbringing congregate, the level of conversation at Löwinger's Rooming House was earthy to say the least. No respect whatever was shown for the Löwinger ladies, very likely for the simple reason that Jewesses were not considered ladies. They themselves had long since become accustomed to the fact that everything pertaining to the human body, particularly its sexual aspects, was openly discussed in basic terms at Löwinger's. The wrestlers were an exception, it's true, and not out of celibate necessity as sportsmen but out of genuine purity of spirit. Only Costa Popowitsch, who couldn't deny a hearty female following, would reply vaguely and in a general way when approached on the subject, but he never quoted personal experience. The Greco-Romans' reticence was more than made up for by the salesmen, however, who delighted in giving detailed descriptions of their latest conquests. The rear end of the horse—his name was Dreher, I remember—gave lectures on sexual repression and emancipation; the students were content to listen, risking only occasional contributions; whereas the uncrowned king in this respect was undoubtedly Pepi Olschansky, the luckless journalist. It was his boast that he'd never left a well-filled petticoat unexplored.

Sometimes things got out of hand and Mr. Löwinger gently reminded his guests of his mother-in-law's advanced years—a dangerous admonition that usually evoked only catcalls and the Ruthenian adage "Never try and shock Grandma with a flash of your cock; she's had bigger in her day," and the rejoinder that people living in glass houses shouldn't throw stones, as Mrs. Löwinger's constant state of pregnancy was tangible proof of her husband's voracious appetite and he shouldn't make life more difficult than it was already.

This last was a reference to a very real problem with regard to receiving visitors at the establishment. The Löwingers had a small dog, a brown pinscher with cropped ears and tail and the habit of kicking up a tremendous racket whenever strangers appeared at the house, making it hard for the inmates to receive even the most innocent visitor unnoticed. Pepi Olschansky insisted on the right to cohabit regularly, once a day minimum, and his lady friends were understandably daunted by the glaring attention the dog's hullabaloo drew to their furtive flights over the back stairs. Pepi threatened to slit the pooch's throat one day if he didn't shut up, which the dog somehow seemed to understand, for he henceforth bared his fangs and howled at the very sight of Pepi. If Olschansky made even the slightest motion to shoo him away, the yowling beast made straight for his beloved protector, the starveling Cherkunof.

The odd thing was that sexual assuagement was to be had right there on the premises, but no one availed himself of it. It was an open secret that Iolanthe would be only too eager to oblige a friend in need; she was in her mid-thirties and eminently ready for plucking. Nevertheless, for some enigmatic reason, she found no takers, again perhaps simply because she was Jewish; one couldn't "stoop that low" was the prevailing attitude; even Cherkunof had declined.

As was her optimistic habit with each newcomer, she'd welcomed me with open arms, immediately suggested that I take my siesta in her room, as mine overlooked the busy street. But I refused this and all other offers as well, knowing that nothing would remain a secret at Löwinger's for long: it didn't need the dog to pinpoint one's movements on the ancient landings; twenty pairs of cocked ears noted every creak. So although I would have liked to sample Iolanthe's ample charms, my fear of appearing ridiculous in my fellow boarders' eyes and thus jeopardizing my integration into the community was stronger. I was savoring the questionable comfort of conformity for the first time in my young life, little knowing that I was soon to be confronted with it as an apotheosis.

Apart from which there was another female present, the servant girl Marioară, a Rumanian country maid of most extraordinary beauty. She was tall, with a sumptuous figure, wonderful shoulders and breasts; erotic promise emanated from her like a golden aura. As was the custom with girls of her station, she wore traditional peasant dresses; the wide belt that separated the bounty of her wraparound skirt from the thrust of her low-cut blouse was pulled so tight that the tips of a man's ten fingers met with ease around it; inimitable, the grind of her behind when she walked.

It was said that she went to bed with every Tom, Dick, and Harry at the drop of a hat. And with the same vehemence that the male connoisseurs at Löwinger's considered it slumming to steal into Iolanthe's room, they proclaimed it a must to have spent at least one night's dalliance in Marioară's.

Needless to say, I did everything to give proof of my qualities as a seducer. But, to my disappointment, Marioară's only response was the taunting gleam of her smile, as if it came through veils of lust. The fact that I always found her door locked seemed ample evidence to me that she preferred the others' company to mine.

Nevertheless, I was quite popular in Löwinger's Rooming House. I enjoyed the reputation of being gregarious and witty. The days when a wanton masculine assessment of Josephine Baker's charms would make me furious were long past; now, when conversation turned to the fair sex, its various physical and inherent attributes and shortcomings, its needs and foibles, I could chip in with an observation or two, these based not so much on wide experience as on a kind of expedient philosophy. Thanks to my checkered academic career, I had come by a rich repertoire in bawdy jokes and verses and could usually crown each specific erotic circumstance under discussion with a pertinent quotation and thus ascend from the earthy detail to the sublime realms of porn poetry. This facility earned me much applause. The melancholy of my recent past was soon forgotten.

It would be wrong to suppose that an era of vigorous activity now dawned for me: I simply took life as it came. The plaster cast around my neck was no great hindrance—except when tying my shoelaces—and was therefore not a good reason for staying away from some form of study or other useful occupation, but I used the accident as a welcome excuse for a long period of recuperation. Money was no problem; I had saved a little to finance my aborted Abyssinian enterprise, and life in Bucharest at that time, especially under Löwinger's roof, was cheap. I did nothing in particular and a lot in general. To pass the time of day and still my curiosity, I often went with Mr. Löwinger on his gambling sorties to the cafés; the experience I gained there in respect of types of humanity and their behavior was not to be found in any handbook. Sometimes he took me along on his trips to outlying villages, where he replenished local stock in marbled pens, and I still carry with me the vivid memory of dusty country roads, of oxen sauntering home along them by the orange glow of evening as though paddling through shallows of burnished gold, of the resinous smell of fresh-cut logs, piled high in blocks before black forests above which the grass-green domes of the Carpathian outriders loomed like a child's cutout pattern; or, in the midst of this magic, a shepherd boy swathed in sheepskins sitting cross-legged on a tree stump whittling his stick but not looking up; or the dirge of boys' unbroken voices through the open windows of a Jewish school, their pale egg-shaped faces framed by long earlocks; or the stamping of dancers at a peasant wedding, the sweat flying from the fiddler's brow, the girls' plaits streaming out from under their slipping head scarves; of meadows couching the silver of a stream, storks stalking through its marshes, accelerating and then rhythmically pulling themselves up to an azure sky; sparkling drops of water shooting in streaks from green flax whipped by girls hidden by the willows—these and many other priceless memories. . . .

My supple tongue had won me the friendship of Pepi Olschansky, the luckless journalist. I could never quite decide whether I liked or loathed him. He was a small, wiry fellow, reddish blond, with devilishly vivacious brown eyes, a pointed nose, a pointed chin, and a thin-lipped mouth that could twist itself into the most perfidious smile I've ever seen. As a German from the Bukovina, he'd served in the former Imperial Austrian Army, and quite famously, apparently; talk had it that he'd been awarded the Silver Cross of Valor. Some rays of this glorious past were still around him; although I had never seen him in anything but rather shabby civilian clothes—hatless, even in those days; no stick, let alone gloves—I envisaged a first lieutenant's star glistening on his collar when I thought of him, but that may well have been because certain aspects of his glamor aroused unpleasant memories of my rowing relative in Vienna. Olschansky was not so militantly brash as the other blade, though, and was light years ahead in intelligence and education. His literary taste was impeccable. He even composed verses himself, a talent that had led to his dismissal as editor from a German-language newspaper in Bucharest.

A romantic story. A privately printed edition of his poems had found its way into the hands of the Queen Mother, Maria, who was something of a poetess herself. Pepi was summoned to Cotroceni Palace and received graciously, indeed on an equal footing; thereafter her resplendent majesty commanded Pepi's undying devotion. When in the course of a political intrigue a certain statesman persuaded the publisher of Pepi's newspaper to launch a slanderous campaign against Queen Maria, and the publisher in turn commissioned Pepi to write the articles, Pepi adamantly refused. It came to a flaming row, news of which leaked out and caused a public scandal: the statesman resigned, the newspaper temporarily ceased publication and came under public fire when eventually it returned to press; Pepi was sacked, branded a traitor by the Germans in Bucharest, and snubbed by them thereafter. This gave him a rather dubious aura, which he sensed not without guilt and which he tried to make up for with insolence. At the same time, there was something of a martyr about him: after all, if a man is a true outcast, then he isn't much helped by the reputation of being the gentleman who never betrays a lady—especially since the queen could not compromise herself and therefore could

151

not express her gratitude. Which was why she never again received him at the palace. All of this made him intensely interesting for me, of course.

Since he had just as little to do as I, we took to going for long walks together, and I learned a lot from him. He knew his Bucharest, a city I had till then regarded as a sloppy conglomeration of Balkan disorder and faceless modernity, but under Pepi's tutelage, hearing his expert account of its history, I came to see it in a different light, began to apprehend it, as one does a new language. Its jumble of junk came to life and started to speak, told a story of boyars and Phanariots, monks, pashas, and long-haired revolutionaries who had descended from the mountains. I was given the code to the Rumanian arabesque and found much that complemented my own character, by birthright, which till then had been blurred by the stamp of my Austrian education.

Löwinger's Rooming House stood near a park that bears the sweet-sounding name "Cismigiù." I was used to rising early since childhood, and my equestrian period had strengthened this habit. While the Löwinger rafters were still ringing to the snort of snores, I stole away to walk in that park. It was fall. Nowhere in the world have I seen colors to match those of Rumania in this season. It may well have been the fact that Pepi Olschansky came with me on these matinal marches that finally endeared him to me. He was a bad sleeper since the Great War, when a howitzer shell had exploded right beside him and buried him; although the shrapnel had not struck him, the blast had peppered his back full of particles of earth which now, after so many years, still kept festering their way out.

Not that this heroic misfortune alone made his company welcome, but it did prompt me to be civil, and his apparent liking for me did the rest. With the same indulgence I imagined he'd shown with his cadets in the good old days of the Imperial Army, First Lieutenant Olschansky did me the honor of allowing me to pay for his umpteen *tzuikas* in the bars on our way along the Calea Victoriei, winding up with his *marghiloman* at the Café Corso, then returned the compliment by accompanying me to the racetrack, where I nostalgically stuck my nose into the stables, chatted with the jockeys and trainers, and gave Pepi hot tips on how best and quickest to lose my money at the betting windows.

These visits helped me close a chapter of my life; I realized that my career as an amateur jockey was at an end, not so much on account of my fractured spine, not even because the few weeks' participation at Löwinger's *table d'hote* had sent my weight rocketing to a level I knew I would hardly even have the energy to reduce. Even if I had—to ride for three hours at the crack of dawn, drink six cups of hot tea, don a rubber vest, shirt, one lightweight and one heavyweight sweater, a leather jacket, and pound the pedals of a bicycle for an hour, then collapse into a steam bath and eat nothing but potatoes with a sprig of parsley for the rest of the week—I knew that it would be impossible to pick up again where I'd left off. And since turning points have always fascinated me—a change of time's quality, so to say, when a mere change of atmosphere can alter the course of one's own life or that of a whole epoch—this change from the open-air solitude on my roof above the Biserică Albă to the lusty carnivalesque existence at Löwinger's Rooming House became a part of my biography that has recurred in my thoughts ever since. As I'm unable to put my finger on any one circumstance that would logically explain the tangent, I am inclined to think that a new chapter began with the day that I was released from my plaster collar.

Löwinger's was agog with excitement that day, and it was only with the greatest difficulty that I kept the whole company of long-term lodgers from going with me to the clinic. Still, my escort was large enough: all four Löwingers;

Pepi Olschansky, of course; the rear end of the horse, named Dreher; and a salesman who had a car.

"I had no idea you'd such a large family," said the assistant doctor I'd made friends with over the months.

"Yes, a colorful bunch, aren't they?"

"At a guess I'd say that with the exception of the blond one with the pointed nose and the fellow with the gray forelock, they're all from Galicia?"

"No, from Temeshvar."

"Watch out that the doctor doesn't see them. He eats Jews on toast for breakfast, bones and all."

"He can hardly make more of a botch of my neck."

"True, but he can add a couple of digits to your bill."

I can still feel the coldness of the big scissors blade as it slipped underneath my cast. "Please be careful," I requested. "Remember I put a sweater on underneath to keep the cast from hurting. I wouldn't want it ruined."

He applied pressure and began cutting. It went much easier than I'd imagined; there was a dull grating sound and the cast fell apart. The sweater was nowhere to be seen.

"You've absorbed it," the assistant said. "Must have been good wool, pure lanolin. It's protected your skin, all right."

I felt oddly naked and chilly. "Will my head fall off if I nod?" I asked.

"Give it a try."

I did. My head stayed put. I gingerly turned it first to the left, then to the right.

"Keep doing that carefully," he said, "come back tomorrow for a massage, and we'll show you a couple of exercises which will help as well. The doctor will want to see you too, so come without the Semitic caravan, if possible."

Outside in the corridor my Semitic caravan welcomed me with unrestrained joy; all three Löwinger ladies had tears in their eyes, and Iolanthe threatened with a kiss.

"Be careful, for the love of God!" Mrs. Löwinger cried. Her mother took me by the hand and led me to a chair. "Slowly does it now, boy, take it easy, one step at a time."

I felt like a peeled egg: "Like the baby in Philipp Otto Runge's *Morning*," I said to Pepi Olschansky.

He smiled his perfidious smile. "Iolanthe will be only too glad to change your diapers," he answered.

The rear end of the horse shook his wild gray revolutionary's mane. "I trust for your sake that you regard the occasion as one of rebirth. With that shell of plaster, shake off the shackles of the useless and asocial life you've led till now, and apply your energy to a more worthy cause!"

This was not the immediate case. That night, after an evening of revelry and mirth at Löwinger's table—the Greco-Romans showed me all manner of tricks and exercises to strengthen my atrophied muscles—I sat up with Pepi. "I feel weary and very content," I said. "Why on earth shouldn't I complete the pleasure and allow Iolanthe to rock me to sleep? She's really eminently beddable and would certainly show her gratitude."

Pepi reached across and selected a cigarette from my case. "The same thought has often crossed my mind," he replied. "Generally speaking, I've nothing at all against Jewesses, but with Iolanthe it would somehow seem like a betrayal of one's race and creed. I don't understand why it should be so, but everyone here feels the same, even Cherkunof."

"I think I know what you mean," I said, in a flash of inspiration. "Committing a sin, like sleeping with one's mother."

He looked up in surprise, then laughed aloud. "You're dead right, that's it exactly. A strange thought, the taboo in a nutshell. Have you ever thought of writing?"

The thought was alien to me and I somewhat asininely asked, "Writing what?"

"Stories," he said, "perhaps a novel, who knows? You're extraordinarily observant."

I laughed and right away dismissed it from my mind.

I was more preoccupied with another incident. One evening the conversation had—once again—turned to Mr. Löwinger's amazing knack for any kind of game. Olschansky had expressed his doubts. I murmured to him, "Be careful! I've watched him winning money from sly old foxes in various coffeehouses."

"Yes," jeered Olschansky, "at dominoes, or tarot, or poker! But not at games of real skill."

I myself had once tried to hold my own against Mr. Löwinger in morris, which had been a forte of mine in my boyhood. But here too I had lost miserably. Olschansky waved me off with a sneer. He insisted on challenging Mr. Löwinger to a game of chess.

"Now *you* watch out," he muttered back at me. "At the military academy, I used to beat people who wound up on the general staff." Nevertheless, he lost the match after a dozen moves. "One game doesn't mean anything!" he cried, running his hand nervously through his hair. "Would you like to see who wins two out of three?"

"Gladly!" said Mr. Löwinger timidly, peering up at his women, who sat around him with immobile faces. We all formed a thick ring around the two opponents: they had long since stopped being players; a duel was being fought.

It was soon decided. Olschansky lost the second game within a bare quarter hour; insisted on playing the third one and lost it so fast that he leaped up, furiously knocking over the chess board, and stormed out of the room, slamming the door behind him.

"Not that I'm normally a poor loser," he later told me. "But I couldn't stand that nasty lurking and finally that triumph in the faces of those Jewish harpies. Did you see the way they sat there, to the left and the right of that little Yid? That unkempt crone, that lecherous Iolanthe, that screechy anemic bitch with that eternal bun in her oven, those witches, all three of them so greedy to see me humiliated that I couldn't even think about any moves. I had to keep fighting the puke rising in me."

"That's known as psychological warfare, isn't it?" I asked, a bit maliciously. "Didn't they prepare you for that at military school?"

Olschansky ignored my baiting. "You know, I really believe they're capable of certain kinds of witchcraft," he said. "Being lucky in a game isn't sheer chance. A man is lucky if he has a certain rapport with the world, the time, the place he's playing in—"

"Yes, but not in chess," I broke in. "A chess player, as the popular adage so nicely puts it, has the law of action in his hand!"

"What do you really have in your hand?" he said, passionately earnest. "You get to recognize that in war. During the first few years in Galicia, I saw a whole lot of Jews. You can experience all kinds of things with them."

"What?" I asked. "Don't keep me in suspense! Do they really slaughter Christian children to enrich their Passover matzos with protein?"

"No, but they believe in one God!" he blurted out, downright fanatically.

"So do my aunts," I said. "One of them goes to Mass every morning."

"It's different, it's different!" He was working himself up. "They've got their God in their blood. They can't get rid of him. . . ." He suddenly threw up his hand as though to shoo a fly away from his nose. "But what nonsense I'm talking, don't you think? Tell me about betting on horses. You say I can bet on win, place, and draw?"

I'm no longer sure whether this conversation took place before or after the Löwingers took in the new female lodger. It caused quite a stir when it was announced one evening that a young lady had moved into room number eight and would be joining us for meals. Mr. Löwinger, who in spite of his scrawniness had undeniable authority—"the dignity of a microbe" was Pepi's definition—appealed to the male assembly in a few well-chosen words to exercise restraint in the lady's presence, at least for the first few days: she was not only a pure country maid but a schoolteacher to boot.

The suspense that built up as we awaited her entrance became so great that even Cleopatra would have had her work cut out for her, and Miss Bianca Alvaro was no Queen of the Nile. She wasn't exactly nondescript, not unsympathetic, but decidedly not winning either; neither pretty nor downright ugly, more on the small side than on the large, more blonde than brunette. Neither her name nor her physiognomy gave any clue as to where she came from. She might have been Jewish, but then again perhaps not. At a rough guess she was in her mid-twenties. She had been studying German language and literature at the University of Jena, and was preparing for a state examination in order to teach German at the local *Gymnasium*. "The only thing one can say about her with any certainty," Pepi remarked, "is that she has luscious tits. She can try and flatten them as much as she pleases, but a connoisseur will spot them a mile off. They're high-slung with a prominent sideways jut; the nipples probably tickle her armpits, a sure sign of quality. There's not much more than a good handful apiece, but they're as firm and juicy as young melons. One will be better able to judge in summer when she wears lighter dresses."

Mr. Löwinger's appeal proved unnecessary, as things turned out. Miss Alvaro's mere presence sufficed to quell all appetite for discussing sex. The change in the tenor of our talk was so marked that one day when she excused herself and left the table earlier than usual, everyone else, including the three Löwinger ladies, remained seated as if by secret arrangement and simultaneously launched into a heated discussion. The first attempt to explain the phenomenon was offered by Iolanthe, and coming from her, in the form of a mournful sigh, it sounded overwhelming: "That's the difference when you're a lady," she moaned, looked across to her mother for confirmation, realized what she'd said, and lowered her eyes in panic.

"Bullshit!" Pepi Olschansky spluttered, "lady . . . lady . . . she's nothing but a bum-beater, that's all. I've never seen anyone better equipped to become a schoolteacher. She has a way of looking at a man that's more sobering than castration. I'm always expecting her to chide us about our dirty fingernails or the way we hold our forks. If Duday Ferencz were to go up to her and say in his beguiling Hungarian way, 'Miz Alvaro, eet would geeve me great pleasure to screw the ass of you,' she'd simply look up and answer, 'Dear Mr. Duday, you surely mean you'd like to screw the ass *off* me, at least I hope you do; you're mixing up your prepositions and adverbs again, and in so doing you completely alter the meaning of the phrase and express a desire to perform an act of sodomy on my person which is generally confined to pederastic relationships. So if, as I trust, the heterosexual method is more to your taste, I suggest that until such time as you have grasped the finer points of our language you'd do better to avoid risking embarrassing misunderstandings and stick to straightforward, basic phrases such as "*Miss*"—not *Miz*—"*Miss* Alvaro, how about a fuck?" ' " We all burst out laughing, and the matter was settled for the time being.

A few days later Miss Alvaro was to cross my path directly. Pepi and I passed through Cismigiù park on the way back from our walk one morning and stopped by the chestnut tree in front of our temporary home; its fruit was thumping to the ground. I stooped and picked one up, peeled off the knobby skin; the nut was shiny and immaculate—"Rather like me when they took off my cast," I remarked to Pepi.

"It doesn't stay that way, unfortunately."

The Löwinger house, which dated from the mid–nineteenth century, was distinctly rural in style, one-storied with a tin roof. It stood facing the road, a narrow courtyard alongside.

Just as Pepi and I entered the yard, Miss Alvaro emerged from the front door and the little brown dog scampered out between her legs, spotted us, and shot forward, yapping furiously, recognized Pepi, gave a howl, and shot back again. For fun I threw the chestnut at him. I hadn't actually intended to hit him, had thrown the nut high, but the dog must have seen the movement of my arm, for he accelerated wildly and ran straight into the missile's trajectory, taking the blow squarely in his exposed rectum. He was even more surprised than we were and let out a scream as though Lucifer himself had raped him. Pepi and I roared with laughter.

Miss Alvaro marched up and planted herself in front of us, glared at me with her big brown eyes, shook her head slowly and incredulously, and said, "*You?* How could you do such a thing? I would not have thought it of you."

I was very embarrassed. Olschansky came to the rescue: "That's his hunter's blood coming out," he said maliciously. "Didn't you recognize it from the precision of the trajectory?"

"Nonsense," I said. "It was pure chance; I didn't aim at him. I'm very sorry." And, although I had no liking for the dog, it was sincere.

Miss Alvaro said no more and was just about to turn and go when we heard Iolanthe's voice through the open kitchen door: "Oh, do stop laughing, you silly goose," and out tumbled the servant girl Marioară, doubled up with laughter, her hands to her face, wiping away the tears. When she looked up and saw me, she controlled herself long enough to say, "I'll never forget that for the rest of my days, never, never," and doubled up again. Her beauty surpassed the superb autumn day, and as she drew a deep breath, straightened up, and gazed at me again, I knew that her door would not be locked that night. Pepi knew it too. He said "Two birds with one stone."

With which Miss Bianca Alvaro also got the message. She turned on her heel and left.

So I was all the more surprised when two days later she spoke to me. "I should like to ask something of you. Will you come to my room for a moment?"

We were alone. She dipped her hand inside her blouse, pulled out a bunch of tiny keys hanging from the chain about her neck, opened a valise, and took out a case wrapped in silk paper. When she'd finally unwrapped and opened it, she

160

held it out to me. "I should be very grateful if you were to tell me whether this ring is valuable or not. I inherited it, but have no knowledge of jewelry. I come from a very poor family. I've heard of such things only in fairy tales."

It was an unostentatious piece, no more than a setting for a single stone. The stone, however, was huge and green; if it were a genuine emerald, it would be worth a little fortune.

"I know nothing of jewelry either," I said. "The best thing to do is to go to a jeweler and then double the price he names you. He'll think you want to sell it and start the bidding low."

"Would you do me the favor of coming with me?" she asked. "I'm from the provinces, a village near Kishinev, and I don't know another soul here in Bucharest I could ask."

I went with her not to one but three different jewelers. The values they quoted varied only slightly and were much higher than I had calculated. This seemed to confuse Miss Alvaro greatly, but she remained reticent. "Thank you very much," she said, as we parted in town—she had already made it clear to me that morning that she didn't want Löwinger's to know about our undertaking, for she had asked that we leave the house separately—"thank you very much, you were as friendly and cooperative as I expected of you."

This drove me to the brink of forgetting my manners. What on earth gave Miss Bianca Alvaro the right to "expect" anything of me at all? What standards had she applied to me and my character, what yardstick of behavior was I obliged to live up to? I for my part gave her no second thoughts whatsoever. By now, I had summed her up and knew which pigeonhole to pop her in. Iolanthe had not been wrong in calling her a lady, but the veneer of her acquired graces couldn't hide her background from me: a drab little Jewish girl from a village near Kishinev—that she was indeed Jewish now seemed fairly certain; Pepi had been prepared to bet on it from the beginning. I couldn't have cared less one way or the other—at all events, I knew her sort. They were a dime a dozen on every village street, all over Rumania; they spent their childhood skipping among mounds of horse dung and flocks of gay sparrows, warbling Hebraic words of wisdom in Jewish schools, chewing Mr. Löwinger's marbled pens and poking their ears and noses with ink-stained fingers, disappearing then to the next town. They returned gangling, cheeky, precocious, and self-confident a couple of years later, unfurled little red flags, and chanted socialistic marching songs; then they went off again. The next time they came back they were unrecognizable—polished, poised, coiffed, and manicured, lugging doctorates on their proud shoulders; they dug themselves in and became dentists, high-school teachers, professors of music, and God only knows what other intellectuals, married similar solid burghers and produced streams of progeny, teaching them to speak refinedly through their noses, packing them off to the Sorbonne to get equipped the better to meddle with the course of the history of civilization. I had witnessed pretty near every stage of these developments in the Carpathian village where I came from, and surmised that Kishinev could not be so very different. And whereas Miss Alvaro no doubt regarded me as the epitome of a smarmy, once-velveteen-suited, governess-tutored youth, cutely twittering away in French, when the time came, my undivided attention to horses and hunting restricting my vocabulary to a fund of some three hundred words—but not hesitating to entrust me with her priceless heirloom!—I on the other hand couldn't help seeing in her the snotty-nosed Jewish guttersnipe we were always in danger of running over when driving through the dusty village streets. It was on the tip of my tongue to tell her she could think, say, or "expect" what the hell she liked of me for all I cared as long as she left me in peace.

I was even more reserved toward her in the days that followed. Besides, I didn't see much of her. Under Pepi's guidance I had begun to read more systematically and selectively, so my time was taken up, added to which the weather broke at last as the *crivetz*, a wind from the steppes, howled across the open marshlands surrounding Bucharest and hit the city, whistled remorselessly through its streets and alleyways, presaging the bitter Balkan winter, discouraging all desire to set foot outside the house. I holed up.

Miss Alvaro wasn't so fortunate; she had to go to her class early each morning, came home then for lunch and disappeared again right afterward, spent her afternoons in some library studying, most probably; and at the dinner table she usually sat with an absent look on her face, seldom spoke, and retired as soon as she finished coffee.

Only once did she take part in a conversation, and that quite heatedly. We were discussing the political situation in Germany. The wrestling troupe had had to cancel a tour in southern Germany and Saxony at the last minute, for the Third Reich authorities had questioned their right to the world championships they claimed, the Nameless One with the Black Mask had been unable to furnish proof of Aryan descent, etc., etc.—the usual story of petty difficulties and preposterous formalities, hardly conducive to showing the "new" Germany in a favorable light. Pepi Olschansky defended the Germans vehemently and ended up by calling the wrestlers "a bunch of loudmouthed fairground barkers," which wounded Haarmin Vichtonen, the Finnish world champion, so cruelly that tears came brimming to his eyes. Radu Protopopescu rushed to his mighty brother's aid and boomed that the Rumanians' sorely tried patience would soon be exhausted if the current megalomania of the "Fatherland" were to increase the already insufferable pretentiousness of its stepchildren living here in their country.

This was just the beginning; the discussion really got under way when Dreher, the putative circus-horse backside, began to question the sincerity of the Nazis' clarion calls in the cause of socialism.

"Do you consider Russian socialism more social?" Olschansky asked.

"That's not the point!" the backside bellowed. "I am debating socialism in principle!"

"Without principle would be nearer the mark," Olschansky answered viciously. "Professing to stamp out poverty but only doing away with the fruits of free enterprise, above all those of the mind. Sacrificing life for an abstract theory. Reducing everything to the lowest possible denominator."

"You've no idea what you're talking about," scoffed Dreher grandly.

Olschansky grinned. "Well, up till now I've always kidded myself that my field of vision at least stretched as far as Sidoli's circus ring."

"What do you mean by that?" Dreher snorted.

"I was attempting to compare our limits of horizon." Olschansky grinned provocatively.

"Explain yourself!" Dreher demanded.

"Oh, do I have to?" Olschansky sighed, looking round at the others. "I don't really think anyone here needs an explanation."

"Well, I *do*," Dreher barked, and his gray forelock bobbed dangerously in front of his eyes, which looked daggers at Olschansky.

"Since you insist," Olschansky spat back, equally venomously, "I'll put it to you straight: I meant that when one has spent half one's life with one's nose up the ass of the man in front, it's hardly surprising that one thinks as you do."

"Slander!" Dreher screamed. "I know you all believe this ridiculous story that I was once part of a circus number. It's all Cherkunof's doing: he invented it. I shall go to him this minute and demand that he come down and own up right away!"

We had to restrain him from dashing upstairs to get the unwitting sculptor. "Leave him alone!" Iolanthe begged in the midst of the melee. "Dear Mr. Dreher, all these years we've thought of you as a horse's ass and loved you none the less for it. What difference does it make if you're a professor?"

But Dreher was a difficult man to quieten down.

"I will bring proof of my claim," he said, threatening

Olschansky. "I will force you to corroborate my evidence and make a public announcement reinstating my honor!"

"If only you knew how little I cared," replied Olschansky wearily. "You could be Lenin himself as far as I'm concerned. You'll convince only fools and small children that that which is taking place in Germany is not an attempt to do something of decisive importance for the history of man. The salvation of the individual within a socialist structure— no more and no less. If you opened your eyes and exercised your brain instead of letting your emotions run amok, even you would be bound to see it."

"You really don't have the slightest idea what you're talking about," Miss Alvaro suddenly commented.

Olschansky fixed her with a stare. "Do you perhaps know more?" he demanded.

"I've just come from there. I was studying in Jena until two weeks ago," she answered.

"They allowed you to study in Germany even though you're Jewish?" Olschansky asked incredulously.

"You are mistaken. I'm an Armenian Christian," she replied, then blushed and bit her lip. After a moment's obvious unease, she raised her head proudly and said, "I won't deny that my parents were Jewish, but the fact remained undetected in Jena. And it has nothing to do with the point in hand."

"In one aspect it certainly does," Olschansky insisted, "in that one identifies Nazism with the Jewish question. One uses it to divert public attention from the very real revolutionary steps being taken in Germany."

"It's my belief—or rather my conviction, based on personal experience—that exactly the opposite is the case. The Nazis are using the so-called Jewish question to cover up far more questionable issues."

Olschansky grinned his provocative grin again; the points of his nose and chin trembled toward each other; he looked for all the world like a demoniacal Punch. "You mention the so-called Jewish question and more questionable issues in the same breath; an admirable play on words, to be sure. But tell me, do you regard the question itself as a mere red herring, or as being indeed in need of a resolution?"

"The question is of valid importance inasmuch as a small, harmless religious minority is now being held responsible for a thousand years' faulty German policy. And, as though that weren't enough, the Nazis pretend that the golden future they promise their countrymen depends solely on the question's being solved."

"With our extermination," Mr. Löwinger added softly.

"Exactly!" exclaimed Dreher, the professor and former horse impersonator. "That's what's so deplorably retrogressive, so abysmally medieval about their whole ideology: it leads to religious fanaticism; it encourages the insane belief that one has only to exorcise the devil for heaven on earth to set in."

"For God's sake don't you start preaching," Olschansky retorted. "If on the one hand you advocate simple rationalism as the new way ahead—you're a democrat, aren't you? Then you believe in the people's right to self-government? Well, then, won't you concede the Germans the right to remove a few Jews from their ranks if the overwhelming majority are convinced they'll be able to manage their affairs better without them?"

Their futile bantering got on my nerves. I knew Olschansky's devious tricks and maneuvers all too well and wanted to put an end to them. The surest method had always been to cite one of my celebrated quotations, so I cried, "Give the masses what they want! Fifty million coprophile flies can't be wrong: eat shit!"

It made a palpable hit, and nearly everyone laughed; even Dreher made a half-grudging, half-acknowledging gesture toward me. Miss Alvaro was the only one who looked at me in outrage; she was at the point of getting up and leaving. Her place at the table was such, however, that an exit to the right would have entailed asking the whole wrestling troupe to get up and let her out, whereas to the left the frail Mrs.

Löwinger had collapsed in a heap. Mrs. Löwinger shook, moaned, and gulped, then grabbed Miss Alvaro's arm and dug her fingers into it.

"What's wrong, for heaven's sake?" Miss Alvaro cried.

Iolanthe sprang to her feet. "God Almighty, she's losing the baby!"

Unfortunately she was right. Mrs. Löwinger was rushed off to hospital, and the next day her mother, red-eyed, told us that all hopes of an addition to the Löwinger family could be buried. When I went to say a few words of compassion to Mr. Löwinger, he looked at me with chill pride in his eyes and said, "I have no regrets; members of our race have no business bringing children into this world."

Soon after this episode, I was flabbergasted when Miss Alvaro stopped me in the passageway, looked over her shoulder in order to make sure that nobody was watching us, and then whispered that she would like to meet me at the Café Corso the next day. She was there before me when I arrived at the appointed time.

"May I invite you to have a drink or something today?" she asked. "I shall be very upset if you refuse."

I accepted and, rather evilly thinking of Olschansky, asked for a *marghiloman*, or what the Italians call a *caffè corretto*—a small cup of mocha coffee with a shot of cognac.

"Do you recommend it?" Miss Alvaro asked. "The thing is, I'm going to ask another favor of you." She smiled shyly, but the smile had a great deal of charm, for she was obviously sure of her ground. "First I must tell you a story," she continued. "The ring you were good enough to help me have valued belonged to an uncle of mine. No blood relative . . ." She hesitated, then went on bravely. "He became critically ill a short time ago, and for this reason I returned from Jena—too late, unfortunately. We had been very close; he had been like a father to me ever since I was a small child. It was because of him that I was brought up an Armenian Christian."

She paused a moment, as though thinking over something

she was reluctant to say. "He was Armenian by birth, from a great family in Constantinople. When the persecution of the Armenians began in the twenties, he emigrated here. Of course he had to leave behind the greater part of his estate and arrived with very little, by his standards. But for my aunt, whom he met almost right away, what he had left was a vast fortune; I told you once, did I not, that I came from a very humble family?

"Would you like a little more brandy in your coffee? Or a brandy all by itself? I know I should." She again smiled her small, shy smile. "I never drink, as you surely guessed, but I find myself unable to tell my story without a lift of some sort. I've never told it before, by the way. . . .

"My uncle first met my aunt when he was ordering new spectacles at an oculist's; she was working there. We're not Eastern Jews at all, not Ashkenazim, but Sephardim, as my name implies, but I'm afraid I can't tell you when my ancestors moved to Bessarabia. Well, as you probably know, among Spanish and Portuguese Jews, especially those who came to Central Europe via Holland, there's a long tradition in oculism, and one of my relatives had continued the practice. This gentleman wasn't exactly a Spinoza, but he seemed to believe in the sovereign rights of the strong over the weak, for he used my poor aunt, who was still very young, quite shamelessly. When she and the Armenian met, it must have been love at first sight. He was probably well aware of her humble origins; he was a man of the world, not only on account of his wealth but through a long family history of intermarriage with the French and Italian aristocracy. However, that she might be Jewish most likely never occurred to him; as I said, their love was spontaneous and unqualified.

"My aunt gave up her job and moved in with him. She was a resourceful housewife and knew how to make life very comfortable, even on their limited means. They became completely self-sufficient and lived happily in splendid isolation for a number of years. Then, when quite unexpectedly both my parents died and there was no one else to look after me, they married in order to fulfill their roles as stepparents respectably.

"I must tell you that my aunt never found the courage to tell him she was Jewish. She knew of the Armenians' general hatred of the Jews, not so much a matter of racial hatred—which would be quite absurd, of course—as a religious rivalry, though none the less fanatical for this. My aunt loved her husband so deeply that she would have done far more than just renounce her faith in order to keep him.

"When I joined them—I was not quite eight years old—she immediately instructed me never, ever to breathe a word that might betray our heritage. I was not with them long before I was sent to an Armenian convent; there, just as had been the case with my aunt vis-à-vis my uncle, my physical appearance aroused no curiosity or comment. Each of the Armenian nuns and the other girls—as indeed my uncle, too—had some facial feature or other that looked just as Semitic to the untrained eye as mine. The only sticky moment was when the teachers found out how ignorant I was in religious matters; they were appalled, but I worked hard and soon caught up with the others. Just as my aunt had done on meeting my uncle.

"I well remember the discussions she had with the priests who came to visit my uncle. They debated for hours the different doctrines of the Monophysites and the Nestorians with regard to the single, double, or composite natures of Christ, or the connection between the vows made for one at baptism and one's own reassertion of them at confirmation. Armenians are extremely devout, and my uncle—who belonged to the United Armenians, the so-called Mechitarists, by the way—positively doted on his church. Can you imagine, he presented his father confessor with a complete first edition of Diderot's *Encyclopedia* because the priest had maintained he daren't possess it since it was on the Index?"

Miss Alvaro took a sip of cognac and then coughed discreetly. "My goodness, that's strong. And I'm not used to

169

it, although I must say I had opportunity enough to get accustomed to it at my uncle's house. He was anything but frugal in that way, loved his food and drink. You know, of course, that Lucullus played an important part in Armenia's history? My uncle jokingly used to say that it was every Armenian's sacred duty to revere his cuisine and his wine cellar, and my aunt used all her considerable guile to make him forget that he could no longer afford to have his salmon sent from Scotland or his wine from Bordeaux. . . . I believe also that their sexual tastes were particularly compatible. . . .

"It broke him when she died last year; he had no desire to continue living without her. Naturally, as a practicing Christian, he did not think of suicide, but there was in any case no need to do so. Only a few months later, although just seventy and in robust health till then, he followed her. His heart simply stopped beating."

She looked at me. "I want to ask another favor of you. As the sole heiress, I inherited not only the ring you saw but the complete contents of my stepparents' apartment. Everything else my uncle possessed—a modest bank account, a few securities, a share in a house, in a word, the remnants of a great fortune, he left to the Armenian Church. I'm very happy; it would have embarrassed me to receive a penny of it. Just the fact that he paid for my education at the convent and later in Germany—quite apart from countless other tokens of generosity—always made me feel, under the covert circumstances, something of a fraud. I have always had a bad conscience that my family concealed our Jewish faith from him. Naturally my aunt made no attempt to have me baptized; she simply let it be assumed that I was a Christian. And perhaps we were in our hearts, but not by right. I often found the conflict hard to bear and was more than once on the point of confessing everything to my priest, then suffered all the more afterward for not having done so. I saw myself as a criminal, not so much before God and my new faith, you understand, but before this wonderful, noble man, to whom I had so much to be grateful for, whom I loved as a father.

"Now to my request: can you understand that I cannot go alone to the apartment? There are the usual things to be done—go through the possessions, make an inventory, pack things up. To be honest, I feel unable to manage alone and know of no one else I might ask. Because of the years I spent in Germany I have grown away from the few friends I made here in my childhood, and of my present acquaintances you are the only one I dare impose on."

Again I was tempted to ask her why, but it hardly seemed the right moment. "May I now buy you a cognac?" I said instead. "From what you tell me, I'm sure we shall find all manner of exquisite beverages in your uncle's flat. We'd better get in training."

The apartment was in a high-rise building not far from Biserică Albă. "How strange," I remarked. "I lived round the corner until not very long ago, up there, on one of the roofs. I probably passed your uncle and aunt on the street many times without knowing that sad circumstances would bring us together one day. By the way, there must be a Russian garden restaurant around here somewhere, with a girls' chorus that starts caterwauling every evening on the stroke of nine."

She didn't know it. "My stepparents moved here only a few years ago," she said. "These buildings are quite new. I wasn't here often—not because they kept me away or anything but they were so happy together that I always was a little shy. I felt I might intrude. They were like the lovers in David Teniers' painting, sitting on top of the hay wagon gazing into each other's eyes, oblivious of the emperors and popes being crushed to death under the wheels below; the *Weltgeist* itself spun a cocoon around their love."

As she said this, Miss Alvaro smiled the little smile that was so becoming to her. I could well imagine her as the prim pupil of the Armenian sisters. The line of her neck was simple and lovely, expressing a modest but defiant pride.

The apartment was on the sixth floor of a building that conceded nothing in hideous barrenness to the one I had lived in myself. We went up in the lift, and Miss Alvaro said, "It's a wonder it's working. I'm afraid this too had something to do with my uncle's premature death: nine times out of ten he had to walk up."

We got out, and again she dipped into her blouse to extract the bunch of keys; I turned my head to hide my smile, as I wondered that her uncle hadn't guessed the origin of his womenfolk from such characteristically careful traits, but then again, as with their physiognomy, perhaps Armenian girls had this in common with Jewish girls also.

She opened the door and we stepped in. It was a typical immigrants' flat: a mixture of old and new junk, purely decorative, impractical pieces salvaged from the ruins of former prosperity standing side by side with the banal indispensables of day-to-day life in incongruous equality, creating that atmosphere of improvised coziness which one suffers gladly only in the comforting knowledge that it's temporary. I had seen the same combinations in the dwellings of Russians who escaped the Revolution with nothing but what they could carry in their two hands. At second glance, I realized that many of the objects here were of some value, however, even though everything was either faded or chipped, and some pieces ruined completely. The modern, practical articles and gadgets had been chosen carefully from the middle-price range, not quite top quality but not quite rubbish either; the housewife's dream—but a nightmare in taste. It was obvious whose hand had sought these out. Miss Alvaro's aunt must have found in them a perfect outlet for her domestic zeal, and the noble old Armenian had obviously given her her head. Everything was clean and pedantically neat; nevertheless, as we stood there for a moment, I became aware of the odors of dust and musty materials, of biscuits moldering in hidden tins.

All the doors stood open: hallway, living room, bedroom, kitchen. One couldn't see much, for the shutters were closed

172

and the windows covered with heavily embroidered but decrepit curtains. Miss Alvaro crossed and opened a French window facing to the west, and raised the shutters. The sun had just set. I recognized my lavender-blue sky, paler now, colder, less sentimental. It had been late summer when I lived in the neighborhood. Now it was late autumn. Golden leaves fluttered down from the trees along the Boulevard Bratianu. Miss Alvaro trembled slightly. And for a few moments we both stood there looking out, breathing deeply, rather like divers, I thought, before braving the deep; but then the city below had much in common with the mausoleum behind us, much the same mixture of modern supertransience and flea-market curiosities. For all its Art Nouveau villas and futuristic glass-and-concrete buildings, Bucharest was as Oriental as Smyrna. The Occident, with its many-splendored towered citadels, was far away, there where the sun, dipping in, blood red, from the swamps and steppes and scrawny settlements of the east, would now only be prewarming the slate and copper roofs before melting them with its farewell blaze.

Miss Alvaro squared her shoulders and turned to her inheritance. "My aunt always spoke of their possessions, especially the furniture and glass and china, as though they were priceless. I'm afraid I'm no judge," she said. "I only want to keep a few things for myself, things that are easily transportable. I've no intention of setting up house in the near future."

On closer inspection it appeared to me that her aunt hadn't boasted; there was a French baroque chest of drawers, an early English grandfather clock, a pair of octagonal Turkish tables with superb inlays of mother-of-pearl, silver and tortoiseshell. The rest was run-of-the-mill stuff: mahogany cupboards; a cumbersome fin-de-siècle bedroom suite, expensive at the time, no doubt; hanging flower baskets; a portable phonograph; a radio. Brocades, gold-thread embroideries, and cashmere shawls were spread everywhere, giving the impression of Oriental luxury. Everywhere too there was evidence of former opulence, surfeit: several solid-silver but aggravatingly incomplete sets of cutlery, dishes and bowls and trays of chipped enamel, fragmentary cloisonné, French and Viennese porcelain sideboard pieces, Bohemian cut glass, but each piece minus a spout, a lid, a handle, with the edges serrated, traces of glue.

I took down one of four leatherbound books with gold stamping that were standing squashed in between pulp novels and department-store catalogues on a bookshelf; it was an edition of Choderlos de Laclos' *Liaisons dangereuses*, early enough still to be signed only "C. de L." Between the pages were a number of religious bookmarks; "Holy Brigitte, Holy Anthony of Padua, pray for us . . ."—tokens of penance for disregarding the Index, most likely.

"The best way to go about it will be to do as we did with the ring," I suggested. "You choose the things you want to keep, then we'll invite three antique dealers to come and make estimates, first separately, then free for all, and may the best man win."

"I hope that one day I shall have the opportunity to show my gratitude," Miss Alvaro replied. "There's just one thing—" She hesitated. "No, I'm sure it's not necessary to remind you again not to mention this business at the boarding house."

I managed not to for about a week. Then Olschansky confronted me: "You're fraternizing with the Alvaro filly. Don't bother to deny it; my information is irrefutable. You meet her in town; you've been observed several times. Why should you deny it? She's not *that* ugly, no cause for shame. Or do you want to shut me out? That's not very nice between friends."

I was obliged to tell him the truth, if only to avoid compromising Miss Alvaro, although I knew immediately that this was but a welcome excuse: I was only too glad for the chance to talk about it.

"You can't imagine what it's like," I said. "We're as complete strangers now as we ever were; apart from what she tells me in connection with her dead relatives, I know nothing about her whatsoever. And she nothing of me, since I've had no call to tell her anything. We still act with the same polite formality as we did on the day she first spoke to me, still keep our distance, partly on purpose and partly because we no longer have any choice. Just think of it: never a personal word, no confidences, and of course, God forbid, no intimacies. It would never occur to either of us to ask the other where or how we were going to spend the evening when we part at the door; our private lives could take place in two different worlds. In reality we simply take separate routes and come straight back here to be under the same roof, sit at the same table twice a day, and watch carefully that no one gets a hint of our relationship, the secret we share—like partners in crime. Then, when we meet at the apartment the next day, we again negate our other life at Löwinger's, never mention it. As a result, instead of becoming easier with each other, the tension builds. The sense of intimacy I feel with her—and she with me, I'm sure of it—grows stronger by the day, our hearts are continually in our mouths, so to speak, and all generated by a purely vicarious experience, by the exploration of two other, dead people's lives. What we find there grows into a monstrous secret between us.

"I say 'monstrous' because no one should be allowed to delve into another's life in the way we're doing, into the remotest nooks and crannies of intimacy. Each one of us has something we prefer to keep hidden, from ourselves just as much as from others; we shut it away and pretend it's not there. But here we are, Miss Alvaro and I, digging out every last morsel and examining it minutely. We know the lives of these two superb, consummate lovers to the last detail, down to their underwear and toilet articles, their hairbrushes, their soap and *eaux de cologne*, the racy magazines and jam recipes they read as they reclined on the sofa digesting a good dinner, the dentures they popped into a tumbler beside the bed when they went into their lovemaking routine, less and less passionately over the years, possibly, after decades of experience and experiment, but still with heavenly appeasement; the suppositories they needed to ease the passage of their sumptuous fare, probably giggling and thrusting them up each other's flabby backsides—each day we unearth some new dimension that again adds a new dimension to the intimacy between us. We sold their whole wardrobe, complete with everything from his bedroom slippers to his tails and white ties, from her corsets to a moth-eaten mink stole—his Christmas present in 1927—to a secondhand dealer, so that little chapter's over and done with, thank God. Sorting out their clothes gave us an indelible impression of their physiques. We came to know their collar and hip sizes, the shapes of their feet, their body odors, the peculiarities of the stains their sweat left, the irksome sphincter and bladder weaknesses of the people who wore these shirts and pants, shoes and jackets, dresses, overcoats, dressing gowns and nighties, and pressed the contours of their bodies into them. . . .

"They're ghosts, and because they're ghosts, they take possession of us, enter us like astral bodies. We politely shake hands and take leave of each other every evening, Miss Alvaro and I, but even if the one lies in bed in room number eight and the other in room number twelve at Löwinger's Rooming House, we are in fact lying together in that big double bed near the Biserică Albă, holding each other, making love, taking a sip of camomile tea, then embracing again, lulling ourselves to sleep. We no longer know which is the real existence: that of ardently united lovers, acting as if they are superficial acquaintances who happen to live in the same rooming house; or that of people who are briefly drawn together by chance and who pretend not to realize they are lovers for life. And the next day we crawl a little deeper into the souls of our phantom matchmakers. . . .

"At the moment we're going through all the drawers in the living room. Piles of documents, letters, diplomas, invitations to all manner of festivities, stacks of photos, all dating

176

from Uncle's glorious Constantinople days, of course, before
he met the little Jewish girl from Bessarabia. I have a
thorough knowledge of the financial status of this Armenian
from the Golden Horn, right down to the last sou, both
before and after the momentous day of Mussadegh. He must
have been immensely rich, but the way he ran his business
affairs is of a naïveté that would make a bookkeeper weep.
Even after he had to emigrate, he should have been in a
position to live a life of considerable comfort, but he allowed
crooked little lawyers to take him for a ride. The deeper one
goes into his papers, the more his innocence touches one's
heart, the more one is warmed by his open-handed generosity and his love for the woman who meant more to him than
anything he'd lost or still might lose. And all the more
intensely, almost violently, does the woman herself take
possession of us with her total, heartrending, never-
despairing humanity. . . .

"I hope you know me well enough by now to believe me
when I say that I'm not normally given to sentimentality.
Normally the story of a Jewish woman from the sticks who
lives in dread of losing the man who raised her to a certain
affluence and security, who gave her a vestige of elegance
and social prestige—her efforts to make herself indispensable
with her sickly-sweet attentivenesses, his slippers toasting
by the fireside, the goose crackling in the oven—wouldn't
touch me in the least, nor Miss Alvaro, I think. But the
passion this woman invested in her sole *raison d'être* is of such
force that one can't help being bowled over by it; she haunts
us with her dedication to the goal of becoming everything for
her husband, to replace what he'd lost and possibly still
mourned. All these impressions and feelings are transmitted
to us by ghosts; she's no longer alive, he's no longer alive,
they're both dead, and still their love lives on; you can read it
in every trace: her recipes, with footnotes underlined in
red—'Aram adores this!' 'Special favorite of Aram's!' Or in
the lists of presents he made for birthdays and Christmases
to come, with shaky handwritten notes in the margin toting

up his bank balance or the yield of his paltry shares. It's so powerful, it so transcends death, that we feel their presence physically every time we open a drawer.

"What must the woman have felt when she went through his papers or sorted his photographs? What did she think when she saw this evidence of a world that must have seemed like fairyland? Wouldn't you think she'd despair of ever filling the gap when she looked at the pictures of his paradise lost, the thousand and one nights' extravaganza, the complacent indulgence of immeasurable wealth? Tea parties at exquisitely timbered villas on the Bosporus, the guests gliding directly into the reception rooms in their boats; next to the visiting Sultan of Morocco we see Her Majesty the Queen's ambassador half hidden by the duchess of Lusignan's enormous picture hat, the duchess and the hostess vaguely related by marriage since the days of the Rubenides' regency over Cyprus; another photo shows the same illustrious party at a sumptuous picnic in Anatolia—the gentlemen in Shantung suits and ladies in white linen draped between chunks of the ruined pillars of Ephesus, lying on piles of rugs and heaps of cushions; some have come on horseback, a few of the younger women already emancipated, sitting boldly astride their mounts; to one side a spindle-wheeled Daimler, caked with dust, its demon driver and his heavily veiled passenger posing playfully beside a camel bearing the whole Kurd family, father, mother, four children, grandmother with a baby goat and two chickens on her lap; yet another view of the same slim gentlemen in gray walking dress, with sloe eyes and tapering noses, mustaches weighing heavily on their drooping mouths, tarbooshes perched pertly on their delicate heads; here again the ladies, in diaphanous Neo-Renaissance gowns, diamonds highlighting their hair, shimmering from their fingers, stout ropes of pearls trussed around their breasts. . . .

"Just think of her, little Myra from Kishinev, who'd been nothing much to write home about in her prime and was now slowly coming apart at the seams—mustn't she have known it

178

was hopeless to wish to appear desirable and elegant in the eyes of the prince charming who had descended to her world? No, her love is too serene, too humble in its pride. It never occurs to her to compare herself to anything connected with him; she no longer thinks of herself at all—solely of him; she has identified herself with him totally. The instinct of her love shows her how to make an incense of adoration from the ghost of his great past; she builds it into a myth and wafts it around him like a golden aura. For his part, he'd have probably thrown all the claptrap out long ago, the now-tawdry brocades, gold-thread embroideries and bibelots, the frayed, smashed, worn-out fragments of former luxuries, the photos of persons reported missing and never found again, the letters and invitations, birth and baptism announcements of people long since dead, superfluous documents, worthless deeds of holding—it's she who dotes on them like an archaeologist sifting through the dust of a pharaoh's tomb; she documents each photograph according to his identification of the people in them and specifies their relationship to him—'Aimee-Doudou, a cousin of his nephew Dschoudshouoglou-Pasha'—arranges them in chronological order, divides them into annual bundles, wraps them in silk tissue and ties them with silver thread; goes on and does the same with the invitation cards, the stock certificates of Nakhichevanian mining companies that collapsed twenty years ago. She gathers all the tiny splinters of a shattered rose-quartz hookah mouthpiece and beds them on cotton wool in an old cigar box, places one velvet-lined but empty jewel case on top of the other to make a tidy pile. . . .

"But all that may well have been due to some retarded, infantile romanticism of hers; turning a faded world into her dream world. No, I tell you, it's something else. She's building her myth, and she doesn't want it for herself. Far more convincing is the way she made a cult of his Armenian bigotry, the evidence of her studies, her notes on Moses of Khorene and Gregory the Enlightener, the devout little pictures and bookmarkers, the umpteen crosses and rosaries all over the place. And there between the Bibles and *Lives of the Saints* you find hardcore pornographic literature and ooh-la-la pictures from Paris, beside a heap of rosaries in his night table we hit on an arsenal of connoisseur condoms, with roosters' combs on the spunk bags, or harlequin heads with baubled jesters' collars. He must have been a dirty old man, this noble camel driver, and there's not a shadow of doubt that she kept her end up in his respect—on top of all the other specters in the house, the image of a lusty devotion to sex bobs up everywhere, culminating in the beckoning presence of the great, musty, freshly made bed. And there we stand beside it, Miss Alvaro and I, coolly sorting the wheat from the chaff amid death's odors of decay. . . ."

Olschansky seemed to have stopped breathing. "Jesus Christ!" he suddenly hollered, "that's it! I told you you should write, and you stupidly asked me what. This is it. Exactly as you just told it, word for word! It's the erotic situation par excellence! It must make the blood rush to your heads, this walk through the no-man's-land between the realities; you must both be literally itching for each other in that incubator of a tomb. Just think of the moment when you can't stand the suspense any longer, when you fall on each other like cannibals—"

"I think of very little else," I admitted.

"She too, of course. . . ."

"Very likely. Most probably. She gives no sign, of course. . . . It would have to happen spontaneously, if it's going to happen at all. Any attempt to force it would ruin everything."

Olschansky grinned. "Still a lot to do?" he asked.

"Hardly anything. We'll be finished tomorrow; the dealer she's decided on is coming the day after. He's taking the things she's chosen for herself into storage as well."

"So happy hunting tomorrow, then," Olschansky said.

I lay awake for hours that night. To begin with, I had a guilty conscience for having betrayed Miss Alvaro's secret. But, then, what was there for her to be so secretive about, after all? At worst our cloak-and-dagger behavior. Still, I felt I had sullied something that had been pure and should have stayed that way; I was ashamed not so much on her account as on that of her Armenian uncle as I had come to imagine him, and my sense of guilt grew to the extent that I superstitiously began to believe he would reach back and punish me. On top of which I felt I'd perhaps laid it on a bit thick; perhaps the suspense I'd described existed only in my imagination. If Olschansky was so enthusiastic about its literary merits, it probably meant that the reality had already undergone a kind of poetic transfiguration and become pure fiction, all due of course to that powerful imagination of mine. The thought that I could so easily fall for my own hokum made me squirm with discomfort; I pictured myself leering lewdly at her at the supposed right moment and her jumping like a startled rabbit, then withering me with a look of total disgust. My embarrassment would be a fitting punishment for my indiscretion.

I realized too that my feelings for Miss Alvaro had indeed undergone some change, and I analyzed them. I was not in love with her, far from it, but I certainly did want her—especially now, after having described the lurid sparks we threw off—but probably not so much her as a person as the role she played in my little melodrama; any other actress would have done as well, just as any understudy could have stepped in for me. One thing was clear, however: the petite Christian Jewess engendered a mixture of respect and fondness I'd never before experienced with anyone of my own age, only with wise, benign older people. Iolanthe had been right: she was a lady, by no means the simple prim schoolteacher Olschansky saw her as. Her authority stemmed from her noblesse. I resolved to tell him as much: "You once told me about Queen Maria's dignity," I would say. "Try to regard Miss Alvaro as having similar qualities."

This resolution made it easier for me to go with her to the apartment on the final day. Even so, I went reluctantly, as I was convinced that whatever might happen between us was bound to be a disappointment; the tension surely wouldn't build, let alone erupt, to the irrevocable moment of truth, the cannibals' feast; if I hadn't just imagined it and she was really awaiting the onslaught as eagerly as I, we still would have invested too much promise in the fantasy, and the reality could never match it in strength.

We worked silently and swiftly as always, even more resolutely now that the end was in sight. Apart from islands of stacked, covered furniture and overflowing baskets and garbage cans, the apartment was empty.

The love nest was abandoned. We had exorcised the ghosts. The noble old Armenian and his Jewish spouse were dead at last.

I was overcome by a feeling of hollowness, more tormenting than any grief. I stepped over to the window again to look out at the city, over which a gray winter sky merged into twilight. Inadvertently, I peered into the chasm of the street between the building fronts, trying to spot the colorfully lit garden restaurant. Here, during my lonesome, lavender-blue summer evenings, the chorus of girlish voices had risen up to me at the stroke of nine: at precise intervals between then and midnight, they had reeled off song after song, the entire repertoire of Russian evergreens.

Behind me, Miss Alvaro's voice softly asked, "Would you mind answering a very personal question?"

I turned around to her.

"It is very indiscreet of me," she said, flushing slightly with embarrassment. "But I would very much like to find out—I mean, it would help me—"

"Please ask," I said with a throbbing heart. I waited to see how she would ask if I had felt the same feelings as she in these past few days.

"Do you believe in anything?" she asked instead, and now looked me full in the face. "Do you believe in God or something of that sort?"

There we have it, I thought to myself. The crucial question. That's all I needed!

But she wouldn't even let me answer; she went right on: "It's been constantly on my mind these past few days. All the aspects of this legacy must have made you aware of how deeply religious my uncle and aunt were and how strongly the bond between them was forged by their religious feelings. And I cannot help wondering whether my aunt, who denied the faith she was born to and brought up in—our family was extremely Orthodox; it was the only thing that gave them a sense of self and a motive for their existence, an identity and, even more, a *raison d'être*—I cannot help wondering whether my aunt really forgot all that and traded it for something else. How could she have given herself over to a different faith with the same ardor?"

"Isn't that possible *only* if you have faith in the first place?" I retorted—partly because I noticed that she was less interested in a response from me than in speaking her own mind, partly because I could thereby avoid answering, which would have been difficult for me. "Besides, she did it out of love," I added clumsily.

"Yes, of course, of course," said Miss Alvaro, almost irritated, as though not to be diverted. "That is what they try to comfort us with when true faith begins to dissolve. The fragments of the old, strict commandments float about in a whey of general love feelings—that's a condition in which I, too, was led into temptation. Love as a basic religious feeling and as the highest ethical value to strive for—these are Enlightenment notions. I wonder whether I am naïve enough for that—no, whether I am not already too enlightened. Perhaps you're right, and my aunt succeeded in getting at the very essence of faith—and that is not the tidings of love!—simply *because* she believed. But *I* believed too. I was eight when I was torn from my Jewish milieu and thrust into the Armenian convent. At eight one is truly God-fearing—I mean, in a fundamentalist way. Nevertheless, I was more than ready and willing to find my God in the new Word that was proclaimed to me. After all, it was taken from the Old Text and enriched by the Gospels

183

—expanded by the dimension of love. And, listen—I have to say something dreadful now. Precisely *because* I often felt that dimension of love to the point of ecstasy when I was eight and nine and ten and eleven and twelve—the grand, universal love for God's creation and all creatures therein, for mankind and every individual—that was the very reason why I learned that this was the decisive step to the dissolution of faith. I understood why the Jews crucified Jesus—do you grasp what I mean?"

She gazed at me almost in despair: "You must not think that faith is taught with any less fundamentalism in an Armenian convent than in a yeshiva. My schoolmates took every litany verbatim. They had an almost physical need for all the religious exercises—from matins to evensong and finally the prayers at bedtime. But none of this had anything to do with faith. They were marionettes on the strings of their rite. And whenever they truly believed that they believed, they stumbled once again into the lukewarm liquid of love, divine love, brotherly love, the love for God's creatures, for the universe—the love for everything and anything. And at that point," said Miss Alvaro with a dismal smile, "the strength of my faith dissolved. At least, that was how it happened to me."

"And what would have become of your relatives without love?" I asked tactlessly.

"Oh, please don't misunderstand. My aunt's love was a Jewish love; selfish, jealous, wrathful, greedy, not stopping at anything—not even evil, not even denial, deceit, lies. In that way, she remained unalterably Jewish—far more than I. . . ." She had paled, and seemed embarrassed again. "I'm probably still Jewish only insofar as I long for my God, whom I seek like Jacob, after wrestling with his angels. It's useless. I know that he does not exist, my God—or at least no longer exists for me—the severe, demanding, wrathful, greedy, and jealous God. The God of love may exist. He is an earthly God—an idol, to use another word. But He, the severe God of the Commandments, He no longer exists."

"Doesn't what we've found in your relatives' things prove that he can be resurrected by love?"

All the blood shot back into her face. She vehemently shook her head. For the first time, I saw how rich and fine her hair was. "We didn't just find devotional pictures, did we?" she said, staring right into my eyes. "I know it sounds paradoxical, but the love of my kinfolk would soon have become squalid without their bigotry. Their piety prohibited them from interpreting the tidings of salvation through love as if sexuality were the great, venerable motor of creation and thus the crown of all beauty. Were it not for their piety, they would have joined the followers of Saint D. H. Lawrence, if you get what I mean by that: stigmatized barbarians. But their religion demanded that they view sexual love as something ugly, despicable, something to be concealed—in short, as something sinful. If you remember that, dear friend, then this happy union of what cannot be unified acquires a macabre touch." Her shoulders drooped. "That's exactly what disheartens me so."

"Then you still believe in your severe God of shalts and shalt nots!" I cried in foolish triumph. "He just happens to be named Jehovah!"

"No," she said with no trace of bombast. "I believe in the devil."

"You can't believe in the devil without believing in God."

"Yes," she then said, half turning from me. "I know. That's logical. And if I were occasionally overcome by poetic impulses, like Nietzsche, I would reply, 'But God has grown old and no longer has the strength to stand firm against the devil.' But I'm afraid even the devil has grown senile—or is banality his last and most dangerous disguise?" She shrugged her shoulders and turned away.

She was packing a bag with things she'd decided to keep. I had persuaded her to take a large writing case in red, gold-embossed leather with an Armenian inscription we'd been unable to decipher. She looked up and handed it to me: "I should like you to accept it as a souvenir and a modest token of my gratitude," she said simply.

I leaned forward and kissed her on the cheek, sensed her start and draw back. I took her hand, bent and kissed it also. Her lips were trembling. She quickly turned away and closed her bag.

When I got back to Löwinger's, I lay down on the sofa in my room and was filled with the realization that nothing had changed since my days on the roof above the Biserică Albă; I was in the same melancholic state I'd been in then. The release from the plaster cast hadn't meant rebirth after all; I was being born back into my old wayward self again. There appeared to be no way out, only a flight forward, through enemy lines, the same route Miss Alvaro's aunt had taken to escape the specters of the past: making myths of them.

Olschansky knocked and opened my door before I could open my mouth. As he reached for my cigarettes, he noticed the writing case on my desk. "A trophy?" he asked, with his perfidious grin.

"In a manner of speaking," I answered.

"So it worked out?"

"What?"

"Don't act so stupid; you bloody well know what I mean."

"A lot more happened than you think," I said.

"So, come on, give; did you screw her or not?"

"What? Today? Oh yes, yes, today as well." I didn't lie. In a literary sense it had as good as happened. "Lots of times recently, several times a day. . . ." Reality had undergone transfiguration and become fiction.

He looked at me quizzically. "Are her tits as good as I reckoned them to be?"

"Oh, much better. Go away now; leave me in peace."

"I understand: Monsieur wants to savor his memories. Very well, and congratulations. But I think it was unfriendly of you to keep it to yourself for so long. After all, we belong to the same club, don't we?"

I couldn't sleep that night either, partly because the little dog yapped out in the passage for hours until someone—Cherkunof, presumably—opened his door and let him in. I was wide awake. I decided to write my mother a letter, and got up. The case Miss Alvaro had given me was already filled with my notepaper. The blotting paper on the inside covers was crisscrossed with the impressions of handwriting, and on one of them the lines of a letter showed up clearly; judging by the fine, sloping hand, I guessed that Miss Alvaro's uncle must have written them. I turned the blotting paper over, saw, as I'd hoped, that the reverse side was even clearer, fetched my shaving mirror, and read:

> . . . I beg Your Eminence to restrain our good Father Agop from taking these steps. My wife has proved herself a worthy Christian over so many years—and Father Agop, her confessor and my own, can testify to this—that I venture to suggest to Your Eminence that she couldn't have been a better one had she received the holy blessings of baptism and confirmation as a child. I admit to my sinful comportment in not having confessed to knowing of her origin and uncleansed condition. One of the reasons why I did not do so was that, as an Armenian, I saw in my Jewish wife a sister in suffering. She too belongs to a people that, like ours, was a victim of violence throughout the millennia. Pray let this speak to my favor when I ask Your Eminence's forgiveness. May I appeal to Your Eminence's spiritual understanding that no word of this be divulged to her. Should Your Eminence see your way clear to baptizing her without my knowledge, behind my back, so to speak . . .

I could hardly wait to run to Miss Alvaro and tell her of my discovery the next morning. I knocked on her door several times before she finally opened it. She looked at me with an expression of loathing that took my breath away. "I never want to set eyes on you again. Never." Her packed suitcases were lying on the bed behind her. "I shall do everything in my power to erase you from my memory as quickly as possible, and I shall succeed, don't worry. We Jews have had excellent training in this." Then she slammed the door in my face.

A dreadful suspicion overcame me. I went to Olschansky's room, got no answer, searched the whole house, and finally found him in the bathroom we were allowed to use on a rotation system worked out with astronomical precision. He was standing naked under the shower with his back toward me, and I saw the ugly, festering, earth-filled pits all over it.

"You said something to Miss Alvaro," I hissed at him.

He had his face stretched up to the nozzle with his eyes screwed up and his lips sucked in between his teeth. "I took the liberty, yes," he spluttered through the cascading water. "If I'd waited for your permission, she'd still be a virgin."

"For God's sake, don't tell me you have done this to her!" I was ready to jump on him.

He turned his face toward me, opened his eyes wide, and, with the most perfidious smile I'd ever seen, said, "I did, yes. But it was a great help that you claimed to have done so. The argument that good friends and members of the same club must share and share alike was difficult for a school mistress to reject."

I grabbed his throat. He seemed to think I was joking. He laughed as he tried to struggle away from me, spluttered water and soap suds, and groaned. "Don't get so excited, you moron. What's the problem? Are you going to let some Jewish broad interfere in our friendship?" I let go of him.

Miss Alvaro moved out of Löwinger's Rooming House that same day; I followed suit some weeks later. It was November 1937. After nearly four years of the Balkans I'd had my fill and felt homesick for Vienna. I arrived there just in time for March 1938.

I never saw Olschansky again. In the flush of my twenty-three years, I often did battle with him in my thoughts, of course, and reproached myself equally often. What shocked me most about the story was that in telling it to Olschansky, I had unwittingly predetermined the only logical, literary conclusion. But soon, far more shocking events put it from my mind completely, and by the time I came to take my strolls along the banks of the lake at Spitzingsee, twenty years later, in 1957, it was very far away. But it was still as clear as the pictures of the Eiffel Tower and the Castel Sant'Angelo one could see through the little lenses inserted in the holders of Mr. Löwinger's more expensive pens.

Troth

The big something falling from the floor above my grandmother's apartment cast a sudden shadow on the window before it bumped on the cobblestones, and my grandmother's gouty claw reached for the little bell beyond the flowery field of playing cards she had laid out on the table for her game of patience and shook it violently. Decades of strained impatience made her movement awkward, and the thin silver sound seemed to mock her intention to reach the deaf ears of old Marie. Nevertheless, as in a vaudeville gag, the door opened instantly and old Marie appeared, trembling with age and the suppressed contradictions of nearly fifty years of service to a most complicated family.

"Yes, please?"

My grandmother majestically stretched her tortoise neck as if it still were encircled by half a dozen rows of pearls and turned her head toward the window. "Something fell down from the upper floor. The Jews must have put their featherbeds in the windows to air or something of that kind. Go and have a look."

Old Marie pushed her head out of the window and then brought it back into the room. "Please," she said triumphantly. "That's no featherbed. It is the young Raubitschek girl."

I spent part of my youth in this apartment house, which

was in a drowsy residential section of Vienna. When I met the "old Raubitscheks" on the stairs, I greeted them with the same polite reserve they used in saluting my grandmother, whose recognition was a delightful mixture of joviality and distance. Never a word was exchanged. They were educated people, though. Papa Raubitschek being a professor at the University of Vienna, famous artists came to their apartment, and every Wednesday evening the remote sounds of chamber music reached my grandmother's apartment and would make her—she was very sensitive to noise—say contemptuously, "They are playing Beethoven's 'Allergique' again or something equally horrid." Because so many Jews were successful in musical endeavors, my grandmother no longer quite considered it one of the fine arts.

Whether those chamber-music concerts got on the nerves not only of my grandmother but also of Minka Raubitschek I am unable to say. However, she was a high-spirited girl with a strong and stubborn will, and on the occasion I have just mentioned, during a quarrel with her mother, she jumped out of the window. "Exaggerated" was my grandmother's comment. "As those young Jewish intellectuals usually are." Fortunately she didn't do herself much harm. She broke a hip and was slightly lame thereafter, that was all. In later years, when I had been accepted into the circle of her friends, we used to put a mountain climber's cord around her waist and let her down the steep stairs to the ladies' room of the Kärntnerbar. This was necessary not only because of her lame hip but also because her sense of equilibrium was impaired by too many whiskeys. She used to thank us with bits of cultural-historical information. "Do you realize where you are, you drunken swine? This place was designed by Adolf Loos, an architect as important as Frank Lloyd Wright. It is one of the early masterpieces of modern architecture—a room that would normally not be big enough for a dozen ignoramuses of your kind shelters half a hundred. If that isn't progress . . ."

As the grandson of an architect who had done his share to

make Vienna's monuments conform to the taste of the *fin de siècle*, I should have given particular consideration to such remarks of Minka Raubitschek's. Her tastes were exquisite and her knowledge was profound. But at the time I was merely reminded of my grandmother. "It is disgusting," my grandmother would say, "how very much like your father you have become. He is a perfect barbarian, with his monomaniacal passion for shooting. But when I think that I gave my daughters Renan to read in order to have them take up spiritualism . . ."

The two neuralgic points in my grandmother's existence were the marriage of her eldest daughter, my mother, with my father and the "exaggerated ideas" of my unmarried aunts. My grandmother never set foot in the back rooms of her apartment, which, after the death of my grandfather, were occupied by her two spinster daughters; for there, every Wednesday evening, accompanied by the remote sounds of the Raubitschek chamber music, the meetings of the esoteric community of Mr. Malik took place. Mr. Malik was an engineer with supernatural powers that enabled him to massage the souls out of the bodies of ladies who had metaphysical talents so that the emptied vessel could be filled with some free soul of a dead person not yet reborn, who would then use the mouth of the medium to utter mystical nonsense, the theosophical interpretation of which was left to my aunts. The soul massaged out of the body remained attached to it by an astral navel cord, and when the free soul, who came like a guest into your body for the duration of the séance, had left, Mr. Malik would massage your waiting soul along that very same astral navel cord back into your body, and you would be yourself again. In later years, when we were letting Minka down to the ladies' room of the Kärntnerbar, I had great success with what I had learned of Mr. Malik's teachings. "It's only her cursed *materia* that descends," I would explain. "Her soul stays with us and her whiskey."

The presumably free, not yet reborn soul of Mr. Malik

will perhaps forgive me. I was only eighteen years old when I thus profaned his messages, and all during my childhood nobody had done much to make me take him very seriously. "I am sure that man is not an engineer at all but just a cheap crook," my grandmother used to say. "Probably a Jew who has changed his name."

The suspicion that somebody could have changed his name already made him a Jew—provided, of course, he was not an Englishman, like charming Mr. Wood, who one beautiful day became Lord Halifax. But that was quite another thing. It was typically Jewish to change your name, for Jews quite understandably did not want to be taken for what they were. Since their names usually made it quite clear what they were, they had to change them, for camouflage. Had we been Jews, we should certainly have done the same, because it must be painful to be a Jew. Even well-bred people would make you feel it—either by their reserve or by an exaggerated politeness and coy friendliness. But fortunately we were not Jews, so, though we could see their point, we considered it a piece of insolence when they changed their names and pretended to be like us. Part of the certain esteem my grandmother had for the Raubitscheks came from the fact that they had not changed their name. Jews who changed their names, like Mr. Malik, were crooks and swindlers. Their camouflage was but a falsehood to which they were driven by their disgusting greed for profit and their repulsive social climbing. This was particularly the case with the so-called Polish Jews—the prototype of the greedy, pushing little Jew one met so often in the Bukovina. There were crowds of them; you could not take a step without running into swarms. The elder ones and very old ones, particularly the very poor, were humbly what they were—submissive men in black caftans and large-brimmed hats, with curls at their temples, and in their eyes a sort of melting look which the sadness of many thousands of years seemed to have bestowed. Their eyes were like dark ponds. Some of them were even beautiful in their melancholy. They had spun-silver prophets' heads, with which the butcher's face of Mr. Malik would have compared very unfavorably, and when they looked at you, humbly stepping aside to let you pass, it was like a sigh for not only themselves but all the burden of human existence which they knew so well. But the young ones, and especially the ones who were better off, or even rich, showed an embarrassing self-confidence. They wore elegant clothes and drove dandified roadsters, and their girls smelled of scent and sparkled with jewelry. Some of them even had dogs and walked them on leashes, just as my aunts did. When they spoke to one another, it was in a pushing, impatient way, even when they had just met. They asked direct personal questions and looked around for someone more worth knowing. They were not humble at all.

My father likewise hated Jews, all of them, even the old and humble ones. It was an ancient, traditional, and deep-rooted hatred, which he did not need to explain; any motivation, no matter how absurd, would justify it. Of course, nobody seriously believed that the Jews wanted to rule the world merely because their prophets had promised it to them (even though they were supposedly getting richer and more powerful, especially in America). But, of course, other stories were considered humbug: for instance an evil conspiracy, such as was described in the *Protocols of the Elders of Zion*, or their stealing communion wafers or committing ritual murders of innocent children (despite the still unexplained disappearance of little Esther Solymossian). Those were fairy tales that you told to a chambermaid when she said she couldn't stand it here anymore and would much rather go and work for a Jewish family, where she would be better treated and better paid. Then, of course, you casually reminded her that the Jews *had*, after all, crucified our Savior. But our kind of people, the educated kind, did not require such heavy arguments to look upon Jews as second-class people. We just didn't like them, or at least liked them less than other fellow human beings. This was as natural as liking cats less than dogs or bedbugs less than bees; and we amused ourselves by offering the most absurd justifications.

For instance, it was well known that it's bad luck to run into a Jew when you go hunting. Now, my father did little else but go hunting; and since there were so many Jews in the Bukovina that it was impossible to go hunting without promptly running into several of them, he had this annoyance almost every day. It made him suffer, like an ingrown toenail. There were violent scenes between him and my mother because she attracted crowds of Jews to our house. She used to give our cast-off clothing to rag-picking peddlers—Jews, needless to say, so-called *handalés*. You couldn't sell them the clothes—my father was the first to realize this. But it was better to throw the stuff away than to support the Jews in their dirty business, thus possibly helping them in their despicable social climbing. For the Jews dealt in secondhand clothes in order to emigrate to America. They arrived there as Yossel Tuttmann or Moishe Wassershtrom and soon earned enough dollars to change their names. Wassershtrom became Wondraschek, of course, and eventually von Draschek, and finally they'd come back to Europe as Barons von Dracheneck and buy themselves a hunting ground in the Tirol or Styria. And this was a personal affront to my father, for he could not afford a hunting ground in Styria, and thus he believed that all his privileges had been usurped by the Jews. More than anything, he felt it was their fault that he, as an Old Austrian, was forced to remain in the Bukovina and become a Rumanian, which made him too a kind of second-class human being.

He felt exiled in the Bukovina—or rather, as a pioneer, betrayed and deserted. He counted himself among the colonial officials of the former realm of the Austro-Hungarian Dual Monarchy; and it was the task of such officials to protect Europe against the wild hordes who kept breaking in from the East. "Civilization fertilizer" was his bitterly mocking term for the function he ascribed to himself and his kind: they were supposed to settle in the borderland, form a bulwark of Western civilization, and show a bold front to Eastern chaos. He had come to the Bukovina as a young man, after growing up in Graz during the most glorious era of the Dual Monarchy; and everything that had become sad and dreary and hidebound after the collapse of 1918 was, he felt, represented in the land where he had been cast away.

The Bukovina is probably one of the most beautiful areas in the world. But for my father—aside from one tip of the forest Carpathians where he hunted—it was a landscape without character. He even went so far as to deny that I had any character, because I passionately loved the Bukovina. "No wonder," he said with undisguised scorn. "You were simply born into corruption—I mean, the corruption of character. If these borderlands didn't constantly pose the danger of corroding character, then they wouldn't have needed our kind of people as civilization fertilizer."

In my boyhood, I found it very difficult to reach any precise notion of what "character" really was. For my father—he repeated it often enough—Styria had a distinct character. Naturally, I had to assume that this was connected to its "mountainous character," which was always brought up in Austrian books on local history and geography. A propos, instead of "character" or the lack thereof, they occasionally talked about "backbone." "The boy simply has no backbone," I had once been forced to hear when refusing to own up to some prank. Styria had character because of its mountain backbone. Now, the Bukovina did have a mountainous backbone, too, although not quite such a spectacular one as the Hohe Tauern. But rocky peaks did loom here and there from the green cones of the forest Carpathians, and the poetic gentleness of the flowery slopes was all too deceptive in obscuring the wildness of the deep forests in which they were embedded. If the word "character" signified what I sensed about it, then these tremendous, wind-swept black forests had at least as much character as the glacier-crowned massifs of Styria.

Even my father had to admit that hunting in the Bukovina

was better, more adventurous, more primeval than in Styria. Nevertheless, he dreamed of a hunting ground in Styria and shrugged his shoulders when he was sharply reminded that owners of hunting grounds in Styria dreamed of having a hunting ground in the Carpathians. When I finally asked him what character was, he replied without hesitating: "Troth, more than anything else."

Now I thought I understood him. "Troth" was a much clearer fetish than the throat-scratching concept of "character." Since earliest childhood I had been taught to idolize this notion of loyalty, or troth. It was obvious: my father could not love the Bukovina, because he had become a Rumanian citizen after its defection from the Dual Monarchy. He had been compelled to commit an act of disloyalty, like the engineer Malik, who had changed his name. Only in my father's case, the conflict was tragic: through loyalty to the hunt, he had been forced to be disloyal to his flag. And what that meant was urgently brought home to me.

In those years, the first great war was still close by. Traces and evidence of it survived throughout the countryside: shot-up farms, barbed-wire entanglements, ditches and dugouts in the heart of the woods, the wasteland of villages over which the Russian offensives had rolled. When I viewed such things, I was seized with a strange excitement, a mixture of fear and yearning, which—projected out of myself into the world comprising my experiences back then—I found mirrored in certain evening moods. In the oppressively hopeless dove-blue of the twilights, as in the dramatics of blood-red and sulphur-yellow sunsets, I experienced the shock that the war had brought to my parents' lives. Under such skies, the flag of our allegiance had sunk in the tumult of battle and amid the croaking of ravens over the field of warriors. It was the golden flag with the black, two-headed eagle of the Holy Roman Empire which had been carried on by Imperial Austria. And anyone who had not died in the battle around that flag had betrayed his troth and was now living on without character.

With the mind of a child, always open to thrilling sublimity, I kept reviving the catastrophe of that destruction and that unwilling disloyalty over and over again. This alone explained the oddly empty grief of the people in my immediate surroundings, their resigned and only ironically reflective stance: their deadness, which allowed them to continue existing in an everyday rut that was barely aglow with the melancholy of golden memories, kept them going even though they seemed not to care about the present. My father and mother in the Bukovina were as old and as much a part of a previous era as my grandmother and my crotchety maiden aunts in Vienna. Their dogs had gray heads and trembled when they walked, like Marie. They lived only when they talked about bygone days. The golden glow of their memories came solely from that sunken golden flag.

This sunkenness even explained the melancholy of the landscape in which I grew up. Beautifully canopied by the silky blue of a usually serene sky, the woodland was afflicted with melancholy, the melancholy of eastern vastnesses, creeping in everywhere: into the dove-blue of twilight hours as into the summer heat brooding over the fruit-bearing earth, into the submission of the peasants and the Jews to God's will, into the gentle flutes of shepherds from the meadowed slopes of the Carpathians. These flutes died out when the wintry winds began whistling from the steppes and high deserts of Asia, which suddenly shifted close to us. The Jews and peasants then pulled up their shoulders and curled into themselves even more humbly; the earth turned to stone beneath the frost; and the twilight hours were no longer ambiguous stages of the universe, leading to mute and colorful celestial dramas: they now were a deeper freezing and darkening over a grayish-white, skeletal world. This was a landscape of catastrophe: the proper setting for a destruction growing from a mythically ancient dichotomy. For not only *one* empire had gone under with the sinking of that golden flag. Not only we—or, as we said, "our people"—had carried it, but also our adversaries, the Imperial Russians. Not only our emperor had gone down with the flag, but their emperor too.

The myth at the source of this tragedy had been drummed into me like a litany. It was the myth of the Holy Roman Empire of the Caesars, which had split apart. The black eagle in the golden field of the sunken flag had two crowned heads rising from his breast—shielded with coats of arms—because the empire had two capitals and two heads: Rome, and Byzantium, the Constantinople of the Emperor Constantine. A breach of troth was at the beginning of this myth: the defection of a part from a unified whole. Two empires arose from one and soon were bloodily fighting one another. For each considered itself the true descendant of the original one great Imperium. Each symbolized this claim in the same flag. Under this flag, Eastern Rome and Western Rome unpeacefully divided the world, until one of the Asian storms that had menaced Western civilization since time immemorial broke loose once again, and Byzantium decayed and ultimately fell into the hands of the pagans.

Western Rome too had gone through dark and disorderly times, which were historically conjured away, as it were, under the term "Dark Ages" and inadequately bedizened with monarchical figures like Alaric and Odoacer. We leaped across centuries in order to come up all the more sensationally with the figure of light: Charlemagne, whom the Germans call Karl the Great, the reviver of the idea of Holy Empire and the founder of the Roman Empire of the German Nation. I cannot evoke my boyhood without his image. A bronze replica of a mounted statue of him stood on my father's desk, and I often gazed at that replica in deep meditation. The thought that after more than a millennium, his slippers and gloves still belonged among the Imperial treasures filled me with awe.

Nevertheless, I was puzzled by one enigma: how could Charlemagne, who was a Frank, after all, and thus, strictly speaking, a Frenchman (and, as a French governess furiously assured me, still viewed as a Frenchman by the French)—

how could he be the new founder of an Empire of the German Nation? Needless to say, my father had explanations at hand which, while not dispelling my qualms, did divert me from them. In a higher sense, he maintained, one could think of Karl the Great as a German emperor because his descendance was thoroughly German. Germans, with the glorious Stauffers in the lead, had worn his crown and given the Holy Roman Empire an eternally German stamp. Besides, my father added, not quite logically, in medieval times (which had now lightened from the "Dark Ages" to the "High Middle Ages," the epoch of cathedrals and many-towered cities, of knights and ladies, of minstrels, inspired master stonecutters, and altarpiece painters)—in those times, such distinctions had been meaningless. People didn't have national sentiments in the modern sense. You just followed a flag, that was all. Either you were born lowly and were a serf belonging to a lord—you followed him blindly wherever he went, and you never thought beyond your own parish—or else you were born into knighthood and served some count or prince as a true liegeman, which might expand your horizon by a few provinces; but in the end it was all the same. It made no difference whatsoever which of the many nations of this imperium these lords belonged to with their little flags and their liegemen and serfs; it made no difference what language they spoke or what costume they wore. For they were all vassals and subjects of the Emperor and the Empire.

This was comprehensible because it was graphic. The world seemed well ordered to me. The Empire was the epitome of order. From the emperor at the top down through the great vassals and their liegemen with their subliegemen and serfs, it was all as hieratically articulated as a pyramid. This could be enacted. This could be represented in the parades of my tin soldiers. This could also be grasped abstractly. Its mechanism was simple. One person protected the other, the higher one always the lower one; and one served the other, the lower one always the higher one above him. And thus up and down the ladder, like the hierarchy of angels under the Almighty's Heavenly Throne. And that was why the Empire was Holy, said my father. It was God's state on earth. Not just purely and simply a political construction, a state constitution that offered uniform protection, uniform leadership and administration to a gigantic territory that was inhabited by many nations and threatened by many dangers. It was more than that: it was an idea and ideal; an ordered image of the world, of human society striving to make God's will come true. The divine right of the Emperor was not as it would be today, an arbitrary usurping by power-drunk demagogues mounted on a pedestal made up of interwoven interests—financial, mercantile, and political. Oh no! It was the very symbol of what God wanted the state to be. And this state was held together not by material interests alone but by the ethical principle of troth, loyalty, allegiance, the allegiance of vassals, the unconditional obedience that the liegemen had sworn to their lord and his flag, just as we, the immediate liegemen of the Habsburgs, had sworn allegiance to the Austrian imperial house and to the flag of the Empire with the two-headed eagle in the golden field.

Usually at this point my mother got up and left the room. Whereupon my father felt obliged to help me, as a small boy, to understand things better. He explained to me that in spite of the fact that we were of Italian descent and had become subjects of Rumania, we were still Austrians, and that living in the Bukovina meant a sort of unfaithfulness forced on us by unlucky circumstances—one of which was that shooting in the Bukovina was much better than in Styria. Still, as Austrians, we should have stuck to our flag. Unfortunately that flag didn't exist anymore; the imperial flag of Austria had been replaced by the vulgar flag of the new republic, with which, fortunately, we had nothing to do. The old imperial flag was the flag of the emperors of the House of Habsburg, who for six hundred years had been the emperors of the Holy Roman Empire, founded by Charlemagne. For six hundred years, the emperors of the House of Habsburg had worn his crown and defended the world of Christendom against another storm from Asia: the Turks. Under the house of Habsburg most of the nations of southeastern Europe had united in that noble task. That's how we, as Italians, had become Austrians, though we had neither come to Austria in the time of Charlemagne nor come in order, as true defenders of Christendom, to fight the Turks, but arrived only in the middle of the eighteenth century as bureaucrats from Sicily. But never mind. Nobody asked you where you were born. They asked only how you were born, and whether you were brave and just and faithful to your liege lord's flag. If you had been brave and just and faithful to your liege lord's flag, you got a coat of arms that obliged you to be even more brave and just and faithful to your flag. As the son of a knight who had his coat of arms—and we had had one already in Sicily, before we came to Austria—you first served as a page, preferably of a queen. Later, you became a squire and ran next to the horse of a knight, carrying his shield. Then you became a knight yourself, and when you weren't fighting for your liege lord and for chivalry in general, you went hunting and shooting. Now, as there were very few queens whom you could serve as a page, and even fewer knights whose shield you could carry as a squire, you were brought up to become a nobleman just by hunting and shooting, and the only way you could fight for chivalry was to stay where you were and at least see that the Jews did not get hunting grounds everywhere, even in the Bukovina. So, in spite of the fact that we were Austrians—though of Italian origin and subjects of Rumania—and my father's father had done his share, as an architect, to give Vienna its lovely neoclassic, and neo-Gothic, and neo-Renaissance appearance, my father never again set foot in Austria, where he had no hunting ground to defend.

But it was agreed that I should be brought up in Austria, and this I resented very much, because I loved the Bukovina. It seems to be the lot of every good childhood to be lonesome, and I was lonesome in both places. In Vienna I was lonesome as a little boy who came from a now remote country of the Balkans and lived with old people and fools. At home, in the Bukovina, I was lonesome as the little snob with a foreign education who tried to avoid contact with others of his age. As a matter of fact, this was not at all my intention. It was the logical consequence of the isolation into which the monomania of my father and the nostalgia of my mother had maneuvered us.

My mother too felt the Bukovina as a sort of exile, but simply as a woman who, with an unloved husband, lives far from those she loves. As my father's monomaniacal passion for shooting estranged him more and more from family life, my mother's various unfulfilled desires found an outlet in a no less monomaniacal love for me, her child. She watched over every step I took and every breath I drew. Between her terror that I would get pneumonia from running too fast and the suspicion that a contact with the gardener's children could give me lice, or that through the friendliness of a Rumanian officer who had put me in the saddle of his horse I would get syphilis, I did not develop into a very social youngster. In wintertime, on the big public skating rink, I found myself lonely in a corner, cutting my circles and loops into the ice, an enormous woolen shawl wrapped six times around my neck, while all around a whirl of hilarious liveliness filled the sparkling winter day.

The majority of the young skaters were Jews. Among them were some extremely pretty girls, with whom, one by one, I clandestinely fell in love, suffering not only from the overprotectiveness of my mother but from guilt. My mother came to fetch me every day and, in spite of my violent protests, had me wrapped in blankets and furs in order to protect my frail health after the exhausting exercise. My departure became a public amusement so humiliating that I did not dare to look the Jewish girls in the eye even when my mother had not yet turned up. At the same time I felt guilty because my tender feelings were a betrayal of everything that

203

in the geography of my inner world formed the moral massifs, the mountainous backbone, so to speak—the Carpathians, without which that inner landscape would have had no character. Of course, there were some people who, with a dirty smirk, would say, "A Jewess is no Jew." But those were swine. For our kind it was impossible to fall in love with a Jewish girl. It meant being unfaithful to our flag. Love makes you long for intimacy, it leads to the most direct of all human relationships, and it was unthinkable to get into a human relationship with Jews. Jews were human beings, too; that could not be denied. But we did not have intimate relationships with other people, either, just because they were human beings. My father would not have anything to do with Rumanians, because they considered him part of a minority more or less equal with the Jews; nor with Poles, because they usually hated Austrians; nor would he have anything to do with other former Austrians who had stayed on in the Bukovina for mere personal interests, and not for a noble purpose like his, and who therefore had been unfaithful to their flag. That did not mean that we wouldn't regard them as human beings and behave like educated people when we came in contact with them. We answered every greeting more or less politely, with the same mixture of joviality and distance with which my grandmother in Vienna greeted the Raubitscheks, and, when it was inevitable, even shook hands with them, and, should the occasion have demanded it, we would presumably have done the same with the Jews of the Bukovina, the Polish Jews, unless they pretended they could come shooting with us. But that did not mean that we wished to enjoy a closer relationship either with them or with the Jews in general. As a matter of fact, it was not really true that we hated Jews. It was more a *façon de parler*. Hatred, too, is a direct human relationship. If there had been a real hatred for the Jews, it would have been just as much as loving them. No, Jews were simply people of another star—the star of David and Zion. It might be a shining star, but for us, unfortunately, it shone under the horizon.

Therefore, falling in love with a Jewish girl could not be considered a pardonable perversion, like, for instance, that of a sodomite. It was *the* incomprehensible, a sudden gap in one's mind, worse than treason and breach of troth. I had good reason to be ashamed.

I would soon have some more, and better, reasons. Thanks to a few lessons from a skating teacher at the Wiener Eislaufverein, my circles and loops had very much improved. I was even capable of doing a few jumps. Home again in the Bukovina, I performed them in my corner of the skating rink. This aroused the curiosity of a group of sturdy youngsters—Jews, of course—who had formed a sort of wild hockey team. One day I found myself encircled by them. I felt a trifle uncomfortable, for they were tough and I did not know what they wanted. So I pretended not to notice their nearness and continued to perform a tidy eight with a Dutch jump at the conclusion of each circle. This went on for a while, till finally the biggest of them said, "Not bad, what you're doing. How about playing on our team?"

"No, thank you very much," I said.

"Why not? Because we're Jews?"

I did not answer and they came nearer.

"Well, what are you?" another of them asked. "A Rumanian? A Pole?"

"Neither the one nor the other."

"Well, then, what? A German?"

"No," I said. I felt an Austrian; that is: I was no German.

"But you speak German. So what the hell are you? A Jew, maybe?"

Why I did not answer I did not know at that moment. It was not cowardice, for it was obvious they meant me no harm. I did not like them very much; they were not my kind, and they were Jews. But I did not dislike them, either, and that made it worse. They had asked me to join their team, and here I stood and lacked the courage to say simply, "I would have liked to play with you, but I can't, because you are Jews and I am not, and I don't need to say any more.

205

However, I thank you for having asked me." I did not fear hurting their feelings. What I feared was that open words of that kind could have meant the direct contact of which I was afraid. A direct human relationship could have resulted— esteem or hatred, either one, would have meant the same. I didn't answer.

"Well, speak, baby," one of them said and came so near that our noses nearly touched. "Are you a Jew or aren't you?"

I still kept silent, and finally the first one said, "Oh, leave him alone. He's only a stuck-up pissing *goy.*" He threw the puck into the field, and they leapt after it, he with them, and there I stood alone again in my corner, with my beautifully tidy eights, and the huge shawl around my neck.

I believe that must have happened in the winter of 1927. I was thirteen or fourteen years old. In order to have the vagaries of my adolescence corrected, my benevolent and crazy parents, after a slight effort to have me tamed by a couple of relatives, put me in a Styrian boarding school renowned for its severe methods of education. To it I owe—along with the ever since vainly fought habit of smoking cigarettes and a profound knowledge of the porno-graphic folklore of the German and English languages—the insight that all public education's task is to vulgarize the genius of young people in such a way that only natures of extraordinarily strong neurotic tendencies are enabled to escape banality. The holidays I spent, usually, in the Bukovina, grateful for the utter loneliness that received me there, luckily freed for a few short summer weeks from the company of schoolmates in whose minds and muscles manhood fermented and from teachers deformed by their profession into baroque monstrosities. I passed my time hunting with my father in the Carpathian forests and walking the streets of Czernowitz and Sadagura, just watching and listening to what was going on. I don't know how I ever managed to pass my final examinations, for my midyear reports were catastrophic. My father, when he got

the good news, sent me a cable with the single word
"*Ahi!*"—an exclamation of Bukovinan Jews expressing unusual astonishment at the unexpected. Later, he explained
that, in point of fact, the exclamation was a survival from the
days of chivalry. Yiddish, he said, was mainly Middle High
German, with Hebrew and Polish elements. For example,
take the Yiddish expression "*nebbish*," which was nothing but
the "squire" (*neb-ich:* "near I") who runs with the knight,
carrying his shield. "*Ahi!*" was what the knights shouted
when, at a tournament, they put their lances under their
armpits and ran against one another.

This explanation was given to me not without a trace of
embarrassment, for it was rather uncomfortable to think that
the language of our models for a noble attitude of life should
be faithfully preserved only by the Jews. Therefore my
father did not fail to add that a certain decline of forms, as
well as of habits and even of costumes, of the upper classes to
the lower ones is the rule. The caftan of the rabbis, for
instance, and their fur-lined caps and boots were actually the
costume of Polish noblemen in medieval times, and a Jewish
wedding preserved many a custom that originated in the
court ceremonies of the dukes of Burgundy. It is about the
only cultural-historical lesson put into my mind between my
fourteenth and my seventeenth year that remains there
today.

The diploma of a *Gymnasium* is a poor substitute for the
rites of initiation with which primitive societies make a
young male understand that he has become a man; yet in my
youth nobody hesitated to take it as such. When I went back
to Vienna, in order to follow in the footsteps of my late
grandpapa and study architecture, I was merely a boy of
seventeen, but I enjoyed all the liberties of a grown man,
with none of the responsibilities. I could go to bed when and
with whom I pleased, drink liquor to my heart's content and
the revolt of my intestines, and spend my money and time as
economically or wastefully as I felt like. My parents were
not rich; my father's passion for hunting was expensive and

soon devoured what the war had left of a former certain opulence. Yet, in the Bukovina, my monthly allowance would have sufficed to keep a Jewish family of seven from urgent need. Anyhow, I was not forced to begin my studies under the mental pressure of lack of time. But all this did not alter my solitude, which by now had become not only a habit but a deliberate, proud attitude. I did not have a single friend, and I did not long for one. With girls I was extremely clumsy and shy. Besides, my mother, fearing that I would abuse my new status and fall into debauchery, had arranged that I again live with my grandmother. Though my mother knew very well that the old lady was too much of a recluse to keep an eye on a young man, she counted on my aunts, whose theosophical preoccupations and love for dogs were evidence of a high morality that would perhaps keep me from immediately getting lost in a swamp of vices.

It was at this time I learned that we had done Mr. Malik an injustice by calling him a Jew. On the contrary, he was a man of high moral standards. A very important free and yet not reborn soul who had followed his invitation and slipped into the emptied vessel of the body of his sister, Miss Weingruber, a highly gifted medium, revealed to the esoteric community that great things were in preparation. The universe was a big system of perpetual perfection. Everything in it had but the sole wish to dematerialize more and more and finally become pure spirit and unite with God. *Materia* was the contrary of God. It was a burden given as a curse to the fallen angels, a curse put upon their souls, which were longing to be light and free again. Death did not mean you would be freed. When you died, your soul was suspended for a while outside the dimension perceivable to us and, in a sort of metaphysical extra course, was taught what was good and what was evil, and particularly to understand what it had done that was good or bad in the existence it had just left. If, in the former life, it had done much good, it was allowed to slip into a new existence less burdened with *materia*. If it had done a medium amount of good or evil, it had to come back to the same world in another existence and carry the same amount of *materia* and live again, trying to do better. If, on the other hand, it had done a great deal of wrong, it was condemned to a lower form of existence, even more burdened with *materia*, and slipped into a body that was not just flesh and bones, like ours, but—let us say—of stone or iron. Your soul, doing better and better each time, finally dematerialized into pure spirit and united with God.

Not only human souls were under the curse of *materia* but also your pet dog's, as a slightly lower form, and everything else—even the cobblestones on which Minka Raubitschek had broken her hip. And each creature or inanimate object was given the chance of doing good or evil and of dematerializing or materializing accordingly. And, of course, the stars and the planets on which you lived too had their chance, and when all the beings of a lower-grade star had done very well, the star itself potentialized and became a star of a higher category, with thinner *materia* and better souls on it. And this was going to happen to our globe.

My aunts were full of joy and expectation telling me about all this. By the good behavior of those who lived for the spirit, they said, our world had slowly potentialized and dematerialized and was now on the verge of potentializing into a nearly butterfly-like world. For there were very high-class souls—people like Buddha, Plato, and Jesus Christ—who deliberately took on the burden of *materia* in order to teach the others what was good or evil. Each of them was announced by some soul of a high category materialized for this very purpose. And as Jesus Christ had been announced by John the Baptist, Mr. Malik had come to announce the arrival of another dematerializer. His name was Adolf Hitler, and one could already see what enthusiasm he had created in Germany by spiritualizing the Germans and cleansing Germany of the low, materialistic Jews. Mr. Malik was no Jew, in spite of the fact that he had changed his name (as had Mr. Hitler, whose real name was

Schicklgruber—and he certainly was no Jew, either); he had done this for a different reason, for Malik was the name given to him in the outer world—the name of his spirit. The name given to his material burden, which he had voluntarily undertaken to carry, was Weingruber. He and his sister were actually one high-category soul divided in two and inhabiting two bodies.

The potentialization of the world could already be felt in my grandmother's home by the fact that it, too, had to a certain extent been cleansed of Jews. No longer were the séances of the esoteric community accompanied by the chamber music of the Raubitscheks, for on the same day both Professor Raubitschek and his wife died of Spanish flu—a typical Jewish extravagance, as my grandmother said, because there was no epidemic, as in 1918, when many people died of it; therefore there was no cause to do it out of season, so to speak. Anyhow, they both died and left their daughter alone, and—alas!—what had been gained by their disappearance was largely spoiled by the scandalous behavior of Minka Raubitschek. Not only did she have an official lover, whose roadster often stood parked in front of the house all night, but other gentlemen were seen going into the Raubitschek apartment and coming out the morning after. Instead of chamber music on Wednesday evenings, one could hear the noises of carousing nearly every night.

I rather liked Minka. She was friendly when we met on the staircase. Her voice was full and warm, and her smile beautiful. She looked Spanish, with her shining black hair and large black eyes. Her skin was lovely, and she used a lipstick of a most provokingly vivid red. She dressed well, and even her slight limping had a certain charm; she did not try to hide it but limped ahead courageously and decidedly. On Sunday mornings, I was invited by my grandmother to breakfast in her room. From the window I could follow the spectacle of Minka's being called for by her official lover, a tall, fair, athletic chap, for their weekend outing. He was obviously an ice-hockey player. Sometimes he got into his roadster wearing his hockey uniform, vividly striped in red and white and yellow. Minka carried his sticks, knee pads, and shoulder pads. It all looked very smart and gay, and made me feel my isolation.

The courses in architecture at the Technische Hochschule bored me to tears. Instead of giving me a taste for harmony, the instructors tortured me with the theory of statics of rigid bodies, equations, the use of vectors, and so on, and I have always been a hopeless mathematician. Very soon I began to cut classes, and finally I did not go there for months at a time. I was too ignorant to enjoy either a concert or the theater. With the exception, perhaps, of a few operettas starring Fritzi Massary, I saw nothing of the good theater in Vienna of that time. My grandmother still kept a seat at the opera and never went there herself, so I drowsed through *Rheingold* and *La Traviata*, wondering why people sometimes sighed with delight and sometimes expressed their disapproval. But I walked a lot. I crisscrossed Vienna from one end to the other, sometimes walking as far as from Döbling to Hietzing, and then taking the tramway back. I walked, preferably at night, through the inner city, watching the swarms of whores on the Kärntnerstrasse. During the day, it was the most elegant of all Viennese streets, and at night it turned into something like the Canebière in Marseille. Or I would stand and marvel at the beauty of the empty Josefsplatz and Fischer von Erlach's National-Bibliothek, wondering why my grandfather had never achieved this perfection. Nobody cared that I came home at four o'clock in the morning, and old Marie had long since given up trying to wake me, knowing that I usually slept till noon.

But of course I was too proud to admit my solitude to anybody. I spent most of my money on clothes, and when I set out for a stroll in the afternoon I would be most elegantly dressed, like some young dandy who is just about to get into his car and drive out to the golf course at Lainz or to the five-o'clock tea dance at Hübner's Park Hotel in Hietzing. In the evening, I never left the house except in a very smart dinner jacket or sometimes even, when I felt like it, in tails, with a silk hat on my well-brushed head. After a couple of hours of lonesome walking through empty streets and somber parks, along the tracks of railways or the banks of the Danube Canal, I would sit down for a coffee and a brandy in the lounge of the Hotel Imperial, slipping off my patent-leather pumps under the table to ease my sore feet. One would have thought I was a young man with an exquisite social life.

Once, well after midnight, I came home to my grandmother's house in tails and silk hat and found Minka at the door, fumbling in her handbag for the key she had either forgotten or lost. She was amused at the misfortune of having no key, and at my arriving just in time to open the door. She was a little drunk. Her eyes sparkled, and her teeth shone moist between those provoking red lips. But, of course, I behaved like a well-bred young man. I unlocked the door and held it open for her with the particular politeness of a certain reserve, and she smiled at me and said I looked splendid. Where had I been, so elegantly clad? At a dance, I said. Where and with whom? With people she would certainly not know. What was their name? she asked. Oh, Rumanians, I said stiffly. It was typically Jewish, I thought, to be so insistent and to ask such personal questions, and I did not like it. The Rumanians were passing through Vienna, I said, on their way to Paris.

She knew frightfully amusing Rumanians in Paris, she said. Had I been there lately? Not lately, I said, following her up the stairs. The steps were flat and easy to mount, but she had a little difficulty with her lame hip and the one drink too many she might have had, so I offered her my arm, and she leaned against it freely. My elbow registered that she was not so bony as the fashion of the early 1930s demanded. It was delightful, and a little embarrassing, so when we reached my grandmother's floor, I stood still, and she let go of my arm and smiled again. "Thank you," she said. "You are charming."

"Would you like me to accompany you to your floor?" I asked, and then bit my lip at my own clumsiness.

She laughed. "Does it show that I'm drunk? I never realize it myself unless I have to get up these stairs on all fours. Come on, then, my young dandy, give me your arm again. . . . I once broke that silly left hip of mine," she said, leaning trustfully against the length of my body. "Because I was in love—imagine! If I had gone on that way, I wouldn't have a sound bone in my body. How are you making out with the girls?"

"Well . . ." I said, and smiled shyly, as if I were too modest to tell her the full truth.

She laughed. I said nothing more. I wasn't quite sure she hadn't seen through me and just been teasing me. "Would you like to come inside for a nightcap?" she asked when we arrived at her door.

"Thank you very much."

"Thank you, yes, or thank you, no?" She looked straight into my eyes.

"Yes," I said, and felt that I was blushing.

She handed me a key and said, "Fortunately, I haven't lost this one."

Again I unlocked the door and held it open, and she went in, dropping her fur coat on the floor. I picked it up and put it on a chair. "What nice manners you have," she said. "It must be lovely to have you around. How old are you?"

It seemed too silly to say "I'm going to be eighteen next May," so I lied. "Twenty-three."

"Just my cup of tea. There is a phonograph in the corner. Put on a record if you want some music. What will you drink? Whiskey, or a brandy?"

"A whiskey with soda, please." The flat did not look at all as I had imagined it would. She must have redecorated it since the death of the old Raubitscheks. With the exception of a huge library with black carved-wood bookcases that could have belonged to the chamber-music-loving Professor Raubitschek, there was no trace of the particular Jewish-middle-class stuffiness I had had glimpses of through open windows at home in the Bukovina. There were flowers all over the place—her lovers seemed to be quite generous, I thought. Through an open door I could see into her bedroom, gay and feminine, the huge bed covered with a soft, flowery comforter. While she fixed the drinks, I had a look at the records. There were masses of them, piled up carelessly around the phonograph. I put one on with the label "Star Dust," hoping it was Mozart and not as violent as Beethoven's "Allergique." With the first sweet sounds, she came toward me with the drinks. "Here's yours," she said, putting a glass in my hand. "Let's see how you dance." I did not know what to do with my glass, but finally took it in my left hand and put my other arm around her, and we danced a few steps. I could not feel that she limped. "All right," she said, and moved away from me. "A little stiff, but there is hope. I can't dance long, because of my hip, but I love it."

I took a gulp of my whiskey. She dropped down on the couch, leaned back, and shut her eyes. Suddenly she yawned, her beautiful mouth wide open. She yawned with a melodious cry that sounded like a happy weeping and that faded away in a sigh of utter relaxation, at the end of which she opened her eyes and said, "You are sweet. Now go downstairs to your grandma and sleep well." She got up with an unexpected swiftness and went to her bedroom, already unbuttoning her dress in the back.

I stood still in bewilderment, not knowing what to think of all this, not even knowing whether I had imagined something else would happen or what—just simply not knowing how to put my glass down and say "Good night" and "See you soon." She turned and looked at me, still fumbling with buttons at her back. "If you don't want to go," she said, "you can listen to a few more records, if you like. But don't mind if I fall asleep. I'm dog-tired."

I felt humiliated to the core. The situation was totally out of my control, and I wished I'd never accepted her invitation to come in for a nightcap. But, on the other hand, she was so kind, and sweet, and pretty. Her mouth had excited me.

She had turned round fully and stood watching me. Then she came toward me, smiling, and before I could say anything she took my head in both hands and kissed me softly and affectionately. Then she smiled again, close to me, under my eyes, and said, "What's all this? Do you want to stay with me?" I didn't answer. Still looking into my face, she said softly, "Then come!"

She very soon found out the full truth about my worldliness, and it seemed to touch her. She was all sweet understanding, treating me with a tenderness and intimacy I had never known before or even been able to imagine. If it had been possible for me to think such a monstrous thought, I should have called it gay and tender lovemaking with a sister.

I put "Star Dust" on the phonograph again, and we lay in the dark and listened till it came to an end. She laughed and said, "Won't your grandma be upset when she finds out that you've been with me in the middle of the night?"

"She doesn't necessarily need to know."

"Well, certainly not. But she will find out sooner or later. I want to have you around, you are so cozy."

I said, "May I put on that record once more?"

"You do like it, don't you? Well, it's yours. You can take it with you and play it till you can't stand it anymore."

"Thank you."

"I wish I had a little more money, so I could buy you things you like. I have always longed for a little brother to spoil. What is your name?"

"Arnulf."

"What?" she cried, with an outburst of her delightful laughter. "It can't be true. Arnulf! Who ever thought of such a dreadful name?"

"My father," I said, smiling against my will. "It comes from his mother's family; they're Bavarians. I think he thought it would oblige me to behave like a good knight." I sighed. Yet I was very much amused myself.

"But you can't possibly expect me to call you Arnulf," she said.

"Well, I have a few more Christian names. I have about half a dozen. Other people I know have up to fifteen."

"Don't tell me. I expect your other names are even worse. No, I shall call you Brommy—that fits you very well."

"Why, and how?"

"Oh, I don't know. It simply fits you."

"Did you have a pet dog with that name?"

"No. I don't know where I got it from—there was an admiral, I think."

"What have I to do with an admiral?"

"Lots. You are very much like a young cadet who will become an admiral someday. And you don't want me to call you Wilhelm von Tegetthoff."

I laughed. The totally illogical jump was typically Jewish. It sounded like one of the surrealistic jokes that were told in the Bukovina about the merry rabbis of the Hasidim and their shrewdly twisted logic. I could not help feeling very much at home with Minka.

"Now, come," she said. "Be a good boy and let's get some sleep."

She did not send me away. She simply put her arms around me and curled close to me, and instantly fell into a deep and innocent sleep, smelling of well-groomed feminine hair and skin, good perfume, and a little whiskey. I lay for a while with open eyes, listening to the fading sounds of "Star Dust," which was now mine, and thinking how funny it was that at the very moment you got mixed up with Jews you changed your name. Soon I, too, fell asleep, my arms around her.

I have often wondered since whether I had an affair with Minka. Whatever it was, it did not interfere in the slightest with her amorous life, and though it altered my life completely, there seemed not the faintest tie that would have given me the impression that I couldn't do whatever I pleased. From that first morning—when I woke in her arms and watched her face, so fresh and well rested, and she opened her dark eyes and, with joyful laughter, said, "Now, who are *you?* Surely not the boy from downstairs?"—we were together day and night. "I am getting so accustomed to having him in my bed," she would explain to her friends— among whom some were even a little more than friends. "Like a child with its teddy bear. He doesn't kick or snore. He's just sweet and appetizing." And, turning to the nearest female in the circle, "If you really want a good night's sleep, I'll lend him to you."

Of course, there were also moments when she said to me, "Listen, my dear Brommy, there is a certain gentleman who is arriving from Paris, so would you do me a great favor and go skiing with Bobby? He's treating, so you needn't spend your pocket money on that. And please don't show up around here before next Friday."

Bobby was her official lover—the fair, athletic chap who skied and played ice hockey and swam and rode horseback. We had become great friends. "You know, my boy," he would explain to me, "if it were any other girl, you'd become jealous. But not with Minka. First, it would be pointless. Second, she wouldn't let you. She makes it quite clear to you that it's not you who possess her, it's she who possesses you. Now, since she is not jealous of you, what right have you to be jealous of her? It's as simple as that."

There was no use trying to explain to him, or anybody else, that our relationship was, in fact, relatively—and even in great proportion—innocent. When Minka and I went to bed together, it was mainly to curl up in one another's arms and fall asleep. It gave her comfort to have someone near. I have sometimes thought that it may have been an atavism or, let us say, a tradition that she had inherited, like the passion for hunting and shooting among our kind. After all, many of her ancestors must have slept six in one bed, like most of the poor Jews in Galicia and in the Bukovina. But certainly such

217

an explanation would not have helped my grandmother or aunts to understand my affection for Minka; in their eyes it would have made things even worse. In fact, it was all rather scandalous, and I was afraid my father would hear about it—particularly as neither my grandmother nor my aunts gave the slightest sign of knowing what was going on. That they knew perfectly well I could detect from old Marie's trembling resentment whenever I went up to Minka's flat or came down from it, and the resentment increased when the hours I spent downstairs in my room became short intervals between the sojourns upstairs at Minka's. I could only pray to God that the hatred of my mother's relatives for my father would not allow them to give him the satisfaction of saying that it was not surprising I got involved with Jews while staying in their house. He had always warned my mother against her own family, and he would no doubt say that it was her fault for letting me go to Vienna, instead of—as he had wished—sending me to Graz, the capital of Styria, where there were fewer Jews.

There is an old saying that when you change your life you also change your ideas. This is not necessarily so. You can very well change your life and in the meantime send your ideas, so to speak, on a holiday. My life had changed entirely, and though I kept right on disliking Jews, I lived among them—for most of Minka's friends were Jews—from then on. One of them, a monstrously fat and ugly yet highly amusing journalist from Prague, who regularly came to Vienna as a theater critic, gave me the password. Once, after a brief encounter with a well-known actor who was not a Jew and who had treated him with special friendliness, he turned toward me and said, "My mother used to say, 'More than of an anti-Semite, my boy, beware of people who just love Jews.'" Right she was, I thought, laughing heartily. For disliking Jews was not something you could change. It was an inborn reaction that did not hinder you from even liking them in a certain way. I liked Minka tremendously, and if she hadn't been a Jewess, I would have fallen madly in love with her and, in spite of my eighteen years (and to her utter amusement, I presume), probably have asked her to marry me. But even when she woke up in my arms and I in hers, after an innocent night's sleep, there was a taboo that controlled my feelings and made everything even more delightful. I felt so free and unburdened with her. As she said, she liked having me around. She could not take me seriously as a lover. I was her toy, and everything was light and nice and uncomplicated. She could summon me and send me away whenever she wanted. I asked no questions, and she could tell me everything. We would both laugh at our particular adventures and misfortunes, share our joys, our money, our problems. Her girl friends were sweet and of a charming libertinage. I can't remember a time in my life since when I have had such pleasures. She was the queen of a little kingdom that for a while became my universe, and I served her as a page. The day began with her morning bath and toilet, and I either came up to her flat for it or was already there, ready to wait on her. She was severe and not at all patient. Very soon I learned everything a young man can be taught about a lady's boudoir. I accompanied her to her dressmaker, her hairdresser, her shopping, her brief luncheon at the Café Rebhuhn, where the artists and intellectuals who had chosen it for their headquarters were great friends of hers. She took me to museums, to concerts, to the theater, to dinner parties, and to the *Heurigen*—the tasting of the new wine in the vineyards of the nearby village of Grinzing. That little kingdom of hers, which became my universe, was composed of all that was best in Vienna in the early 1930s, the most intellectual and most amusing. Her friends came to her home as birds fly in and out of the foliage of a tree. Among them was Karl Kraus, who at that time was considered merely a satirist but whose life stands as an example of moral uprightness and courage which should be put before anyone who writes, in no matter what language. Thanks to Minka, I had, at the age of eighteen, the privilege of listening to his conversation and watching his face, lit up by the pale fire of his fanatic love for the miracle of the German language and by his holy hatred for those who used it badly. There was also a young man, not a Jew, who was a gifted musician. "Come on, Herbert," Minka would say, "play something on the piano." Many years later, I remembered that his name was von Karajan.

What gave me the right to stand my ground among those people was a rather strange talent Minka had discovered in me. Not for nothing had I passed a great part of my childhood and adolescence amidst Polish Jews. While walking through the streets of Czernowitz and Sadagura and Lvov, I had kept my ears open, and I spoke better Yiddish and knew more of the customs and behavior of the so-called Polish Jews than most of the refined Jews of Vienna or even Prague. I was an expert in all shades of Jewish slang and the way Jews spoke when they wanted to speak select German. And when somebody told a Jewish story, which at that time, and especially among Jewish intellectuals, was cultivated as an art, and told it badly, Minka would impatiently interrupt him, saying, "Come on, don't bore us. Tell your story in a low voice to Brommy, and he'll tell it to us much better than you do." If for some reason she chose not to interrupt the imperfect storyteller, she and I would exchange a short, vague, yet significant look, very much in the way that my eyes would meet those of my mother or father, my grandmother or my aunts, when somebody who was not of our kind committed some lapse of manners or language. If, on the other hand, some master told a Jewish story to perfection, then Minka would pull my sleeve and say, "Pay attention, Brommy!"

Brommy. . . . It was a name of quite another form of existence, which ran parallel to my existence as son, grandson, and nephew—very much as Guru Malik within the esoteric community of my aunts led a life parallel to that of brave engineer Weingruber, who lived his petit bourgeois life as an employee of the Styria Motor Company. Once, when someone called me on the telephone, one of my aunts

220

answered, and afterward she asked me with an expression of amazement, "What do your . . . friends call you? 'Brommy'? But you have such nice other Christian names. What a regrettable lack of taste."

Furious, without knowing why, I said, "You mind your own business!"

"Now, really!" she exclaimed. "Have we come to the point where boys of your age speak to adults in such a way? Don't forget, you're only eighteen, after all."

I certainly did not forget it. It weighed on me that I had lied to Minka about my age. One day I could bear it no longer. We had been talking about some of her troubles, and she said, "It's astonishing how understanding you are for your age, my boy."

"Minka," I said, "there's something I have to confess. I lied to you."

"What about?" she said and smiled. "Oh, I see. You want to tell me that in fact there *is* a drop of Jewish blood in you."

"No," I said. "I am sorry there isn't. But I'm not twenty-three. I am only eighteen."

"What? But you're not serious?"

From then on, she treated me as a sort of wonder child. "Would you believe it? He's only eighteen!" They probably all thought I was Jewish, and were proud of my precocity.

Well, it did not go on forever, alas. Very soon I was nineteen, and at twenty I had to do my military service in Rumania, and my gay time in Vienna was over. But it was soon replaced by another fascinating experience. I now became aware that I knew almost nothing about the country I belonged to, the Rumanian people, or their language. In order to fill that gap, a young Rumanian student was hired to teach me Rumanian and something of Rumanian literature and history, and I not only formed friendships with my tutor and some other young Rumanians which have lasted till today but also learned the historical past of the three

Rumanian principalities—Moldova (to which the Bukovina had once belonged), Muntenia, and Oltenia—and their struggle to unite against their Turkish oppressors and Phanariot rulers and become a nation and the kingdom of Rumania. By tracing some rather remote lineage of my pedigree until it found root in Rumania, I was able to justify my newly discovered love for that country and my claim to belong there not merely as part of a former Austrian minority but by inheritance. Then I exchanged my first name, Arnulf, for the third of my Christian names, Gregor, which also happened to be the Christian name of some half-Greek, half-Russian ancestor originating in Bessarabia and beautifully outfitted with a Turkish wife. My father watched with intense disapproval my Rumanian friendships and my attempts to tie myself genealogically to Rumania, but by that time I had—thanks to Minka Raubitschek—acquired a certain independence of mind, and when my father said that he loathed the Bukovina and if it hadn't been for the Carpathians would long since have left it, I said boldly that, according to my taste, it was better to have a free outlook over a lovely rolling country with a vast horizon than to be always running your nose against some stone wall, as in Styria. Whereupon my father turned his back, and did not speak to me for a couple of weeks.

I came back to Vienna in the summer of 1937 as Gregor, sporting an enormous Phanariot mustache. I hurried upstairs to embrace Minka and break the news that I was in love. It was not a very happy love story, though, for the lady in question was married, and, to make matters worse, I liked her husband very much. Minka, as usual, was full of understanding, comfort, and good advice. We passed a few gay days together, but no night. I had outgrown my teddy-bear stage and, besides, would have considered it treason to my love to sleep soundly in another woman's bed instead of lying alone, sighing for her. I was going to meet her shortly in Salzburg, where she wanted to attend the festival. Minka took me to the station. Looking up at me

222

while I looked down at her from the open window of my compartment in the train, she saw my excited happiness. Her eyes shone tenderly, with a strange, more profound tenderness than ever. "If you were wise," she said, "you would now get off this train and never see that girl again."

"What do you mean?"

"Everything you have had with her so far is beautiful—all promise and expectation. Now come the troubles."

"Oh, don't talk rot. We are going to be very happy."

"I do hope so," she said. "I am very, very fond of you, you know."

The train started up, and I sat back in my seat in a state of bewilderment. It could not be that Minka was in love with me, could it? No, that was impossible. Yet the thought flattered my vanity, and, rather the prouder for it, I looked forward to meeting my adored one.

Minka was right. Things became frightfully complicated, and Salzburg in the summer of 1937 was just awful. It was overrun with Jews. The worst of them had come from Germany as refugees and, in spite of their luggage-laden Mercedes cars, behaved as if they were the victims of a cruel persecution and therefore had the right to hang around in hundreds at the Café Mozart, criticize everything, and get whatever they wanted faster and cheaper—if not for nothing—than anybody else. They spoke with that particular Berlin snottiness that so got on the nerves of anyone brought up in Austria, and my sharp ears could all too easily detect the background of Jewish slang. My Turkish blood revolted. I could have slaughtered them all. I fled to Styria, for a visit to my old boarding school, and then followed my ladylove back to Rumania.

When I came back to Vienna again, it was February 1938, and what I found was chaos. Minka had come to fetch me at the station. She merely said, "Poor boy, I am afraid that your aunts' guru is right and the Weingrubers and Schicklgrubers and Schweingrubers will soon potentialize the world." Most of her friends—Bobby among them—had already gone to Switzerland, she said, or England, or France, or were preparing to leave Austria even at the price of their material existence.

"Oh, don't exaggerate," I said. "You Jews are always making a fuss about something. What in the world is going on, anyway?"

"Poldi will explain it to you. We're having dinner with him. You just listen to what he has to say."

Poldi was the fat journalist from Prague, who, as a theater critic, went regularly not only to Vienna but also to Berlin. He had lost a lot of weight and was not half so amusing as he used to be. What irritated me most of all was the self-complacent way he treated me—and I could not rise to the occasion, because he resolutely kept aiming at my cultural gaps. "I understand that we have sworn off allegiance to the ancestor of the Carolingians," he greeted me, "even though the mustache is downright Merovingian." And when I shook my head uncomprehendingly, he went on, "I mean, we are no longer calling ourselves Arnulf, now, but Gregor. Good, very good. Gregory the Great, as we all know, was a protector of the Jews."

I dryly answered that this was certainly not the reason I had been given this name, and he threw in, "Very well, let's stay with the Carolingians. We are then not far from Bishop Agobard, and we can look forward to a new *De insolentia Judaeorum* or, even worse, a new *De Judaicis superstitionibus* with a few blood libels. Today, you see, there are two schools of thought—two camps, I must involuntarily say: one outside and one inside the concentration camps. And uncomfortable as the latter may be, it is, still and all, the only one for decent people."

"And I would rather end up there myself than let Brommy get in," said Minka. "But just tell him seriously how things look politically. He's straight out of the Middle Ages, you know. That's where his father lives, in the Carpathians."

Now I realized that Poldi's irony was put on in order to

conceal an enormous fear. Most of the things he told us, in a whisper, looking around to make sure he wasn't overheard, did not make much sense to me. In the landscape of my mind, politics had not figured prominently. As a subject of Rumania—that is, of His Majesty King Carol II—I knew, and was expected to know, that he was the sovereign of a constitutional monarchy, and that in Bucharest there was a parliament where deputies represented the party of the peasants and the party of the liberals and whatnot, and that they were a bunch of crooks who did nothing but steal the money of the state. There were also some Jews, who were Communists, and therefore, rightly, were treated as such—that is, as Russian spies and *agents provocateurs*. But fortunately there were also some young Rumanians who, under their leader, a certain Mr. Cuza—which was a good and noble name, though only adopted by that gentleman— beat up those Jews from time to time, thus keeping them in a hell of a fright, and preventing them from spreading more Communist propaganda and provocation. I knew, too, that in Austria there were many socialists, called Reds, who were beaten up by or beat up the Heimwehr, which was a national guard defending the ethical values—such as the cleanliness of mind guaranteed by the fresh mountain air, and the love for shooting goats and plucking edelweiss—of Styria, Tirol, Carinthia, and others of the old Austrian lands. With the help of the Heimwehr, Chancellor Dollfuss had cannonaded the Reds, only to be shot down later by a Nazi. Nazis, in Austria, were rowdies who dynamited telephone booths, but that was not necessarily true of German Nazis, who, after all, had done very well. They had built up a state of order, and justice, and genuine social welfare, in spite of the fact that Adolf Hitler was a frightful proletarian, as my father said, and looked exactly like a Bohemian footman my grandmother had once employed, against his advice. The footman turned out to be a thief and stole my father's cuff links and some other items, including a very nice hunting knife. Only people like my mother's family could be wrong about somebody with such a face, my father said.

The Reds were bad because they were proletarians and wanted to do away with people of our kind, as had happened in Russia. Jews had a fatal inclination for Reds; therefore they ought to be kept in a hell of a fright, so they would keep quiet. Nazis were also proletarians, but they had some very sound ideas, like the theory of breeding, and some exemplary laws about hunting only in season, which gave the game the chance to regenerate and even improve in number as well as in size. And on the whole they were against Jews and Reds, so it was quite obvious that we had to stick with them. I really did not think there was much more to the subject, and I got rather bored with Poldi's Cassandra-like whispering, so I proposed that we go to the Kärntnerbar for a whiskey. If, as Poldi said, the Germans wanted to conquer Austria, so much the better. The German-speaking peoples would be united again, as they had been in the Holy Roman Empire of Charlemagne. And if the Jews were frightened, it served them right. It would keep them from becoming Russian spies and propagandists of Communism and also make them behave a little more decently at the Salzburg Festival. As for the reaction of the English and French and so on, they should mind their own business. I did not see any reason to start a war just because the German-speaking peoples did what the Czechs and Poles and Rumanians had been encouraged to do by the very same French and English. Of course, I did not say any of this to Poldi and Minka, because they were friends and it would have hurt their feelings. So we went to the Kärntnerbar.

When Minka went to the Kärntnerbar, it was the crest of the wave. We let her down to the ladies' room by a rope and pulled her up again, and Poldi became his old self and was highly amusing. At three o'clock in the morning, we found ourselves in the beer cellar of the Paulanerbräu, sitting between a stone-drunk chap—who shouted in a loud voice that he was a former cavalry officer with a golden decoration for bravery and the official title of the Hero of Zaleszczyki—and a shy little tart I knew fairly well from midnight strolls on the Kärntnerstrasse. We had hardly had a spoonful of our gulash soup and a sip of beer when a huge, rather shabby-looking young man roared in our faces, *"Juden raus!"* "Jews out!"

The former cavalry officer got up in stiff dignity and said that he felt offended by having been called a Jew, and would the gentleman instantly follow him to the men's room in the basement in order to fix the place and conditions of the duel. Poldi pushed him back on his stool. The rowdy then, surprisingly, sat down on the other side of the little tart and stared with a dull expression at the wooden table. Suddenly he lifted his head and looked at me. "Don't you remember me, you swine?" he roared. "Arnulf! I'm Oskar. Oskar Koloman."

I could scarcely believe my eyes. He was one of the boys at the boarding school in Styria, a good deal older than I but in the same class. "Where the hell have you come from?" I asked.

He rose to his full height and volume. "You really want to know?" He nearly fell over the table in the attempt to grasp my shoulder. "Come with me to the men's room in the basement. I'll *tell* you where I've come from."

"I think you'd better go," Minka said, in a low voice. "It'll give Poldi and me a chance to disappear."

I followed my schoolmate past a row of gentlemen standing against a tarred wall, showing us their backs, till he found a gap where we could stand next to one another. He had that very day been released from Steinhausen, the Austrian concentration camp for Nazis under the regime of Chancellor Schuschnigg. As one of a group of Nazi students, he had blown up a telephone booth in Graz and had been caught doing it. He had spent three years in the camp. "For a cigarette butt no bigger than this," he howled into my face, showing as well as he could with his thick fingers how small, "for such a tiny little butt, they made me clean the latrines for a week!" Then, hammering his fists against the tarred wall, "They have forsaken us! They have betrayed us—our brethren of the Reich! They left us in the mire while they became great and mighty. Now they will come and take over here, too!" He leaned his forehead against the wall and wept.

So that was Austria. Hadn't my father been right to keep out of it? Again I fled to the clean mountains of Styria to ski for a couple of weeks. I had nothing to do anyway but wait for the lady I still loved. We had made an appointment to meet in Vienna on the eleventh of March. I was there a day earlier, and felt as if I had wandered into a madhouse. A sort of regimented revolution was going on under the watchful eyes of fat Viennese policemen in long bottle-green coats. On one side of the Kärntnerstrasse, people with swastikas in their buttonholes promenaded, shouted *"Heil!"* and sneered at the people on the other side. The people on the other side, young workers—many Jews among them—shook their fists at the Nazis and shouted *"Rotfront!"* I could not get hold of Minka, who was helping relatives in Mödling prepare their departure, somebody in the Café Rebhuhn told me. So I went home to my grandmother's flat, where I found that my beloved had already arrived in Vienna and would be waiting for me next evening at ten o'clock in an apartment house on the Opernring. I did not go out all the next day but spent the day in great uneasiness waiting for the telephone to ring. The cable with that precise information could only mean that something had gone wrong. But no call came. When I left the house at a quarter to ten, the streets were strangely dark and empty. I walked the short distance from the Florianigasse to the Rathaus, and through the Rathaus arcade—one of my grandfather's dubious architectural masterpieces. Coming out, I found myself in the middle of an uncanny procession. In blocks that in their disciplined compactness seemed made of cast iron, people marched by thousands, men only, in total silence. The morbid, rhythmic stamping of their feet hung like a gigantic swinging cord in the silence that had fallen on Vienna. This cord seemed to originate somewhere in the outskirts. I could detect it through the length of the Alserstrasse, then winding round toward the Rathaus and leading down the Ringstrasse. Parades of all kinds were not rare in Vienna. They were nearly always led by a detachment of streetcar conductors and were in protest against something or other— unemployment, or the rise in the price of milk, or the pollution of the city water, brought in from the clean mountains of Styria by aqueducts. But this was different. It had an uncomfortably decisive character. I tried to break through between the blocks, but I did not succeed. Two or three times I asked a bystander what was going on, and got no answer. Impatient, fearing I would be late for the appointment with my beloved, I squeezed myself into the last row of a marching block and marched with them.

"What the hell are we marching for?" I asked the man beside me.

"*Anschluss,*" he barked.

Well, that literally meant "connection," and that was exactly what I was looking for. If I could march with them down to the Opernring and get out of the parade there, I'd be in time for my appointment. But they wouldn't let me. I was pushed out. I had come far enough to see the full height of the tower of the Rathaus, toward which the marchers turned their heads, starry-eyed. The tower was surmounted by the statue of a knight in armor, a statue I had loved as a child, so I turned my head, too, and saw a huge flag hanging down from the tower's peak, attached to my knight's armored feet—a red flag with a white circle, in which there was a black swastika. "So that's it. It's come, finally," I said to myself. "Austria has united with the German Reich."

It was not unexpected. For weeks people had spoken of little else. Yet how did all these people know that it would happen this very night? And how, for heaven's sake, did they know their place in the serried ranks? They must have been drilled for months—but where? In cellars? Austrian Nazis had been underground up to this moment, an underground everybody knew about and spoke about quite openly and—with the exception of Jews and Reds, of course—with a certain sympathy. And now here it was. The whole male population of Vienna seemed to be marching in that silent parade. I felt a sudden resentment at being left out. After all, I was an Austrian myself; I had been born under the flag of the double-headed eagle as well as they, and though I was a subject of Rumania, it seemed unjust to deny me a place in one of their marching blocks as if I were a Red, or even a Jew. Politically, too, I wasn't much different from them. Anyway, the event in itself was something I welcomed, even if I didn't much care for the *Pieffkes* (as we Austrians called Germans). These people probably didn't care for them either. Oskar Koloman had already expressed his disillusion. In any case, the unity of the Reich was restored. The dream of a century had come true. Such a political reversal would change many things, perhaps even the decision of my beloved to get a divorce from her husband, whom, unfortunately, I liked so much. There was a promise of hope in the atmosphere. In spite of that uncanny silence all over Vienna, something was happening, something important, and not merely a protest against the diminishing size of *Wiener Kipfeln*—the beloved Viennese croissants—and the pollution of the city water. Again and again I inserted myself into the marching blocks, trying to keep step so it wouldn't be too obvious that I did not belong, and was pushed out of the ranks each time. At last, I came to the Opernring and hurried up the staircase of a certain house, and there she was. We both burst into hysterical laughter. "Can you imagine!" we said. "What an effort to celebrate our union!"

It wasn't a union, though; it was the opposite. With great emotion, and not without tears, she had to tell me that in spite of all her love for me she couldn't divorce the man

230

whom we both liked so much. She had been married to him for too many years. It was the old story of an engagement more or less arranged by their parents; then, suddenly, she had felt that she could not marry him, and was about to tell him so when he went on a trip, and while she was waiting for him to come back so she could tell him how she really felt, he wrote her such charming, loving letters that—well, she finally married him. And he had been sweet to her and decent, and everything I knew so well, too, and—well, that was that. I had to accept it.

Next morning, we stood at the windows and looked down at the Opernring, now empty, where all the night through there had been ecstasy—a sudden ecstasy that had its source in the silent marching blocks, and that drew people out of their houses and made them run toward the marchers, shouting, roaring, embracing one another, swinging flags with swastikas, throwing their arms to heaven, jumping and dancing in delirium. It was an icy-cold yet gloriously sunny day, quite unusual for the middle of March. It was so cold that you would not allow your dog to stay outdoors for longer than five minutes. There was nobody as far as you could see except two or three of the old hags, wrapped, onionlike, in layers of frocks and coats, who sold flowers in the New Market. They were running across the Ring and throwing their roses and carnations in the air, yelling *"Heil!"* What did they have to do with it, anyway? Over the radio we had learned that Austria was about to unite with the German Reich, and the Germans were expected to come here triumphantly, as our brethren, in a huge parade, under a rain of flowers. And that the great unifier and renewer of the German-speaking peoples, Adolf Hitler, was also about to arrive in Austria any moment and would come down the Danube, the old stream of the Nibelungen, to Vienna, the former capital of the Holy Roman Empire.

She stood at one window, I at another. I turned my head toward her and saw her face, pale and suffering. I knew it was not only because we had to part but also for that clear, icy-cold emptiness outside. Out of a sudden intuition, without even thinking about how cruel it was, I said, "I know how you feel about what happened out there last night." She swung her head round and looked coldly at me. "You feel," I said, "precisely the way you did on the day of your marriage." She covered her face with both her hands. "I can't help feeling the same," I said. "We are at a wedding day of sad promise."

I could have gone back to Rumania or somewhere else. But I felt that, at last, I should do something properly. I had wasted so much time, never finishing—if you could say I had ever seriously begun—my studies. Also, there was promise in the air, even if the appearance in Vienna of the great Führer of the now Greater Germany had turned out to be sort of a flop. His voice blared through the loudspeakers, over the heads of some million ecstatic listeners who were crammed together in a compact mass that covered the Heldenplatz. But the voice was choked by emotion (or by the rhythmic uproar of some million voices' *"Sieg Heil! Sieg Heil! Sieg Heil!"*) and could only stutter, "I—I—I—I—I am just so happy!" In spite of all that, as I say, there seemed to be born a new reality, clearer, more transparent, more energetic, more dynamic. It felt as if the fresh mountain air of Styria were blowing through Vienna. Then several divisions of the German Army came down the Danube, in marching blocks that were even more solid, more resolute, more dangerous, in their silence and gray metallic hats, than the ones on the night of *Anschluss*. After that, German civilians swarmed in and took everything into their administering hands. They filled that mountain air with their snotty Berlin slang and, to our utmost surprise, cynically mocked the great Führer and the Nazi Party, so that the Austrians had to take over the task of enthusiastic confirmation that everything was wonderful, really great, marvelous—particularly my aunts, who had now interrupted their *Anschluss* with the world beyond and entirely devoted themselves to the Nazi Women's Union. Mr. Malik, I learned, not only had become the leader of his department at the Styria Motor Company (which very soon united with a German company and disappeared) but also was a *Sturmbannführer* of the SS—a very mighty position, so I had better make friends with him and stop saying that his real name was Schweingruber. Old Marie, for whose senile eyes the victorious symbol "SS" read "44," insisted that he would be made a colonel of the 44th Regiment of the Imperial Infantry, which, as a young girl, she had very much admired. My grandmother shut herself in her rooms and received nobody. Coming back from Mass, she had been laughed at and shouted at in the open street, and nearly manhandled, by a handful of young rowdies who were forcing a group of Jews to wash slogans for the Schuschnigg regime off the wall of a house. Among those Jews, my grandmother recognized a physician who had once cured one of my aunts of a painful otitis media, and she interfered, attacking the young rowdies with her umbrella and shouting that this was going too far. Only the interference of Sturmbannführer Guru Malik saved her from serious trouble.

As for Minka, she was in despair. Of course, I had seen her immediately after the first big events. We were together a few days later when *Anschluss* was officially declared, in an impressive ceremony that we followed on the radio. And there was a rather embarrassing moment when, for the first time, we heard the "Deutschland, Deutschland über Alles" and she burst into tears. "Listen, old girl," I said to her, "it's not all that bad. It's just the first letting out of an old hatred that will soon calm down. Don't be afraid. It appears they really want to build discipline and order."

She turned to me and shouted, "Don't you realize, you imbecile, that it's the 'Gott Erhalte,' our old Imperial Austrian anthem, composed by our Haydn, that they've embezzled for their dirty anthem of Greater Germany? Why, it's a breach of . . . troth!"

Troth. She must have used it quite unconsciously, without a second thought as to the word's immeasurable profundity. This made me rather pensive for a couple of days. She was right: an incredible breach of troth was taking place all around us, but which troth was actually being broken? One already sensed that the faith, the pure enthusiasm with which this transformation had been yearned for and then greeted, was being betrayed. Troth itself was betrayed, I thought. For instance, the troth to the old empire. This Reich had no more to do with my dream of the Holy Roman Empire than with the glorious dream of the Habsburg Dual Monarchy. But I was soon tired of brooding about it. After all, I was a Rumanian, and even if I had been an Austrian, how could I have prevented what all the other Austrians obviously welcomed? I felt frightfully sorry for Minka and all our friends, but it was not my fault that they happened to be Jews, and in the event that they got into serious trouble I could use my connections with the SS to help them out again.

These connections were by no means limited to Sturmbannführer Malik. I had run into my old schoolmate Oskar Koloman again, and this time he looked prim and tidy, in a splendid black uniform, with the insignia of an even higher rank than that of *Sturmbannführer*. "*Heil*, Arnulf," he greeted me. "How is it you're in civilian clothes? Don't you want to join us?"

"I am Rumanian, you know."

"That means nothing. You were born an Austrian. Sooner or later, all German-speaking people will come home to the Reich. I can easily arrange for you to change your nationality."

"I'll think it over," I said. "Thank you anyhow."

"You were a fairly good skater, and not bad at horseback riding, as I recall. We need sporting types, you know. We have some excellent horses at the Mounted SS. Come and ride them, if you want. What are you doing otherwise?"

"Well, I'm trying to get on with architecture. But it bores me stiff."

"You see! Studying bored me, too. That's why I amused

234

myself blowing up a telephone booth. It cost me three years, all right, but look what I've become now. Not bad, hey? You can have the same if you want. But tell me"—he looked at me mistrustfully—"don't you have contact with Jews? I remember that dark girl you were with when we met again for the first time."

"Oh, she's a Turk," I said, and laughed.

"A Turk. I understand." He laughed, too. "However, a Jewess is no Jew, and a Turkish girl even less. I do understand, you old swine. Now, don't be a fool, and come riding one of these days?"

I did. They had excellent horses. I rode one that had belonged to the Rothschilds, and was very good indeed. The cavalrymen were fantastic yokels. They clicked their heels and threw up their arms and shouted *"Heil Hitler!"* every time they saw me. Sometimes I had the impression they did not take it seriously themselves, because they tried so hard to *do* it seriously. On the whole, they seemed quite harmless, happy with their uniforms and their obsolete importance. Oskar, in order to avoid silly questions about my riding there without being a member of the SS (also, perhaps, in order to give himself an air of clandestine importance), had told them that I was a Rumanian engaged in some special intelligence work, and I did nothing to destroy this legend, so I was treated as if I were the bearer of top secrets that would soon enable Adolf Hitler to unite the Carpathians with the Styrian Alps. I knew I could certainly count on Oskar, because, in a drunken moment, he had confessed to me that his group of Austrian Nazis had been deceived by the men of the Reich. He and his friends had not at all wanted *Anschluss* but a separate Nazi Austria under their own leader, Dr. Rintelen. The next day, he came to me and implored me never to mention what he had told me. I grasped his arm and said, "Well, Oskar, after all, we have always been friends. Let's not fuss about how reliable we are," whereupon he grasped my arm and said, "Arnulf, I always knew you were a fine fellow, though you sometimes"—and here he laughed heartily—"have a trifle too much to do with the Turks. However, I would very much like to meet that Turkish girl of yours. She has something that appeals to my particular taste. If you don't mind."

Of course, Minka knew about all this, and laughed when I told her that she had only to smile at Oskar and he'd immediately make her an honorary Aryan. "Aryans," she said. "I can't stand the sight of them any longer. The sooner I get my affidavit the better. I want to get out of here. It breaks my heart, but I simply have to." She was waiting for her affidavit for England, as most of our friends were. It was not easy to get an affidavit. The English would take only people who wanted to be employed as servants, so very soon some clever man opened a butlers' school on the Prater-strasse, where Jewish bankers and intellectuals were taught how to wait on the British. I once went there with Minka, and we laughed our heads off. Old stockbrokers were waddling around with aprons about their hips, balancing trays and opening bottles of champagne. My talent for imitating Jews made me invent a sketch in which a Scottish laird, reading in the newspapers about the sad destiny of the Viennese Jews, decides to dismiss all his wonderful High-land servants and replace them with Dr. Pisko-Bettelheim, Jacques Pallinker, Yehudo Nagoschiner, and such. Minka's house had become a sort of center for the few Jews left in Vienna and some Aryans unfaithful to their new flag, like myself. My sketch was a great success.

During that summer and autumn of 1938, most of the Jews I knew went away. Some of them were arrested and locked up for a while, and came home with some rather gruesome stories about what was going on in the prisons of the Rossauerlände. Some disappeared, and we did not know whether they had been put in jail or had just fled at the last moment. All this was pretty awful, I had to admit. But one knew, after all, how people were—some being horrid, others really very nice—and those who got arrested were not always entirely innocent. A Jewish lawyer, telling about his cruel treatment at the hands of the SS, said proudly, "But I was not arrested for just being a Jew. I am a criminal." However, I was becoming bored with the Nazi attitude of promise, hope, and expectation, as nothing really happened, and the whole thing was nothing but a great mess with some sordid highlights. Vienna had become a dreary place. Even Oskar complained; he didn't enjoy the *Heurigen* anymore, God knows why. Then he said, "Do you remember our school library? Well, there was a book called *The City Without Jews*. Actually, I never read it. Have you? Anyway, I sometimes have the feeling that Vienna is just that. There's nobody left to hate."

There was a young boy of great musical talent around Minka in those days—not Herbert von Karajan but a little Jew by the name of Walter, whom I had come to like very much. He was intelligent, and funny, and extremely well read. Minka protected him, as, in happier times, she had protected me, and he showed me a touching affection and confidence that I could not resist. Since he had relatives in America, he got an affidavit rather quickly, and we decided to give him a farewell party. We chose an out-of-the-way place—a small winegrower's cottage behind the Kobenzl—with the poetic name, in the Viennese dialect, of Häusl am Roan (Cottage at the Edge of the Vineyard). We were a party of sixteen, and there were some pretty girls. Someone still had a car, and it took two trips to get us all out there, and we were gay as in the old days. Walter played the nice old Viennese *Heurigenlieder* on the piano. I performed the butler Yehudo Nagoschiner, serving the wine and the fried chicken. Below us, beyond the hills that smelled of mown hay, lay the sparkling lights of Vienna. Suddenly this idyllic happiness was interrupted by a voice that roared, "I've finally caught you in the very act, you scoundrel!" I felt the marrow of my bones freeze. In the door stood Oskar, with a group of sturdy men in civilian clothes behind him. My poor Jewish friends stood or sat motionless as he came toward me, followed by his silent men. Then he threw his arms up and said, "But don't let me interrupt your good time. I'm a schoolmate of Arnulf's, and I wanted to show a few friends from the Reich what a true Viennese *Heurigen* looks like."

It was true. He had not come to arrest me, or anything of the kind. When I asked him how he knew where I was, he said with a smile, "Old boy, there are very few things we don't know."

"Come on, don't give me that. Who told you, really?"

"Your grandmother."

"My *grandmother*?"

"Well, that old witch with the trembling voice who answers the telephone at your house."

Old Marie, then. I was a fool. For months I had told her where I could be reached when I went out, hoping that a call might come through from Bucharest to tell me that things had changed again and that my beloved was getting a divorce. I was more than a fool; I was blind to what was going on around me. I felt this very strongly when Oskar poked his elbow into my side and said, in a loud voice, with a glance toward his companions, "Now, how about introducing me to your beautiful *Turkish* girl friend?"

"She is my wife," I said. "We are celebrating our wedding."

The Germans were very pleased to hear this, and clicked their heels and congratulated us, shaking our hands so hard they almost pulled our arms out of their sockets. One of them sat down next to Minka in order to tell her about a cousin who lived in Istanbul. Oskar clapped my shoulder and said with a wink, "Don't look so frightened. Tell that little Jew there at the piano to play some *Heurigenlieder*."

The Germans soon got very drunk. The one with the cousin in Istanbul flirted with Minka, in competition with Oskar. The others danced with the pretty girls, and finally one of them performed a most courageous jump over a small stone wall in the garden, misjudged the distance to the ground, fell, and broke his leg. The Germans made a stretcher for him, so they could carry him to the nearest hospital, and then, in a great hurry, they shook our hands, clicked their heels, threw their arms up, shouting *"Heil Hitler!"* and "Long live Kemal Pasha Atatürk!" and disappeared as spookily as they had come, with Oskar waving and calling good-bye.

"You bastard," Minka said to me. She went out into the vineyard and sat down on a stone. I followed her.

"I'm sorry, Minka. I know I am a mindless ass."

"Never mind. After all, it was funny. Did you see darling little Walter playing the piano as if the devils were standing over him?" She laughed her enchanting laugh. "But still . . ." She sank back with a deep sigh.

It was dawn. Out of a mist in the valley Vienna rose, the peaks of its towers first, then the Riesenrad, the Ferris wheel, in the Prater, the monuments, the roofs, the streets. I sat beside Minka, looking down at all this. Suddenly I heard a strange sound coming out of Minka's throat, and thought she was going to cry, but she was laughing instead. "Do you know what happened to Friedel Süssmann?" she asked. "I told you that in order to get her affidavit she got married at the British Consulate to an English sailor she had never seen before? Well, when she got to England, she was met by some gentlemen in black. They had come to break the news to her that her husband had fallen from the mast and broken his neck. She now has a widow's pension—one pound a month."

"Listen, Minka," I said. "After all, I am a Rumanian. My hands are not tied. I need not tell you what it would mean to my parents, and you know that I love somebody else, but if it would help you—I mean, just in order to get you a passport that would enable you to get out of here, and, of course, with an immediate divorce afterward—if you want to, we could bloody well go and get married. You won't get a pension, though, if I break my neck."

She drew herself up slowly till she was looking into my face. Then she took it in both her hands, as she had done when I first came to her flat, and kissed me. "You know, my darling Brommy," she said, "that you are the dearest person on earth to me. I could never have felt closer to a brother, if I'd had one. You are a bastard, it's true, but I am more fond of you than of anybody else. Just kiss me, once—and kiss me tenderly." Her mouth was as beautiful as ever, and I could even feel more than the tenderness I would have felt for a sister. In that moment, it appeared to me that if she had not been a Jew, I could have loved her even in the same way, or perhaps more than, I loved the one I had lost. Still, I felt a twinge of bad conscience, as if I were being a traitor to my flag.

"All right," she said. "That's that. And now don't be afraid that I'll say yes to your kind offer. I couldn't possibly marry you. Apart from the fact that it would hurt your parents and that you love somebody else—we could certainly get an immediate divorce, but that is not the point—I would not want to marry you, if you understand what I mean. Because of certain goyish qualities of your soul. But still, you are the dearest to me. Come, let's see how the party is getting on."

A few days later, she got her affidavit, and within a fortnight she had sold her things, even Professor Raubitschek's carved-wood bookcases, and gone to London.

There I saw her once more, in the year 1947. God knows how she had found out where I was living—near Hamburg at that time. Anyway, I got a letter from her saying that she was all right, and married to a man—not a Jew, by the way—who had left Austria in 1938 and who was as sweet and decent as could be, a professor of philology and a great admirer of Karl Kraus. They were about to emigrate to America, and she would very much like to see me once more. She enclosed in the letter a ticket to London and all the papers necessary to get me, as a former Rumanian, a visa for Great Britain. I accepted all this more than gratefully. I was as penniless, as starved, as miserable as any displaced person could be in the rubble of Germany in early 1947. As she had known how—and where—to trace me, she must also have known that my father had fired his last shot into his temple when the Russians took the Bukovina in 1940, and that, two years later, my grandmother had died in Vienna. I had not had a chance to build up a life or settle in a place for all those years.

There was only one difficulty: I had no valid passport. But Minka had even thought of that. A friend who was with the British Military Government arranged to get me a travel document. It defined me as an "individual of doubtful nationality" but brought me to England, all right. Her husband fetched me at Victoria Station, took a closer look at me, and said, "Let us go to have lunch first. She doesn't know that you are arriving today. I have not told her, in order not to excite her too much."

"Why?" I asked. "Is there anything wrong with her?"

"That trouble with her hip seems to have affected her spine. She is in great pain, and you will have to be very patient with her."

They lived in a nice house in Cadogan Square. Minka's husband showed me in, fixed me a drink, and then called up the stairwell, "Oh, Minka, would you mind coming down? There is a friend of yours." She came down the stairs, a middle-aged woman with gray hair, bent and torn by the atrocious pains of cancer of the bone. "Who is it?" she asked sharply. Then she saw me. "Brommy!" she said, and covered her face with her hands, her poor, tortured body shaken by her sobbing.

On the evening before their departure for America, all of our old friends who had managed to emigrate to Britain came to their house to bid them good-bye. Even though they had been told I would be there, they marveled at seeing me, as if I were a creature from another star. They could not stop asking about Vienna during the war, and how it had looked when I last saw it. They remembered things I had long since forgotten. Had Oskar survived? Oh, he had been hanged in Poland? Poor chap. And Guru Malik, the spiritualist I had told so many funny stories about? No! Had he really been

241

dematerialized by a bomb? Great success, that one. Every one of the guests had brought me a gift, things I badly needed at that time—mostly secondhand clothes. And when, at the end of the evening, I had kissed Minka good-bye—forever, as we both knew—and had shaken hands with everybody, I went back to my hotel carrying two large suitcases full of old clothes that I hoped to sell in Hamburg like a *handalé*, to make enough money to follow Minka to America.

She died there a few months later.

Pravda

"As if he were lost among the lotus eaters, he seemed to have forgotten his fatherland. . . ." What was this? Where did it come from? It had the rhapsodic intonation of memory, but he was not sure whether it was *his* memory, although grammatically it sounded as if it were: even his memories could no longer be narrated simply in the murmuring imperfect tense, they required the resolutely indicated "as if," the subjunctive, the mood of possibility, in any case the shift into the indefinite; even if occurrences had occurred from occurrences, the chain of motifs reached so deep into the past, reached back to the beginning of recorded time, the dawn of history, the golden haze of myth where everything was open, any possibility. Only one thing was certain: time was passing, had passed even if occurrences had not assumed a visible shape, time had slipped, kept slipping through the grip of memory, a great, great deal of time—and he had lived from the fullness of days as if they were inexhaustible, he especially: for it was not just one life which, these days, formed and would go on forming (not for much longer, he told himself, perhaps for ten more years, at best fifteen), but a half dozen different lives, lived in different eras, in different countries, in different languages, among totally different people; his name had had a different ring, had been pronounced in different ways, his costume had changed with his tailors and barbers, with the fashion of his environment, people he had met frequently twenty years ago could not for the life of them recall having made his acquaintance, he certainly looked different at sixty from what he had looked like at forty, at twenty, a man with totally different characteristics: in the south, his gestures were livelier than they had been in the north, there he had smoked a pipe, here cigarillos, there he had drunk whiskey, here wine, there a woman's shiny black hair had electrified him, here it was the fragrant mane of a blonde. . . .

to be sure, through all this, he had unshakably said "I" to himself, he had never felt any doubt as to his identity. He raised his eyebrows ironically whenever he heard or read the phrase that someone was "seeking his identity" like some lost or never possessed object that was rightfully his; it gave him a sardonic pleasure, when someone expressed perplexity or unfulfillment or disconnectedness, to ask that person in the broadest American accent, "You're lookin' for your lost iden'ity, aren'tcha?"—even though he himself could scarcely have indicated what constituted his own identity—:

what did this properly dressed, gray-haired man, walking along a deserted Via Veneto on a drizzly winter morning, with a large box of *marrons glacés* under his arm, on his way to pay his respects to a Russian great-aunt of his (present, third, Italian) wife—a regular visit he had been paying once a week for years now—what did he have to do with the boy who, fifty years ago (half a century—and what a century!), had lain in the grass on a hilltop somewhere in the forest Carpathians, dreaming up a life in Jack London style: a prosperous farmer in East Africa, the bougainvillea around the farmhouse reaching into luxuriant plantations, the plantations into the Masai Plain, ostriches and vast zebra herds, thousands of antelope, sometimes the blacks running up to get the bwana with the unerring elephant rifle because a lion has broken into the ox kraal . . . such dreams were not at all extravagant or impossible back then; the reality they evoked truly existed, as late as yesterday even; today they are anachronistic, purely romantic, even as a mere boy you make a fool of yourself with such daydreams, you place yourself in the category of those who live in the golden haze of myth. . . .

well, he had learned to adjust to such changes in the world: as a child in the Bukovina, within walking distance of the Dniester River, beyond which Russia began, he had been awakened in the night—the Austrians had marched out, the Rumanians had not yet marched in, people were afraid the Bolsheviks might attack or at least maraud, hordes were already passing through the countryside and plundering the military depots. He had retained the images of that time all his life; above all, trembling hands—the trembling hands of the nanny waking him up and dressing him, the trembling hands of his mother putting the jewelry in boxes to hide it, the trembling hands of the servants to whom his father—an eternal Don Quixote—distributed pistols. . . .

had he fallen into a deep slumber back then like Rip Van Winkle and awakened only in the world of today, he would go crazy with despair: what has happened to this world between then, 1919, and today 1979, is so incredible, has changed it so radically that one can scarcely believe the same person lived in both epochs. Whatever his parents, the people of that world of yesterday, were afraid of—today's reality is much, much worse than anything anyone could have imagined then. The red, the blood-red reality of the Bolsheviks was bursting with life compared to the gray anemic reality of the crumbling democracies. Yet, blood still flows today as it did then; blood has always flowed, in torrents, all through his lifetime; that it was not his own blood was due to random circumstances that one cannot even call fortuitous: the only dignity to be maintained in our time is the dignity of being among the victims.

Experiencing such highly varied conditions, he said to himself, one inevitably goes through many metamorphoses. What, for instance, would seem to indicate that he, the distinguished, gray-haired, well-shaven man in a dark blue overcoat, walking down the Via Veneto in drizzly winter weather, is the same person as the newcomer here twenty years ago: the mustachioed, happy-go-lucky, Capri-shirt-sporting lothario who, with a hunter's skill and sharp eye, manages to grab a seat at the small, crowded tables outside one of the now vanished cafés, and sits round-eyed at his *granita* seeing the protagonists of a breathtaking *Dolce Vita* in every gigolo and movie floozy strolling by: he himself, for all his apparent sophistication, an utter simpleton, for whom Rome is a daily festival, as for an enthusiastic tourist—the sight of the Castel Sant'Angelo in floodlight a revelation, the Pantheon in the mist of crepuscule, the Campidoglio at sunrise impressions as deep as the glory of a Christmas tree in childhood, at night, by starlight, he takes visiting friends to the Piazza dei cavalieri di Malta like children to a crèche, has them peep through a keyhole in a garden gate to see the dome of Saint Peter's in the vanishing point of an avenue of cypresses, shows them the cloister of the Quattro Coronati as if it were the spot of his own martyrdom, talks about it as eloquently as Gregorovius. . . .

it doesn't take more than two decades for this to change completely, the man and the city. Eternal Rome is eternal only in its constant change, perhaps what allows him to feel unalterably himself is also his perpetual changing. "I" is a notion that requires the immediate present. Yesterday's "I" is mythical, a mere possibility of today's "I." Where has this "I" of twenty years ago gone now? Well, where has the glamor of Cinecittà gone that brought him here? The grandeur of swinging Italy back then? Prince Massimo marrying the film starlet Dawn Adams: an epochal connection. Fleeting the epoch, like the many others he has lived through: the echo of the Habsburg Empire in the Balkan operetta world, the entrance and dying fall of the roaring twenties in Berlin; the elegant thirties in Vienna, in Prague; the entrance of America into the core of Europe: Barbara Hutton marrying Count Haugwitz-Reventlow, the king of

England marrying Mrs. Simpson, a sporting and shooting club at Mittersill Castle in Austria attracting the most frivolous specimens from a newly formed café society on both continents; and at the same time: Adolf Hitler expanding his Berghof at nearby Berchtesgaden, Reichspropagandaminister Dr. Joseph Goebbels compromising the actress Lydia Barowa—the scandal shocks public opinion more than the shooting of Röhm . . . altogether, everything, the events, concentrating more and more on Germany, on Berlin; it whirls together there, the suction pulls him in too: soon an epoch of ration cards and air-raid shelters begins, cities crumble, what is left of Berlin's high society attend dinner parties with stiff upper lips and toothbrushes in their pockets in case they might not find their houses standing when they come home; and even this passes, gives way to a short and violent epoch of women-raping Russians, the division of Germany and Austria into zones, icy rubble-cities, a black-market time, hunger time in Germany while Italy begins to swing, Existentialism triumphs in France, Juliette Greco sings before Jean-Paul Sartre in Saint Germain-des-Prés, Italian *musica leggera* erupts, Dior's New Look conquers Brindisi, the khaki uniforms of Americans are visibly withdrawn from circulation and, instead, the city-scape of Rome is dominated by a gaudier sort

—and where have *they* gone, the swarms of crinkly-mouthed climacterials with black, butterfly-wing-framed glasses like carnival masks, cobweb-fine matron's coifs for their laundry-blue-rinsed hair and ants in their pants? Where have their Mennen-drenched, corpse-washed escorts and consorts gone with their raspberry-colored slacks, violently checkered clown jackets, snow-white moccasins on huge feet, and toilet-bowl-white porcelain teeth in their kissers, the Supermen of America's short-lived supremacy? . . .

to be sure, one must bear in mind that anyone born then, twenty years ago, is now twenty years old: for anyone at the outset of his life, a decade is enough to change a world, and certainly more so two decades, or even four; but seen from the end of a life, the decades went by like last week—and yet the *fusti* of Trastevere, so much liked by the American climacterials, with attractively swollen thorax muscles under skintight T-shirts, are now dyspeptic postal workers and fat espresso-bar managers; Anita Ekberg and Gina Lollobrigida hint at their not sharing the secret of Dorian Gray, in their cases the news has leaked out; meanwhile, the babies born in Lollo's and Anita's heyday and now twenty years old are crippling one another with monkey wrenches and bicycle chains, mowing down dutiful government servants and unpopular judges in broad daylight with sheaves of machine-gun fire; yet the epoch is not lively and dynamic, but oddly stagnant, not colorful, gaudy, but utterly gray like the winter weather—the closer the Molotov cocktails and homemade bombs explode (philanthropic publishers offer how-to instructions at a low cost in paperback editions), the more blood flows across the sidewalk into the gutters, the more hectically the *pantere* of the Carabinieri race around corners with howling sirens and flashing blue lights, then the more life becomes provincial, a drab Biedermeier: the cities are quiet, dead quiet, anyone with an eight- or nine-digit bank account (lire are such a flimsy currency) fears to venture out after the stores close for the night, bodyguards with machine guns, safety catches released, stand in front of building entrances, the children are in Switzerland (and most bank accounts too, of course), the evening's entertainment on television is both suspenseful and paralyzing: it shows you highly exciting events of no consequence whatever, a most romantic standstill, a still-life of chaos, so to say, of scandals, of corruption and continuous crises—government crises, oil crises, supply crises; the national passions for soccer and bicycle racing are gradually replaced by a national passion for strikes; the more visible the mechanisms of behind-the-scenes wire-pullers become, thanks to the indefatigable educational efforts of (bribable) journalism, then the more

248

anonymously these selfsame wire-pullers withdraw into obscurity. . . .

meanwhile, clouds of poison gas escape accidentally and turn children's faces into cactus blossoms, the coasts rot under the beached dead fish, the climate of southern Italy becomes like Scotland's but scientists assure us that this has nothing to do with the increasing density of jet planes in the stratosphere . . . it may be understandable that the twenty-year-olds today are restless, more restless than even we were at their age, the pressure bothers them more than it bothers us, our generation has gone through so much it can put up with this, too—above all, we have learned to put up with things, to make the best, even of the worst; but the young people, born back then when he first had come to Rome—in a word, his son's contemporaries, if the son had survived, the poor little thing . . .

he instantly pushes the thought aside: he stops thinking of his son, forbids himself to think of him—what was I thinking about? Yes, the young people of today: why are they so restless? We were restless because of our dreams—dreams of the future. Do they have a future? What do they dream about? socialism come true at last? heroism in the adventure of the Revolution? or simply world fame as a rock singer? as a hero of Formula-I racing? . . . Certainly not about love, as we did when we were their age; they've got it too easy in this respect, they're already copulating at the onset of puberty, in short pants and pinafores, so to speak; at twenty, they have acquired the sexual experiences of an active man in his mid-forties; enviable but of course detrimental to eroticism; the feelings are sure to deaden with such an unresisting, such an insensitive, such a semi-involved possibility of sexual activity—or at least so our envy encourages us to presume. As for great love, the very notion of which in our time made all the feelings in the forehead and the pit of the stomach and the Venus mound contract in poignantly sweet ardor—the unique great *love* with which life is fulfilled and bliss on earth attained, the *one great love* that is the attained goal of troth, loyalty, allegiance to the banner that waves over a life—they, the young ones today, most likely never dream of that. So they say, in magazines, anyway; and polls, surveys, and statistical analyses confirm it. . . .

Be that as it may: they must dream about something, they too, these young people, even if only about finding their identity. For what made him, the man with gray hair and the box of *marrons glacés* under his arm, walking along the Via Veneto to visit a Russian great-aunt of his (present, third, Italian) wife—what made him identical with the forty-year-old of twenty years ago, here, outside one of the now vanished cafés, Rome-hungry and future-minded, freshly divorced from his (second, Jewish) wife, and expecting his little boy to be awarded to him; what made him one and the same person as the adolescent on the hilltop in the Carpathians half a century ago and, even further back, the child who awakened at night (because they feared the Bolsheviks were coming), or the air-raid-shelter sitter under the hail of bombs in Berlin, and the freebooter in the intellectuals' interregnum during the Ice Age of the German rubble-cities, and the writer of screenplays for Cinecittà during the fifties—what made him one with all these characters and various other forms of his diverse metamorphoses? Yes, there was an answer. The thing that made them all one and the same person was: dreaming. When he thought *I*, he felt as if he were dreaming himself up: *Somnio, ergo sum*—I dream myself up, therefore I am.

Notwithstanding that his dreams had been different with every change and had sometimes taken on the character of nightmares. Dreaming per se had remained the same, whether a boy's conjuring up a vision of himself as a white hunter or a world-famous artist or champion amateur jockey, or the eternal dream of a man whose love is fulfilled, or other banal wishful thoughts that scarcely suggested originality. Indeed, what had allowed him unswervingly to feel himself as *I* through all the real and dreamed-up transformations was not *what* he dreamed, but *how* he dreamed—an outwitting of self developed to a fine art, with the help of which he eluded any out-and-out collision with reality.

The first time he had seen a bullfight (not in Spain, which events of world history had prevented him from visiting until quite late, but in Mexico, where he lived during a transitory stage as a car salesman), wearing a tremendous sombrero and sitting with a breathtakingly beautiful gum-chewing American girl friend in the shady parabolic section of the arena, he watched as the matador made the black dart of the bull aim at the red cloth of the *capa* over and over again, and the matador over and over again steered the bull past by a hairbreadth. The first time he watched this, he realized with amusement that he himself employed the same tactic with himself, and that he had developed equivalent mastery. Elude an out-and-out collision with reality. . . . No, sir, this was not cowardice about life, not escapism—rather the contrary: he, too, could look reality in the face, better than most other people, for he knew how dangerous reality was. But the artful feat of always holding up a new possibility of himself, a fiction of himself, and the knack, the balletic skill, of eluding reality, withdrawing the fiction at the last instant before colliding with reality—those were talents no one could emulate.

Indispensable talents, if you wanted to survive. For otherwise, how could you stand the look of your face of yesterday? For instance the reddened face of the teenager in the Carpathians, eyes burning, lips trembling in the greed to kill something, a dove, a hare, a roe deer . . . or the face of the young man in love, not dry behind the ears but scandalizing the *beau monde* of prewar Bucharest with his sentimental performances, who, while the world around him is about to crumble, Europe preparing to commit suicide, welcomes the Nazi invasion in Poland just because he loathes Poles, since the lady whom he happens to love (one of the several unique *great loves* of his life, each of which promised fulfillment, bliss on earth attained, the very goal of troth and loyalty)—well, she has had a Polish lover before him and sometimes seems to mind that he has left her . . . or the face of the hideous fop who, under the hail of bombs on Berlin in 1943, leads an idler's life, cynically watching a world in flames, millions of people dying, being crippled, suffering unutterable grief, but he, in the midst of a panicking crowd that rushes toward an air-raid shelter even before the sirens have howled their warning, pulls a watch from his pocket, looks at it, then up at the sky, and with an ugly sneer says in a loud voice, "They're late today. Do let's hope nothing has happened to them on the way!" . . . or the face of the man who sleeps, sleeps for days in a Munich room whose door leads into a corridor that leads, in turn, into space—half the house is missing, piled up in a heap of brick and mortar, broken window frames and splinters of glass and slate where once a charming street in Schwabing gave out on to the Englische Garten, now a narrow path across the rubble, glittering in the frost winter of 1947, and he doesn't care whether there is coal for the stove in the corner of the small room where his (first) wife, a refugee from East Prussia, sits in a mangy lambskin coat staring hatefully at him, despising him for his refusal to find a job or do the least work to make their improvised habitation habitable or try to get into some petty black-market racket in order to procure a bagful of potatoes or half a pound of rancid butter . . . or the ridiculous, mustachioed face of the would-be lothario who, after all this and two divorces and a pitiless fight with his second wife over their little son (a fight that ended with the poor boy's death) sits outside a café on the Via Veneto eagerly trying to adjust himself to the glory of Cinecittà. . . .

Well, go on with your biography. Jump a decade forward, or backward if you please. Examine at random this or that possibility of yourself: you always come across someone you would be embarrassed (or even outright ashamed) to identify with, someone you'd refuse to frequent if you weren't forced to live with, because he happens to be yourself. . . .

yes, but there's always another dimension, another possibility. . . .

this "yes, but" which allows you to admit that all these dubious characters were you—or, in any case, possibilities of yourself—that all these faces (including the face in your shaving mirror) were undeniably yours, what else is this "yes, but" but a bullfighter's slight, elegant, perfidious twist of the *capa* that makes the bull's horns miss him by a hairbreadth? . . . "yes, but" the boy in the Carpathians was brought up in a peculiar, anachronistic world, a feudal world, a strictly traditional education that used the lust for killing—shall we call it, less emotionally, the pleasure of hunting—as a way of strengthening the heart for equally exciting and far nobler feelings, all rooted in the rules of chivalry, such as one's duty to defend the oppressed, the feeble, and the poor, the readiness to die for the sake of troth and flag or for one's lady—infantile notions, you'd call them, yes, but notions on which our civilization is based . . . and as for the creature who, out of sick jealousy, welcomes the assassination of a small and very noble people by the power-drunk followers of a lunatic: well, "yes, but" consider the utter violence of the love that led to such sick jealousy, a love in which all that pent-up romanticism broke loose; at last, after a childhood, an adolescence, of craving to be a good knight, at last he could realize an unconditional commitment to a flag, a cause—his lady . . . mind you, fanaticism was in the air at the time; supposing instead of falling so violently in love, he had committed himself to the SS? (though, strangely enough, their view on Poland didn't differ much from his) . . . "yes, but" take the same face a few years later, in Berlin in 1943: that look of cynicism is but the fruit of suffering, he is sick with hatred, hatred not only for the Nazis but for everyone and everything, for the Germans as a whole and in particular the remnants of their old high society, now apathetically attending their *Götter-dämmerung*; equally, however, he hates the British for their hypocrisy and shortsightedness, the French for their *rêverie* of lost glory, the Italians for their greed and vanity, and most of all the Americans for their devious self-righteousness—did all these imbeciles not see that their glorious war was not for or against a man called Hitler, or a nation, or an ideology, or a political system, but against themselves? couldn't they admit that this was the class war they were bound to lose, that would destroy the very things they pretended to fight for: ideals, holy traditions, values handed down from generation to generation; couldn't they understand that every bomb that gutted a house—here, there, on this side or that side of a front line (a front line that in reality ran through the social structure of each of their countries)—that every one of those bombs simply opened the cellars and set the rats free, the profiteers, the greedy, the uncivilized, the illiterates, the oppressed and offended who wanted their share of the cake no matter how—perhaps through revolution that would, conceivably, bear fruit in the future . . .

"yes, but" is it worth the price of a destroyed civilization? I don't give a damn for the future! Fuck the future! I live for today and will not live long enough to see those liberated rats produce a civilization of what they think to be social justice . . .

and that's why the man in the half-ruined house in the icy Munich of winter 1947 does not give a fuck whether his wife (whom he has married the year before, whom he has promised to take in his arms and carry from the misery of postwar Germany into the dream world of Argentina or some such place of sparkling, starlit nights, of whispering palm trees, of mild air pulsating with cha-cha-cha and tango rhythms) slowly but steadily starves herself to death while her blue frozen fingers stuff a pipe with tobacco extracted from butts of cigarettes already made of cigarette butts, while he, her husband, just lies there on their bed, sleeping or pretending to sleep: isn't that a shameful, cowardly, self-pitying attitude from someone brought up to be a good knight? . . . "yes, but" even the very best knight has moments of despair, think of Perceval or Tristan the fool; you are likely to lose faith in yourself and in mankind when you see the survivors of the cataclysm trying to build up a new world by building into it all the same structures that have led to the decomposition of the old; he, at least, would have no part in it, he was not guilty of helping bourgeois capitalism to revive and find its most fertile soil in bomb-cratered Germany; his hands were clean: his son—had he survived, the poor little thing—could nowadays consider papa a pioneer, an evangelist of dropouts, long before the idea of criticising the consumer society was dreamed of . . .

anyhow, what counts is not the moments, the days, perhaps the weeks and months when you are downhearted or defeated and want to give in for good (those moments of cowardice that *did* count for his first, East Prussian wife, that so shattered her confidence in him that he could never, never regain it); what really counts is what you salvage from your defeats. . . .

What, indeed? the career of a screenwriter for the most mediocre directors on the tattiest productions of Cinecittà? . . . "yes, but" a writer who dreams himself a genius of motion pictures, someone who would use images as the greatest writers use words—for words are no longer adequate for today's reality, words are for awe, for beauty and veneration, for noble and refined feelings, for precise and differentiated thought, for minds sensitive like seismographs, for ears used to silence; today's barbarians can't cope with words, in their mouths words seem too big, they choke on them with too many pretensions; yet on the other hand they are too small, too narrow to hold the rapidly increasing, hybrid growth of their meaning: try to put the horror of a discothèque into words—a glimpse of a rock'n'roll-drunk teenager's face does it; try to describe a concentration camp—how many thousand words would you

255

need?—the photograph of a man hanging electrocuted in the barbed wire needs no comment; or try to explain the possibility of the various metamorphoses of a man's character, the changes of his beliefs, convictions, points of view the while he feels no loss of identity—well, take his pictures as a boy, a young man, a grownup, a man shortly before and shortly after his midlife crises and have a close look at them, you'll see it all there clear enough to give you goose bumps. . . .

in short, with all his yes, buts, he told himself, he did not lie to himself more than anyone else. Parallel to the way he was dreaming himself ran his feeling of guilt—and that was what made him feel *I* through all the changes. It was no personal guilt but a sort of collective guilt, a guilt shared by everyone belonging to so-called Western Civilization, a guilt that was immanent in the epoch, in this civilization's present, particular state and shape. To be conscious of it, as if it were a personal guilt, was his dark privilege. *I* could not possibly act in a way other than to become guilty by it—yet *I* was responsible for it. That was his heavy keel. With that it didn't matter what sails he set to what winds. The others believed in being strong characters, formed once and forever. Their identities (assuming they believed they had them) had, at best, grown over their faces like iron masks. He shed his own identity at will, studied it, put it away, put on another one, in which he studied himself again, as watchful as ever, always finding himself guilty in one way or other. His identities were forged not from the iron of a steadfast lifetime but from extremely light, virtually experimental and interchangeable materials, and they had not become second nature to him; although they were merely hypothetical, like molecular models scientists construct, he would find himself in each of them. Every one was undeniably *I* to him. In other words, with all his yes, buts, he knew he was lying to himself. But he also knew why he was lying to himself. And by knowing it, the better he knew it, he lied to himself no more.

Nor did he lie to others. He had indifferently left it up to his (present, third, Italian) wife to fathom why he regularly visited her almost ninety-four-year-old Russian great-aunt every Wednesday afternoon. It was not pure pleasure. For years now, she had been bedridden, surrounded by dusty, tattered, worn-out junk. She was shapelessly, inordinately fat, with a tiny turban on her bald head—the ephemeral crown on a pear-shaped face with enormous jowls, the eyes of a bloodhound puppy and the thin white mustache of an old Mandarin. And he did not care to picture what was wobbling under the ruff of her nightgown, what was running riot and to seed. Ninety-four-year-olds have a more indisputable commitment to their bodies than younger oldsters, whose decay often seems almost unethical; beyond the biblical age the body becomes sovereign—after all, we are then dealing with a corpse that has been virtually whisked away from death, with all the paraphernalia, the fermenting, flatulence, wetness, degeneracy; a corpse is an object of reverence even in its putrefaction . . . nevertheless, *her* corpse still very clearly put forward the demands of living matter: there was something mystical about the greed with which she grabbed the box of *marrons glacés,* tore open the wrapping, snatched out the kidney-shaped, sugar-frosted balls, stuffing one after another into the munching mouth under the Chinese mustache, claiming while she munched that she had never had much of a sweet tooth—something mystical, the feeding of a primordial toad. Then, she usually drowsed off. Less and less often did she tell him about St. Petersburg and Tiflis or Paris and London before the turn of the century. But this did occur now and again, and that was the reason he visited her: she too had lived half a dozen lives, some of them in grand brilliance—as a girl, at the court of the tsar; as the wife of a diplomat at posts in the capitals of the picture-book-happy world before the Great War; as an impoverished émigré in Paris of the twenties; as an ironical observer of Roman society before and after Mussolini. She presented him with the colorful plunder of her memories, with which he could then garnish his own memories more vividly, like someone adding an imaginative touch to his home with objects purchased at the flea market.

Thus the memory of his childhood, his adolescence in Rumania, his isolation in Berlin, his misery in the ice-rubble cities after 1945, gained new dimensions. His biography gained historical perspective. Each phase of his metamorphoses was enriched by anecdotes, descriptions, observations, ways of thinking, and turns of expression which this model White Russian bequeathed him. Thanks to her, his own life story became more complete, livelier, more credible, more true—the biography of a model White European, so to say: moth-eaten survivor of a bygone splendid world.

When, in depicting an Easter celebration in the Bukovina or a ball in Vienna of the thirties, he used some decorative detail that his (present, third, Italian) wife recognized as usurped, it did not matter when she broke in: "You got that from my Aunt Olga!" Why not? He had a rightful claim to such details, for they belonged truly to his world, a world he shared with Aunt Olga, a world that had sunk into oblivion anyway: Imperial Russia and the folkloric gaudiness of the shepherd of the Carpathians both had long since passed into the twilight of myth and fairy tale. So if he was describing an Easter festival in a village in the Carpathians a half century ago (which had created a much larger historical distance than several earlier full centuries), then it was proper if this description took in something of the gold of Resurrection Masses and the floweriness of the spring mood at Tsarskoye Selo; the Opernball in Vienna 1937 (the first and only one he had attended) resembled a rout in an English peer's house in 1911 that Aunt Olga had described to him. Details were metaphors anyhow—on the one hand ermine, diadems, braided uniforms, on the other embroidered blouses and lambskins, crocuses and primroses. After all, his aim was not to color in the preciousness of his personal background but rather to enhance the hallowed mood of an exotic religious act; here in a chapel, there in a ballroom. He borrowed a little pigment for his palette and, shoulder-shrugging, ignored anyone who regarded this as sheer embellishment or even flim-flam. Such a reaction struck him as not only seriously philistine but also quite simply stupid.

And that was it. That was one more thing—among several—that he could not forgive his former, second, Jewish wife. Already the previous, first, East Prussian wife had soon discerned his habit of incorporating other people's memories into his own when they were suitable and colorful enough; but she had held her tongue, just as she had held her tongue about everything, especially about her contempt for him: for she had loved him and been disappointed; and to avoid sharing the guilt of this disappointment, she had to keep his defects in mind. But the second, Jewish wife (whom he viewed as a mere intermezzo between the first, East Prussian, and the third, Italian wife: the marriage had not even lasted a year, had been entered into only because she was pregnant and refused to abort the chance product; two days before the delivery, they had finally gone to the justice of the peace, an utterly ridiculous, disgraceful act; then they had spent another four years fighting over the divorce and the unfortunate child)—his Jewish wife attacked him from the very start for his heedless outlook on biographical property, and she was so rabid about it that he was offended. At first, he could not understand the vehemence with which she championed authenticity, documentary truth for every autobiographical detail. ("Even at the expense of vividness?" he had once asked her ironically, and she had answered fanatically, "Yes! Yes! Yes!") This trait of hers clashed with her passion for art, her fanatical devotion to art, any kind of art: she would tiptoe up to a Pollock drip painting as worshipfully as to Michelangelo's *Pietà* in St. Peter's; she would listen to an atonal tone poem with her forehead lowered as devoutly as to a symphony of Beethoven's; she would follow a play of Beckett's with the same breathless suspense as a deadly performance of Schiller's *Wallenstein*; a poem of T. S. Eliot's would throw her into the same ecstasies as the Bolshoi's *Swan Lake;* and in between, she devoured any number of novels, Grass as greedily as Canetti, Bellow as ardently as Muriel Spark. "You get drunk on the stuff the way other people get drunk on beer," he would say, to bait her, and she promptly fell for it and gave him, the lowbrow, a lecture on the novel from *La Princesse de Clèves* to Robbe-Grillet; and he listened to the end in order to say, "You consume all this: it is your drogue. I invent myself in my own novels: that's *my* way of escaping an unbearable reality. And as for what you tell me about the necessity of identifying with the hero or, more recently, the antihero, I manage to do that effortlessly: I am my own protagonist from the very start."

He had loved her and been disappointed, and to avoid sharing the guilt of this disappointment, he had to keep her defects in mind: she was quite simply stupid. That was it. Beautiful and stupid. And a pseudointellectual in the bargain. He hated the Beckmesserish nitpicking, the fundamentalism, the blind obedience to rules in her "intellectual interests." Needless to say, one of these interests was depth psychology; she had mastered its rules the way a convent schoolgirl learns catechism. Only her belief was more ardent, and never for a moment did she hesitate to form an everlasting judgment by means of the Freudian grid. He would not even listen to what she had to say about his loose relationship to "Truth": "Leave me in peace. I'm my own best lunatic-keeper. And you can't expect too much of me: a child of sleepwalkers—growing up in a dreamed world, sometimes nightmarish—I was predestined to lose every kind of reality by all the things that happened around me before and certainly during my lifetime; realities like the Viennese Opernball and Treblinka are incompatible with what *you* mean by 'Truth'—they can only happen in a surrealistic dimension; you of all people ought to see that, as a Jew—but you are the most goyish Jew I know. Still, I'm not going to let you talk me into a psychosis like yours by abandoning my need for delusions and hallucinations about myself, even though that need is certainly libidinous in origin—I was a master masturbator before I met you to do the job—and marked by trauma, like meeting with idiots who believe in reality."

His bile was in proportion to his disappointment, for he had loved her very much; there had been moments when he had knelt before her, for instance, when she told him about how she had been forced to hide during the war; this had not been possible in her small Thuringian home town, everyone knew her there, knew her background, her parents were already running around with the yellow star; and she would not have succeeded in going underground in one of the bigger cities, even if she had managed to cope with the problems of police registration and the necessary food-rationing card: she was too striking, too beautiful—people turned around to look at her in the street: she was splendidly tall and voluptuous, dazzling in the freedom of her laughter, in the radiance of her gray eyes, in the lush fall of her rust-red curls . . . wheedling a doctor to certify her as tubercular, she withdrew to a tiny sanatorium high up in the Allgäu mountains, the head doctor was in on the secret, for a few weeks she could rest from her pillar-to-post dashing from hideout to hideout—but only for a few weeks: one morning, she looked out of the window and saw a city of tents in the meadow, it was teeming with SS men, who had pitched camp there . . . panicking, she dashed down a back stairway, hoping to flee through the kitchen and the service entrance into the open, out to the forest, the mountains—but she was caught by a giant in a black uniform, the *Kommandant* of the echelon, he clutched her hand in an iron grip, pulled her out to his men, ordered them to fall in in a square, had a table placed in the center, lifted her upon it, and shouted, "Men. So you can see what a German girl should look like!"

he had worshiped her when she told him this—at such moments, he was ready to make any sacrifice for her. He understood how important it was to her for him to be "genuine" and "true." But was what she meant indeed the truth of such reality?

When she finally overcame her resistance to marrying him (for the sake of the child whom she had not had the courage to abort), she had instantly done a one-hundred-eighty-degree turn: had expected the utmost spiritual rapport from their marriage, a total mutual devotion, an exclusive, unconditional dedication on both sides; the least misunderstanding, perhaps due simply to hearing something wrong, the slightest divergence in opinion, whether about the moral justification of the United States in the Korean War or the choice of curtain material, brought pain to her eyes as though he had hit her; once, she wept an entire day because he had failed to switch on the same evening radio concert when they were separated for two days—"But you promised me, and I thought of you at every note, I believed I could feel what you were feeling. . . ."—she set store by being able to trust him blindly, by relying on him no matter what; after what she had gone through during the twelve horrible years of her youth, now she could settle only for the absolute.

Naturally, she had had an affair with the SS man who had presented her to his men as the very model of a German girl, and when she then confessed to him that she was Jewish, he was crushed. He said he could not spend another minute with her, he must never see her again, never think of her again. His honor was troth, he had sworn total loyalty to his Führer, to his flag, to the Third Reich, allegiance to his Faith in the Purity of the German Race—it was his obvious duty to report her to the authorities, he said, but he could not, because of his hapless love for her—the tragedy, the catastrophe of this love—he writhed under it as under a disastrous stroke of fate, as under a curse. He might overlook the fact that his flesh could be so mistaken as to desire her, a Jewess, but that he had to love her, "genuinely and truly," that he had to see her as "his female counterpart," that he was "in spiritual bondage" to her—this drove him to

262

despair. He drew the inevitable conclusion: volunteering for the front that very day, he hurled himself into the thick of battle and was dead within a few hours—but he had saved her life, obtaining papers for her, food, a secure hiding-place. . . .

The gray-haired man with the large box of *marrons glacés* under his arm (a box whose contents would suffice to kill a horse, if the horse tried to consume them at one swoop, not to mention a ninety-four-year-old woman) pulls up his coat collar: it is drizzling, he has no hat, headgear never suits him, under hats, caps, hoods, his face looks oddly asexual, his masculinity must be located in his forehead and in the short-cropped iron-gray hair above it, his mouth is effeminately soft with his mustache removed, even though the not-all-too-full lips have narrowed over the years. He knows it: it's the mouth of an old crone. Not a pleasant face, he has to tell himself, even though he has been told there is a great deal of charm, a great seductiveness in the way he speaks, in his liveliness, alertness, and even at times lascivious malice— "your goddamned charm," as his second, Jewish wife used to say, "your abominable, disreputable charm" . . .

yes, but behind this disreputable charm, which sometimes strikes even him as abominable, he sees an often astonishing naïveté—more distinct (because of the contrast) in the mustachioed lothario who sat here twenty years ago on the Via Veneto, elegant in the by no means unintended, not unflirtatiously selected, unconventional, vacationlike casualness of his clothing (as though the blue Mediterranean lay right behind the walls of papal Rome; as though the palms of Hammamet were growing right there), to all appearances blasé and urbane, a man who wasn't born yesterday, who can do anything, and who throughout his checkered career has pretty much learned all the tricks of the trade—and yet a childlike, round-eyed believer in miracles like the one that you could change the world by filmmaking. . . .

that's how he sees himself here, among all sorts of whores and pimps: ready to transfigure the surrounding world for himself, redreaming it into the world that was promised him in earlier stages of his existence—although promised only in his dreams, promised only as an eternal wish. Nevertheless he never tires of reinventing it for himself; he sits here, knowing he is surrounded by nothing but different varieties of prostitution: the straightforward, unadulterated prostitution of female flesh, of boys' flesh, intellectual prostitution, the prostitution of talent, of ambition, of faith, of enthusiasm—he sees all this accurately, he has no delusions about it. In this respect, he only knows he will draw his nourishment from the wealth of images which he takes in like a whale taking in plankton, the pigment with which he can transfigure Rome—

for he is prepared to love this city, he has sought it out as a final refuge, as the last colorful nook in a leukemic Europe. All through his life he had felt alive only to the extent that the world around him seemed alive. And Rome in its ancient decay appears alive as a compost heap. This is the only legacy he has for his son, and he is determined to will it to him. The unhappy little bastard should at least become a European. In other respects, the boy resembles his father only in a shadowy, ghostly way. Then at least in this one respect there is to be semantic harmony. He is prepared to fight all the more energetically for this random son (still and all his only son!), now that the divorce has been granted and the child awarded to her. He wants to use any legal and, if necessary, illegal means to get him here, to Rome, into his custody. He even considers kidnapping him if all else fails—

for he wants to defend the child against her, against her restlessness, her insecurity and stupid insistence on the absolute, her (as he puts it, "not always housebroken") fanaticism. Once, when they were making a halfway peaceful attempt to agree on the boy's upbringing, she screamed at him, "I'm the mother!" and he himself lost his composure and screamed back, "That's precisely the kind of lie I want to protect him from!"—whereupon, disarmed by her incomprehension, thrown back on his irony, he shrugged and

264

turned away while she hurled back at him with a sonorous theatrical laugh and thespian gestures, "You?! You?! . . ."

"Well, I'm waiting," he snapped maliciously over his shoulder. "You can't just stop at two dramatically meaning-ful 'You!'s. You ought to drop from your high-toned theater German to the yiddling level and blurt out, '*You!* Of all people! . . .' Your sense of style should have obliged you to do so: Neo-Realism instead of Weimar."

Too bad. But stupidity is unforgivable. Besides, their being at daggers drawn, mangling one another furiously, had begun very early, right after the child was born. He remembered the pang in his heart when he learned it was a boy and not a girl. A girl would be *she*, would be *her* likeness increased by him, a creature to be worshiped. He had ardently wished it would be a girl. That it had to be a boy struck him as fateful: he could not say, then, why he regarded racial mixture as a boon in a girl and as a curse in a boy. Today he knew: a boy was he himself as a Jew; a monstrosity, a kind of curse—he had felt that, back then, but had not dared to admit it to himself. Nor had he understood back then that the quarrel erupting between them had concerned only one thing: the conception of "Truth"; they had never come to terms with what this actually meant.

Not even when the argument had assumed outright criminal proportions. He recalled a certain day: the little boy, five years old, had contracted a childhood disease, measles or something of the sort—he tended to make light of such matters, he also wanted to spare the boy the torments caused by his own mother's maniacal anxiety; the circum-stances were very different, of course: while he himself had been a fairly robust child, his little son (he almost said resignedly, "Naturally!") was frail, susceptible—in any case, the child was in bed and had been looking forward so much to the father's visit that his temperature rose steeply; the father was no longer living with the wife but visited the boy as often as he could, though his work kept him so busy that he seldom managed to come; now he was sitting by the sick child's little bed, telling him stories—talking into the disquieting, huge, belladonna-black eyes, telling him stories from the forests of the Carpathians, from his own childhood there: many wonderful and dreadful tales about deer, weasels, and falcons, about bears and lynxes, about flute-playing shepherds and poachers and brigands hiding out in the immense woodlands . . . and she, the mother, hatefully called to the child, "Don't believe a word he says! He's lying!"

The crux of it was Pilate's question, he thought ironically: "What is truth?" It wouldn't really have been worth more than a shrug, if he hadn't felt that it "represented itself," that beyond the motives, the arguments, the logic and logic-chopping of their disagreement, there was a fundamental conflict that virtually lifted their fight about the theme of "Truth" into a different dimension and gave it metaphysical weight: as a question of spiritual, moral existence, the decision between damnation and salvation. Even today, when he knew and saw so much more than in the past (he was more judicious in his judgment both of her and of himself, purged of passions), even now he still could not quite discern the meaning of their struggle, only suspect it, sense the momentous "beyondness," the way one senses the ocean beyond the dunes of a coastal landscape, the way he, as a child at home in the Bukovina, had sensed something vast and menacing beyond the woodland on the horizon: Russia and, beyond it, Asia.

Nevertheless, it fills him with a ridiculously vain little satisfaction, which he registers ironically. He can say to himself, it was not just the banal story of a swiftly abortive marriage, it was a theme for classical tragedy. He tried to see it with the eyes of others. The fighting with her soon became unbearable for everyone and poisoned five years of his life, driving him into a different country, a different city. For oddly enough, the people around him seemed to have sensed the transcendent quality of the conflict: his friends, his acquaintances, her friends, her acquaintances, took passionate part in it, took sides, split into camps. Suddenly he found himself being snubbed by previous well-wishers because they had allegedly discovered that he was a confidence man, his name was not what he claimed it was, he was probably Jewish himself and, typically, anti-Semitic toward his charming wife; then again, others came to him privately to confide that everyone knew she could not be regarded as normal, she had been in psychotherapy for years, had spent long periods in sanatoriums, and would probably soon wind up in an asylum. This horribly embarrassing, shameful quarreling that could not be hushed up and, naturally, called the stupidest people into action took place at the expense of their child and within its bewildered soul, and it probably killed the boy in the end. But at least it was not just about something personal and private. It was fought out for something general, crucial. One could define it by asking the same simple question twice with a different meaning each time: is it possible for two human beings to communicate? Fine: as far as the spiritual needs of Jane Smith and John Doe might be concerned, it's merely a question of semantics, of the similarity of social background, of intellectual level, emotional harmony; but put in a general context, the question whether it is possible for two human beings to communicate strikes at the foundations of human existence.

One thing was certain: between him and his quondam second, Jewish wife communication had unfortunately become impossible; and the more he pondered how it had come to this after their initial, frequently stupendous rapport on every directly human issue, the more incomprehensible it seemed to him that the cause of their estrangement and ultimately their hate-filled opposition should have been theological—yes, indeed, to put it bluntly, a theological argument. They had never lacked rapport about plainly human issues; at times, this rapport had reached a state of ecstatic connivance. He remembered holding her in his arms and cradling her like a child when, trembling, she told him

267

how her father had been arrested: friends had hidden the father in a country house, strictly impressing upon him that he was never, never to leave a certain room, because they wanted to show that he was not in the house; but he had panicked and crept into a different room that struck him as a more effective hiding-place, and indeed it probably was; when his friends, in order to show that even a room so obviously suitable as a hiding-place was empty, brought his pursuers, whom they wanted to lead astray, to the door and opened it—he was crouching inside. . . .

trembling, she had told him this, and he had caressed her, waiting for her to calm down and to say what he must not say, and she had said it finally: she had looked up at him and asked, "Do you think my father was very stupid? Even my mother, who almost went crazy because of that, even she said he died because he was always such a stupid second-guesser. And of course, the friends who wanted to save him, they perished too. . . ."

Thus had the rapport between them reached a dangerous level, and he wanted to understand how it could have been destroyed by an abstract disagreement that was in no way supported by anything concrete, a disagreement about two different conceptions of "Truth," moral alternatives that neither of them had thought of as relevant—and naturally he had been unable to push away the thought of race, as a normal person feels morally obliged to do nowadays, after Auschwitz and Buchenwald. Why deny it? After all, he believed in the possibility of a mental legacy in the blood: a psychological heritage specific to the race and passed on from generation to generation—why, if crooked or pug noses are inheritable, if dark or light eyes or dark or light hair keep recurring, stubbornly following Mendel's laws in bigger and bigger chess-knight leaps—his little boy, for instance, had much lighter hair than he himself as a child, and yet also those amazingly shiny, pitch-black eyes, melancholic in their childlike expectancy, even though, as far back as he could remember, his own family had always had dark hair and bright-blue eyes; and she too, the little boy's mother, as Jewish as she may have been to all intents and purposes, had two radiant, clear eyes—what utterly mournful Talmudic student in her gallery of ancestors had shone through? . . . why—in the face of such disagreeable facts, one could, after all, ask with impunity—why should not spiritual and psychological structures, or at least a disposition to them, also be inheritable? Environment and education are not everything that forms a human being; it was nonsense to deny this, even if, thanks to the Nazis, it was now taboo to say so: in fact, because of those asses, one could no longer think about the Jewish problem in any halfway reasonable manner, one had to act as if there were no such thing; yet he was convinced that it would have to be possible to make characteristic distinctions quite unpolemically, altogether scientifically, between Jewish and non-Jewish mentalities, as detached as possible from the sociological conditions that normally shape them, determine them psychologically . . . especially here in Rome, where one has all the test material at hand, from the finest biblical scholar to the most knowledgeable Talmudist, it would have to be possible to draw the information from the purest source—but who would go to the trouble of being so thorough: the closer one lives to the sources, the more indifferently one lets them bubble—an old experience, alas—how often had he gone to La Scala when living in Milan? How often to the Louvre in his Paris days? . . .

besides, that would have been irrelevant in the case of his (former, second, Jewish) wife, for she was not typically Jewish in any respect, quite the contrary: truly the most goyish shikseh he had ever encountered: no Jewish upbringing whatsoever, of course, being the child of emancipated parents; as her father was an art historian, she had been surrounded from the start by reproductions of religious works of art, imbued with Catholic culture; she, in contrast to him, her husband, the alleged anti-Semite, had never seen the inside of a synagogue, had not the foggiest notion of

Hebrew ritual; the mother was once a member of the Laban dance group and needless to say a devotee of some freethinking nature cult, sandals her religious belief, so to speak; she knew about Moses and David only because of Michelangelo; long before being made conscious of belonging to the Chosen People, she could reckon herself among the chosen few for whom the mosaics of Ravenna and the Baroque jubilation of Ottobeuren were as natural as shoe polish and toothpaste for other people; then, of course, she was made conscious of the other chosenness so emphatically that unconsciously she scorned it. In her schooldays, a teacher had summoned her to the front of the class and exclaimed, "Just have a good look at little Ruth, she belongs to the nation that crucified our Savior!"—of course without mentioning how much Christian art owed to that event. Unfortunately the Aryan self-awareness of the Third Reich was not exactly conducive to the creation of Jewish national pride; even with the hatred for her Aryan classmates which she inevitably developed, she could not help resenting being different from the others, to wish she too would be one of those blond grain-harvesters in trim white blouses, laborers participating in Germany's renewal, marching along with them when they sang their dear songs; she herself, after all, as the Allgäu incident proved just a few years later, had perfect physical requirements, not to mention the willingness of conviction; and it was no coincidence that in her rebellion against his own lax relationship to truth, she fully concorded with his first, East Prussian wife, who could have been accused of anything but not being Aryan, having the purest Pruzzian blood. . . .

But then the ghastly thing had happened, which he called "invention of reality" and because of which he never for an instant doubted the correctness, the "Truth" of his own conception of truth (it was a frequent event in his dynamic life, an event he observed with the thrill of the uncanny, which refortified his bent for mystical notions): because they had started hating one another, they strove to know one another more clearly—after all, they had to give their hatred nourishment, reasons, arguments; and by seeing each other more and more sharply, more and more relentlessly, they invented each other in a new and more merciless shape—and that shape became reality. He had tried fully to comprehend the trauma of her childhood, adolescence, and youth as a pariah, a Jew in the Third Reich; he had tried at first out of love, in order to understand her all the more intimately, to identify with her all the more deeply; now he did it in order to find weapons against her, weapons she herself forged for him. He invented her as a Jew with the inevitable mental damage, and that is what she turned into, visibly turned into, more and more each day, each hour . . . it happened more and more often that one of his or her friends said to him, "You have to understand her: she's got awful complexes —she *has* to have them, poor thing. If someone's as Jewish as she is, it's a miracle she survived!" And the voices accumulated, admitting to him, "Yes, you're right, unfortunately. She's awfully stupid. It's too bad—she's so beautiful. But when stupidity is added to the Jewish complex, then it's really unbearable." It was eerie: one could invent reality so that it became real; for example, one could invent Jews for oneself, in order to hate them. . . .

As for him, certain frosty responses of certain people, occasional irony, open baiting, and insolence made him notice more and more plainly that she had succeeded in depicting him as a disreputable personality with a shady background and an unreliable character; at times, he recognized with pale terror that her invention was visibly gaining reality: he caught himself telling fibs that were meant to give his background a brilliance that could scarcely lay claim to credibility; to correct this mistake, he took refuge in a flimsy self-irony that made him all the more suspect; incidentally, with his irregular income, he lived far beyond his means, often finding himself, shamefully, dunned by creditors, reacting in a cowardly way at times and a foolishly arrogant way at others—in short: he became the person he was taken for. One day, they ran into the prince—the prince in whose father's castle they had met and fallen in love, under absurd circumstances, incidentally. . . .

He had encountered the prince's father in a Munich hotel, it was long past midnight, he was sitting in his room, at the typewriter, almost naked because of the dreadful heat, expecting someone to knock on the wall because of the clatter—then someone really did knock, but on the door; when he said "Come in!" an incredibly tall, haggard figure appeared, exuding antiquated nobility like a half-ruined tower overgrown with ivy and fanned by jackdaw wings. The figure named an historic name going back to the age of the Stauffers. He covered himself as best he could, named his own name, asked in what way he could be of service, apologized that his typewriter clatter had disturbed His Highness's rest—No, no, the old prince protested, sheer curiosity had prompted him to knock: "You see, I was walking along the corridor and I saw your shoes outside the door, they are the shoes of our kind. Then I heard the typewriter; now that is something which our kind cannot do, I mean type—so I had to see who it was staying here. . . ."

very flattering, to share a passion for custom-made shoes with someone from the first section of the Gotha Almanac of German Nobility, even though one risked being taken for a con man; but it turned out that there were other common features: the prince knew the Carpathians, had hunted there himself; they also found common ground by remembering that in the good old days when one could hunt to one's heart's content in the headwater region of the "swift" and "golden" Bistriţa River, the villages had teemed with Jews. The old prince did not regard the danger they posed as now entirely averted, despite the cleansing that had taken place there, too. His son, the heir apparent—endangered on his maternal side (the old prince took it for granted that one knew who the heir apparent's mother was and what dubious legacy she had brought into the family: "Well, the Lützelburg line, as we know, has always had a proclivity for dangerous friendships, hence the unfortunate connection

272

with the Hohenzollerns")—the heir apparent was in the hands of a Jewish conspiracy, had allowed himself to be talked into investing his money (a great deal of money, by the way) in a film production, was going about with Jews, and had, incidentally, invited not only the Greek shipper Niarchos to go shooting but also the Baron *de* Rothschild; the old prince, who spoke fifteen languages, had indulged in the jest of addressing the shipper Niarchos in ancient Greek and the Baron *de* Rothschild in Hebrew: "The surprise was delightful, I have never seen such round eyes!" The old prince now went on in Rumanian, although not altogether intelligibly, since he had learned it, like most of his fifteen languages, from books, but nevertheless it sufficed to communicate what he had on his mind: "I am gaining the insight that you, writing film scripts here at midnight, are personally involved in the cinema business"—one could put it that way, yes, indeed—and the old prince went on in German for the sake of simplicity, "Well, would you be kind enough to come to our place in the next few days, to have a look at the crew my son is surrounding himself with? These people have been camping in the Gundlach Wing for weeks, and it can't be locked, there are all sorts of valuable items in it, who knows? . . ."

He then visited the historic castle, three hundred rooms, more than fifty alone in the Gundlach Wing, to meet the heir apparent—tall, blond, round-faced, slightly jittery head movements, but merrily sparkling eyes, a keen sense of humor, a malicious, black humor—and to meet the Jewish conspirators: a movie weasel, very imaginative, eccentric, plucked as a child in Buchenwald from the breast of his mother, who had starved to death, brought to an orphanage in Reims, outstanding pupil at the *lycée*, then the École Normale, assistant director to all the kingpins of the *nouvelle vague*, now production head of a new, evidently serious company; yes, and she, first impression of her wonderfully free, radiantly happy laughter ("I can be so happy when I'm happy!" she once said about herself rapturously)—

273

the luncheon with the prince's father in the Loitpurg Wing; behind the thronelike seat of the old prince a gigantic canvas darkened like smoked meerschaum: a knight in armor lying in a landscape full of mountains, castles, cities, hamlets, a landscape filled with huntable creatures; growing from his genitals like a weathered oak the family tree of the princely house, the coat of arms clustered like cherries, hanging in the branches, row for row, generation for generation, heavenward . . . the old prince speaking only with him, the new guest, the heir apparent quite openly amused at the movie weasel's deliciously unabashed, occasionally even insolent behavior toward his father, at times it gets critical, he expects the old prince to order the whipper-snapper to leave the table, but an iron upbringing keeps the situation under control even in the most precarious moments, only the old prince for his part becomes quite bluntly suggestive: after speaking in detail of family history, he shifts to the Holy Roman Empire, pointing out the catastrophic influence, which historians have as yet inadequately recognized and which is still to be investigated, that the emancipation of the Jews exerted upon the decay of the Reich: the Austrian Tolerance Edict of 1782 was suicidal, one need go only a bit further to see how the Jews profited from the dissolution of the old Empire, the further recognition of their civil rights step by step—1808, under King Jerome ("Well, typical!") of Westphalia; 1814, in Prussia; and by 1850 complete equality there ("Krauts, it stands to reason!"); then the foul play of Bismarck's founding of the German Empire under Jewish patronage: "According to the Imperial Law of 1869, all still extant limitations of civil and civic rights are hereby declared null and void. . . ."

he knows all this, has known it by heart since childhood: if he shuts his eyes, he might think he was at home; even the voices, the diction, the unembarrassed smacking of lips while eating are the same . . . and he is ashamed when the heir apparent takes up the threat with merrily sparkling eyes and explains the family tree on the wall to him and to the movie weasel, to his personal guests, and begins a simple arithmetical calculation:

"Now every last one of us has two parents, four grand-parents, eight great-grandparents, sixteen great-great-grandparents, and so on, *nicht wahr?* As a child, I once figured out that since our family tree goes back thirty-five generations, that would make quite a number of forebears: a total of thirty-three billion, five hundred thirty-six million, five hundred thirty-eight thousand, one hundred sixty-eight people—the very opposite of this painting, where we all spring from one single man and spread out into an oak tree. If we keep counting back, let's say sixty generations—which would reach all the way back to the birth of Christ, then the number of ancestors would run into the trillions. But until the eighteenth century, the population of Europe totaled hardly more than some hundred fifty million—am I wrong, Papi? Please correct me if I'm not making sense!—So every single one of them must be our ancestor, thousands of times over. And the Jews of Heidelberg were exempted from persecution by the Inquisition because they could prove by their tombstones that they had not been in Jerusalem at the time of the Crucifixion, they had already been in Heidelberg at that time, they had come with the Romans—*nicht wahr*, Papi?—so our veins must be carrying at least the blood of all the Jews who were living in Europe back then. . . ."

he envies this son for his courage, his independence, his freedom toward his father: he himself would never have had the nerve as a young man. He admires the young prince's hardness against himself: the young prince drags one leg, the result of childhood polio; the physician, having little hope of saving him without serious paralysis and atrophy, suggested a transfusion of his own blood, which, because of his constant dealings with polio victims, had presumably developed good antitoxins and would therefore strengthen the child's blood against the pathogens, but the prince's mother strenuously protested: commoner's blood in her son's veins, and a Jewish commoner's to boot—she would not suffer it even with the risk of seeing her child crippled. . . .

he becomes a friend of the young prince, lives in the Gundlach Wing; in the evenings, they drink very heavily, the movie weasel the most, but holds his drinks badly, reels through the vaults of the arsenal, and flaps his arms in a kind of bat dance, singing, "They see their death in us, the princes and the dukes and counts! The descendants of the knights fear us—We are the worm in their family tree—Ha, I am the angel of death for the master caste, the master race, the death of all masters—I am the Malakhamoves of the self-styled masters. . . ."

and *she* laughs her beautifully free laugh, throws back her head with its chestnut-red curls—he does not know what she is doing here, what function she has in the film project they are tinkering with—anyhow eighty percent of all film projects are cloud-cuckoo-land —she might be the costume designer—anyway she is very beautiful, no better reason for her presence. . . .

and the heir apparent, who makes a point of drinking his guests under the table, lets his wicked eyes sparkle and says to him, "Congratulations. You have charmed my father completely" (they are using the familiar form by now, have begun their third bottle of whiskey); "Poor Papi is totally isolated: he's had a falling-out with the family, he can't stand other aristocrats, he can't go about with the philistines, as he calls them; what he lacks are perfect toadies, he must be very grateful to you. . . ."

and he himself is silent to this perfidy, merely exchanges an ironic glance with her: it is the first glance of rapport between them—

then the heir apparent, beads of sweat on his forehead, with the first signs of difficulty in speaking, expatiates on his family's anti-Semitism, tells about a grandmother in the Lützelburg line who could not be moved to set foot in a Jewish house—a refusal that might involve occasional problems in Berlin during the 1870s; once, however, it could not be avoided, and she went, eating her way through a pompous dinner without uttering a syllable to the host, next to whom she had been seated, she did not even perceive the hostess; on the way home, she was asked by her husband, "Well, it wasn't all that bad, all in all?" She cheerfully shook her head: "No, because I had a clever idea. I paid for the food. I pushed the money under the plate before leaving the table."

whereupon he got up, saying: "I believe it's time for me to go." And, turning to her, "For you too? If you like, I'll accompany you back to town."

he held out his hand and she took it: they went away, hand in hand—

and now they are once again facing the young prince, more than three years have passed—naturally, the heir apparent had sent a gigantic bouquet of roses with profound apologies for his inexcusable drunkenness ("I knew it: he is the most chivalrous man I know. Once, I felt sick during a meal, I was horribly embarrassed in front of the old man, but I couldn't help it anymore, I barely managed to get to the dining-room door, and there I had to vomit—and he, the young one, put his arm around me and said, 'You're perfectly right. One can't really eat what the cook expects us to put up with these days! . . . ' And once, we were strolling in the park, and Jacques, whom you call the movie weasel, had drunk too much again and had to pee just when the old man came along. Naturally, the old man pretended not to notice anything, but his scorn was so tangible I became dizzy—and the son instantly stood next to Jacques and peed too . . .")—they saw the young prince, the chivalrous man, less and less after their marriage, and lately it had been a good while; now his attitude makes it plain (these crowned heads have an astonishing way of expressing themselves without words) that he is informed about their quarreling, and also approves of their mutual reinventings, as something he has always believed and articulated, his forte is his

277

knowledge of human beings. They run into one another in a theater lobby, she is wearing a black dress, her only adornment an emerald brooch which he gave her at the birth of the child, and the young prince compliments her on it—"It is a very early present from my husband," she says meaningfully, and the prince returns the smile and says, "Oh, and the stone is genuine?"

and he did not slap him in the face, he simply turned on his heel and walked out of the theater, and, coming home (or at least the apartment they called home at that time), he packed his bags and went off, ultimately landing here in Rome after several detours and provisional sojourns, divorced from her at last, and resolved to do everything he could to get his little boy away from her baleful influence.

Today, after twenty years (the boy would be going on twenty-five today—he cannot imagine him a twenty-five-year-old, he would not like to imagine him a monstrous replica of himself, he still sees the pale childish face with the enormous black eyes, and he feels a sharp pang in his heart each time, alleviating the pain with the thought that in many ways, in every way, it is better that the poor thing died . . .), today he looks back on all that as if it were not really his own story: in fact, it did happen to someone else, not the man now walking along the Via Veneto with a box of *marrons glacés* in order to pay the doubtless final visit to the ninety-four-year-old aunt of his (present, third, Italian) wife; for she probably will not make it much longer, *la cara zia Olga*, even the last time her life spirits were drooping critically. . . .

seldom does one feel the power of the present so strongly as at this moment, he thinks: the past is always fairyland. How could she fail to understand this, his quondam, second, Jewish wife? Granted: a past in which you are presented to schoolmates as the crucifier of Christ and then to a pack of SS bulls as the model German Girl while you think you are about to be raped eighty times and then strung up on the nearest branch, this cannot be shaken off lightly, this cannot

278

lightly be reinvented into a fairy tale; likewise, his first, East Prussian wife could not rid herself of the images of the flight from the Russians; yet that should probably not be compared to the other. . . . Well, he too has a number of horror images at his disposal—Germany under the hail of bombs provided a wealth of them, but they belong to another existence, probably because even when those images were being stamped upon him, he saw them as though someone else were seeing them. . . .

to be sure: now, with the detachment of the sixty-five-year-old (although still with that certain childlike naïveté in the sky-blue gaze, the naïveté that is part of his compelling charm), he senses that his strength for reinventing reality is beginning to wane, the reality-forming reinvention of the present as well as the transfiguring fairy-tale reinvention of the past. It is drizzling over Rome, one cannot even get a decent winter in this lousy town: a negative plate of a town, in every respect, a ghost town of thick-blooded vulgar human flesh and ghostly rubble of the past: the traffic hectic as if it were an industrial center in the Ruhr, yet nothing happens here, absolutely nothing: a town of abstract administrators, of lawyers, even in cardinal's red—sheer luck that his little boy was spared having to grow up here—just imagine what might have become of him: a young bomb-throwing radical—a Jewish leftist intellectual like the ones who helped the Bolsheviks in Russia. . . . well, they are being recompensed by the Russians nowadays, those stupid wretched Jews, always seeking the truth, the absolute, the Eternal Holy Empire. . . .

if she were here now, his former, second, Jewish wife (she had loved Rome so much, he had probably moved here to spite her by living here without her), if she were with him now, he would take her to Doney, one could still sit there, not very cozily, of course, on a kind of inverted summer terrace, but she could eat the typical tartuffo ice cream of Rome there which she liked and he could take her hand and say to her:

"Do you know why—why we quarreled? Don't say a word, I too know it, and I too know that it was not so harmless, so irrelevant as I made it out to be. I knew you were stupid, my darling, and I loved you very much for what I often tenderly and often with hatred called your stupidity; yet you should have understood that as someone lost among the lotus eaters, like yourself, I couldn't believe in the truth of reality. One can't believe in a reality that comprises Auschwitz and the Opernball of Vienna at the same time. One simply has to escape into possibilities that make it appear possible. Yet, one must not fool around with the dreadful power of invention: a fool can create a reality that drives millions to madness, I know, I know. . . . Only, you must admit that it was grotesque when, between the two of us, you, the fervent art-consumer, the glowing admirer of art-creators, should believe in the reality of facts, and I, the lowbrow, the pedestrian, should be elevated by my powers of invention . . . isn't it ridiculous? And even more so, that you, the Jew, defended the absolute, the unconditional, and I the goy defended the relative like a rabbinical student. . . . Look: my betrayal of pure truth—isn't it also a possibility for the fallen angels to make the world lucid? You who believe in art the way St. Cecilia believes in resurrection in God, you ought to have known that my transfigurations, the fairy tales I wove out of images from my and other people's past, were an act of love; love—as we both always knew—is identification. Well, this was the only way to identify with a world one was bound to hate and a mankind one loathed and despised. Transfiguration as the alchemists' who strove to change vulgar metals into gold—I could even identify with myself; had I not done this I would have denied myself. But I did make something lucid with my love and my hate, didn't I? . . . Yes, I know," he would have quickly said, "we shouldn't get at it psychologically, the thing's too general. What is truth? Naturally not in the sense of whether it's true that this waiter already has flat feet at a young age, but rather in the metaphysical dimension—the way the Russian aunt of my present wife understands it. The way she feels truth when she utters the word with her heavy Russian accent and cracked Slavic voice. When she says '*pravda*,' the word is virtually surrounded by a nimbus, by the pealing of Easter bells—just as I told you when we were still in love the word *skushno* means not just homesickness or yearning but far, far beyond it, way beyond the dusky horizon, the homesickness, the yearning for God . . . but, honestly, my beautiful, once so tenderly beloved wife, are we Russians? I mean, do we believe in God? Or do we only occasionally act as if we did, out of despair because we really don't and also because we enjoy doing so, as artists: as actors of ourselves, for the sake of the "as if," just as we enjoy acting as if we were Russians when we drink vodka or listen to the Don Cossacks. . . . Look into my eyes and tell me what truth is!"

and she would probably smile now and repeat what she would have hissed back then: "You're always right when you talk. But the instant you leave the room, nothing is true anymore!"

Exactly. As when you put down a book. As when the curtain falls in the theater. . . .

Never will he forget the pain in his little boy's eyes when he was told "Papa's lying." "Perhaps," he would say to his wife, "it was even more than pain; it was fear. And it lingered in our darling boy's eyes, for it might have been the fear that Papa could seek truth—for instance in those huge belladonna-black eyes of our little boy the Talmud student, and in the susceptibility of the eternally sickly child, the Jewish shack in which his mother's ancestors had lain in the same bed by the dozens, coughing tubercles at one another . . ." but that would have been too cruel to tell her: cynicism, even as an act of self-defense, has its limits—he suffers, he feels sick at the thought of what an unbearable intellectual snob the boy would most likely have become under his mother's pretentious, exalted bluestocking ways. And how he must have suffered from her cruelty. The cruelty of the really stupid: once, when she tried to be ironical, asking him whether he had invented himself in his earlier phases as so fine, so good, so courageous only to set an example for their little boy, and he had nodded, she shouted scornfully, "He'll respect you more if you confess what you really are! . . ."

"What?" he then asked, "an anti-Semite?"

No, it was good that the boy had died early, they would have mangled him in their mutual mangling; he, the father, would have turned him into a psychopath with demands in which the boy would have caught not even unconscious, inadequately concealed expectations and she, the mother, would have openly given him the hidden meaning; the poor little brat would only have needed to prolong the sentences: "Don't tell me you're scared to jump off this little wall" (it won't make your little Jew-legs crooked); or: "You don't like ham? Since way back, or did your mother talk you into it?" (not because she'd like you to be kosher but because her intellectuality yearns for vegetarian purity); or: "That kind of thinking, my boy, is not our kind of thinking" (back home in the Bukovina, at least, only junk-shop Jews think like that—not the rabbis, mind you, I have nothing but respect for the rabbis, hats off to the rabbis—no, that's wrong too: hats on to the rabbis—whatever you do, it's wrong for those bloody Jews). . . .

his little son would have prolonged any sentence like that compulsively—assuming, of course, that along with the keen, nimble, distrustful mind of the Talmudic students he had also inherited the self-destructive proclivities of the fallen angels . . . from her the Jewish woman he had doubtless inherited his beauty: a stub-nosed Aryan beauty despite the belladonna eyes, like a Raphael infant Jesus (although here too one can hardly speak of a pure Aryan background) . . . that was poignant, no doubt, but it was questionable whether it would have persisted beyond puberty: he does not care to think how the Raphaelite infant Jesus might have developed into a Maoist—

for that must be what they dream about, the now twenty-to-twenty-five-year-olds: another absolute truth, socialism come true, the world revolution that shall bring about God's kingdom on earth—that is what they identify with, that is why they kill one another and others who believe in the relativity of things; they would like to invent this reality for themselves the way, in his time, a generation wanted to invent the reality of the resurrected Holy Empire for themselves, with the same fanatical will for the absolute, with the same unconditional quest for the great life-fulfilling love of the great, ultimate truth for which one dies, for which one kills, especially those who ask whether it is really the only truth. . . .

No, he would rather think of the small, anemic boy with the tremendous dark eyes, eyes that grew bigger and bigger the closer the poor suffering thing approached his early death: he would rather think of the idolatrous love with which the boy clung to him, his papa: never will he forget how they walked through a park one winter, and the little boy held out his hand to have the father lead him along; he gave him his forefinger, and even today, he can still feel the little fist closing around it and clutching it—

and even today he can still feel it: once, in Berlin, in the year 1943, in a trolley car, he gave his finger to an elderly man, well beyond his fifties, he had been struck by the man's intimidated behavior—wearing a knapsack, the man had asked for Tiergarten Station several times, and when he made an awkward move, he knocked aside his lapel and exposed a yellow Jewish star he had tried to conceal; he had understood that this was one of the poor devils who had to gather at Tiergarten Station to be sent "to the East"; he had rolled up a fifty-mark bill and stealthily passed it to the man, and the man had held his finger, all the way, until Tiergarten Station. . . .

that, my son, was my good deed: I can book it to my credit. You can believe me: it is the truth. . . .

283

Even though Pontius Pilate most likely treated that question in the only possible form—philosophical challenge. Should the ninety-four-year-old aunt of his (present, third, Italian) wife have a lucid moment today, he would talk to her about it: in regard to memory; his focusing more and more pointedly on his childhood, washing up more and more flotsam of a distantly lived life—and this focus had made him feel he was preparing to return home; in the past, he had dreamed ahead, now he dreamed himself back—and he had *actually* returned home.

One day—just a few days ago—he had taken a plane and flown to Bucharest: home. Not really his home, for his home no longer existed there, but the moment the airplane landed, he knew he had come home; even though the landscape around the airfield did not look at all like what he remembered—it was much flatter, much more elementary: when he had lived here, had he not perceived how sober, how unromantic and unpicturesque, how unemphatic the countryside was? Only the vastness was impressive, but he had expected that. . . . And although the soldiers all over the place—wearing thick earflaps on their Muscovite fur caps, automatic rifles at the ready, as they stood guard when the plane discharged its passengers—in no way recalled the uniformed red-cheeked peasant boys whom he had commanded as an operetta lieutenant during one happy peacetime summer more then forty years ago, nevertheless, he knew: I'm home.

He knew it also because everything went as a matter of course. He was not the least bit excited. He thought, it's been forty years since I was last here. No doubt a couple of things must have changed, but he was afflicted neither by expectation nor by curiosity. He now knew, he had three days to convince himself of the truth of his memories. And that had happened the very instant he set foot on the ground.

Bucharest—yes indeed, there was the Shossea Khisseleff, fairly unchanged. Only instead of the racetrack where he had ridden there stood a gigantic building in Stalinist style. Downtown: more space had been cleared around the old royal palace, the Café Corso was gone, the palace was confronted by a newer, mightier one (in proper Stalinist style): the seat of the Party. Biserică Albă was unchanged; the house he had lived in just a bit shabbier.

"That was the truth behind my dreams of forty years," he wanted to tell the ninety-four-year-old woman. "*Vous comprenez, ma chère:* it was all so overwhelmingly banal. Certainly, the colors of the past are missing. Do you know why they deploy their strength to industrialize a rich country of farmers, an agricultural land? Not to manufacture consumer goods but in order to create a proletariat. Rumania, my farmland of the past, has become a country of class-conscious proletarians. Naturally, this changes the picture a few shades. But the land is unchanged—the land I was born in, lived in, loved, and have dreamed about for forty years—unchanged in essence, I mean to say, and therefore, to me, of an overwhelming banality. Oh, you should thank the Creator that He has not brought you back to St. Petersburg. . . ."

needless to say, he had had to look up his childhood sweetheart—the great love of his life, a cousin, flesh of his flesh (although marked by a gigantic hooked nose from their common grandmother), of course not as fresh as forty years ago, but unchanged—that is to say: unchanged in essence, therefore, to him, banal. Then, she had rejected his tempestuous courtship, marrying late, only after the war; the husband was Jewish, originally highly respected in the Party, then arrested and locked up for years; she did not care much to see him, she still had the same proud neckline, her aquiline nose boldly cut the air as in the past, yes, she had a son, twenty-five years old now. . . .

she had wanted to avoid meeting him where she might be seen with a foreigner. Picking as neutral a place as possible, they went to the "Village Museum" on Shossea Khisseleff.

285

"Our youth is preserved here. Do you remember the girls leaning on fences like these when we rode by?" She remembered. The embroidered blouses those girls had worn were now valuable collectors' items; of course, the state confiscated them from private collectors. "Were there really such wooden houses in our part of the Carpathians?" Yes, it was true. What else? . . .

on the third day, she sent her son to take him to the airport. He was frightened at how Jewish the boy looked. He had the hooked nose from their common blood. As well as the dark hair and piercing blue eyes. The young man was cordial and utterly indifferent. The old man from the West concerned him not at all. No use pointing out to the boy that he might have been his son. When parting, they barely shook hands. Then the airplane spiraled up over the bleak landscape, in which countless ponds were glittering.

"Thank the good Lord, *ma chère*, that you will never see Tsarskoye Selo again . . ." he would say to the old Russian woman.

When he arrived at the old lady's building, the concierge was standing there as if awaiting him. "I just telephoned your wife," she said, peering at him as though expecting consternation before she even told him the bad news. "The old contessa vanished," is what he heard, for the woman said, "*La vecchia contessa è mancata.*" Only a fraction of a second later he realized that this was a euphemistic expression to avoid the rude word "died." Aha. Well, they had been expecting it for weeks.

The concierge had been taking care of her during the last weeks. Things had gone downhill rapidly. "I wanted to get in touch with you a couple of days ago, but you were out of town, your wife told me." This morning, the contessa had sat up once again and gazed straight ahead and loudly exclaimed, "*Pravda!*" And then she had crumpled up, dead.

"It's a Russian word," he said, removing the wrappings from the box of *marrons glacés*.

"I know," said the concierge. "My husband's been in the

286

Communist Party for thirty years. It's a Moscow news-paper."

"Yes. Truth. Here—would you like a chestnut? Take the whole box, I'll just eat one, I really mustn't, you know—at my age, one has to be careful."